The
EVERYTHING®
Einstein Book

Dear Reader:

Thanks for picking up *The Everything® Einstein Book*! Einstein was one of the most important scientific figures of the twentieth century, and his theories touched many areas of physics. However, did you know that Einstein was also an ardent humanitarian, and that he spent much of his later life lobbying for human rights around the world?

Einstein is, of course, most famous for his theory of relativity, which showed that time and space are not absolute. Relativity also proves that space is actually curved! But Einstein also developed a series of other theories—from the famous equivalence of mass and energy that makes up the formula $E=mc^2$ to other, more arcane theories on topics including quantum theory, the motion of microscopic particles, and why the sky is blue.

If you've ever wondered what black holes are, or what $E=mc^2$ really means, then this is the book for you. It's written in easy-to-understand language, with minimal equations and simplified technical explanations. You don't need any math background to understand the theories of one of the world's all-time great scientists.

Thanks, and happy reading!

Cynthia Phillips

Shana Priwer

D1297046

The EVERYTHING® Series

Editorial

Publishing Director	Gary M. Krebs
Managing Editor	Kate McBride
Copy Chief	Laura MacLaughlin
Acquisitions Editor	Eric M. Hall
Development Editor	Michael Paydos
Production Editor	Khrysti Nazzaro

Production

Production Director	Susan Beale
Production Manager	Michelle Roy Kelly
Series Designers	Daria Perreault
	Colleen Cunningham
Cover Design	Paul Beatrice
	Frank Rivera
Layout and Graphics	Colleen Cunningham
	Rachael Eiben
	Michelle Roy Kelly
	Daria Perreault
	Erin Ring
Series Cover Artist	Barry Littmann
Interior Illustrator	Christopher Speakman
	and Dover Publications

Visit the entire Everything® Series at everything.com

THE
EVERYTHING®
EINSTEIN
BOOK

From matter and energy to space
and time, all you need to understand
the man and his theories

Shana Priwer and Cynthia Phillips, Ph.D.

Adams Media Corporation
Avon, Massachusetts

To our children Zoecyn and Elijah

An Everything® Series Book.
Everything® and everything.com® are registered trademarks of Adams Media Corporation.

Published by Adams Media Corporation
57 Littlefield Street, Avon, MA 02322 U.S.A.
www.adamsmedia.com

ISBN: 1-58062-961-X
Printed in the United States of America.

J I H G F E D C B A

Library of Congress Cataloging-in-Publication Data
Phillips, Cynthia.
The everything Einstein book / Cynthia Phillips and Shana Priwer.
p.   cm.
(An everything series book)
ISBN 1-58062-961-X
1. Einstein, Albert, 1879-1955. 2. Physicists–Biography.
3. Relativity (Physics) I. Priwer, Shana. II. Title. III. Series:
Everything series.
QC16.E5P48 2003
530'.092–dc21
2003009085

This book is available at quantity discounts for bulk purchases.
For information, call 1-800-872-5627.

Contents

Acknowledgments

Special thanks to our children for their patience,
to Dr. Marshall Gilula for love and support,
and to Raven for proofreading.

Top Ten Impacts of Einstein's Life and Work

1. The theories of general and special relativity changed the way we view the physical universe—space and time are no longer absolute.

2. The equation $E=mc^2$ relates mass to energy, and while it is not a formula for creating an atomic bomb, it did help lead to the development of nuclear energy.

3. Einstein, a lifelong pacifist, suggested that the U.S. government develop an atomic bomb before Germany could do so during World War II, but lobbied against its actual use.

4. Einstein's work on the photoelectric effect laid the groundwork for quantum mechanics, and earned him a Nobel Prize.

5. He also laid the groundwork for the field of cosmology, the study of the universe as a whole, and his work led to the discovery of black holes, wormholes, gravitational lenses, and other weird astronomical objects.

6. Einstein assisted many Jewish immigrants in fleeing to the United States or other countries during World War II.

7. Einstein also helped with the establishment of the state of Israel as a safe refuge for Jewish people from all over the world.

8. He created the iconic image of a genius—even today, he is still referred to as the top symbol of intelligence, and his name and face grace T-shirts, mugs, movies, soda commercials, and baby products!

9. Einstein's work for world peace and world government, though idealistic, helped make the world a better place.

10. His final quest, for a "grand theory of everything," was ultimately unsuccessful, but this and his other theories laid the groundwork for much of modern physics.

Introduction

▶ALBERT EINSTEIN WAS ONE of the most important scientists of
all time. The impact of his work was not limited to the realm of
science, however. Einstein's discoveries and humanitarian causes
affected people all over the world, from all walks of life. In fact,
Einstein was named "Person of the Century" in 2000 by *Time*
magazine, beating out such historical figures as Franklin Delano
Roosevelt and Mohandas Gandhi!

This book examines the impact that Einstein had throughout his
lifetime, from his birth in Germany in 1879 to his death in the
United States in 1955. Einstein's work was a reaction to the changing
scientific times—from the simple, elegant view of the universe of the
nineteenth century to the more complex picture that began to
emerge at the turn of the twentieth century.

Einstein's university years and his difficulty finding an academic
post following his graduation from a Swiss university led to his
accepting a job at the Swiss patent office. It was while he was
employed in this position that he married his first wife, Mileva Maric,
a fellow student, and published an astonishing series of papers.

These papers, all submitted to scientific journals in 1905,
included one on the photoelectric effect, one on special relativity,
one on the equivalence of matter and energy, and one on Brownian
motion. Einstein became established as one of the pre-eminent
scientists of the twentieth century, and in fact he won the Nobel
Prize for his work on the photoelectric effect. These papers also laid
the groundwork for much of Einstein's later career; one of these
foundational works included his famous equation $E=mc^2$ as well as
special relativity, which Einstein would later expand into the theory
of general relativity.

Einstein also had an important role in the development of quantum mechanics, a theory with which he was never completely comfortable. While quantum theory describes the universe in terms of probabilities, Einstein believed that the behavior of particles and energy should be able to be uniquely determined.

By using his theory of general relativity to model the entire universe, Einstein also laid the groundwork for the new field of cosmology. In the course of his studies of the universe, Einstein predicted the existence of dark matter and black holes and laid the foundation for the Big Bang theory of the origin of the universe. His theories also predicted the expanding universe, although Einstein originally included a term in his equations to keep the universe static in keeping with the ideas of the time. He would later call the addition of this term one of his greatest blunders.

Einstein's later years are also fascinating. After he moved to the United States in the 1930s to escape Hitler's growing threat in Germany, Einstein became increasingly involved in humanitarian concerns. He was an outspoken advocate for Jewish people who needed a safe place to live and also was a lifelong pacifist. Despite or perhaps because of his commitment to pacifism, he wrote to President Franklin Roosevelt to suggest that the United States should work to develop an atomic bomb before Nazi Germany had a chance to do so.

Einstein's complex role in twentieth-century science can be seen in the scientific quest he spent the rest of his life pursuing, a unified field theory that would unite all of physics into one simple, elegant relationship. Ultimately unsuccessful, this quest was also reflected in Einstein's desire for a single united world government, which he saw as the only way to ensure peace.

Einstein's legacy is further seen in the way that he has become the icon of intelligence in popular culture. From "Baby Einstein" videotapes to his appearance in soda commercials, Einstein's disheveled appearance has become the standard image for a genius.

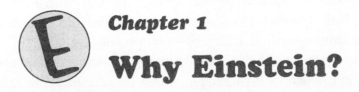

Chapter 1

Why Einstein?

lbert Einstein is perhaps the most famous scientist of modern times, but he was not only a scientist. He was also an ardent humanitarian who worked for peace and for equal treatment of all people. His theories changed the scientific world of the twentieth century, and his work on humanitarian issues helped change the lives of many people whom he helped find a better life.

Einstein's Impact

Albert Einstein was, without a doubt, one of the most influential people of all time. He was a scientist, a humanist, and a father. While he is best known for his special and general theories of relativity, Einstein contributed much more, both to the scientific community and to the world at large. His interests were varied, and his intelligence immense. With a natural capacity for both thought and reason, it is no surprise that Einstein had such an amazing impact.

Have you ever heard of the Big Bang theory of how the universe began? Thank Einstein for laying the groundwork. Did you know that Einstein first proposed the building of the atomic bomb to Franklin Delano Roosevelt? He did, and then later tried to retract the idea. Einstein was not accepted at university when he first applied! He also had his share of layperson drudgery—before making his most important contributions to science, Einstein worked a nine-to-five job in a patent office.

People often think of scientists as highly educated folks who spend all their time holed up in an office. While Einstein certainly spent his share of time in research, his life's work extends beyond the laboratory. Religion was also important to Einstein. He was a deeply spiritual Jew whose thoughts on religion influenced his ideas about the creation of the world. He spent much of his later life involved in humanitarian concerns, campaigning to convince the United States and other countries not to develop nuclear weapons. He also spent much time writing affidavits and otherwise helping Jews who wanted to immigrate to the United States from various European countries in the years leading up to World War II.

How Did He Become So Famous?

What is it about Einstein that makes people worldwide know his name? Why is he such a familiar figure, even to those who don't understand his theories? How did one person come to be so widely known? A simple answer to this question doesn't exist, but one of the goals of this book is to explore all the elements that created the icon everyone knows as Einstein.

Part of Einstein's fame and recognition was circumstantial.

He developed his theories at a time when the world was ready to accept them. The scientific community of the early twentieth century was ready and willing to receive new ideas, and without this support, Einstein's ideas might have done nothing more than gather dust. The general public was also ready for some good news in the late 1910s, especially after the depression and stress caused by the war years. When Einstein's theory of general relativity was beautifully confirmed by observations of bending starlight taken during the 1919 solar eclipse, Einstein received international acclaim.

Accessible Science

In addition, the nature of Einstein's work was such that it could be accepted by those who did not understand it. Einstein didn't challenge common religious beliefs or attempt to overthrow societal norms. While his work was complex and not readily comprehensible, it also wasn't blatantly offensive to most people. Had his goal been to prove that God didn't exist, for example, Einstein's name probably wouldn't be known as fondly as it is today, if at all.

FACT

Perhaps one of the most famous equations in the world is Einstein's $E=mc^2$, which refers to the equivalence of matter and energy. In this equation, energy (E) is related to mass (m) by a factor related to the speed of light (c) squared.

Einstein's major scientific works can also be easily stated in terms accessible to the general public, even if the physics and mathematics behind them are far beyond all but the most advanced scientists. Such ideas as the equivalence of matter and energy, as expressed in the equation $E=mc^2$, can be understood by just about anyone. So can the idea of living in a four-dimensional universe, with the fourth temporal dimension (time) in addition to the three spatial dimensions (length, width, and height). It is also fairly easy to picture the idea of the warping of space, or the speed of light as a universal speed limit, or a black hole with gravity so strong that nothing, even light, can escape from it. All these concepts are results of Einstein's work, yet they do not require advanced physics to understand intuitively.

Why Does Science Matter?

A larger issue, of course, is the question of why science matters. Why do nonscientists care about science? From the perspective of the human race as a whole, it is obvious that science is valued. If it weren't, no one would have ever heard of Einstein. There would be no Nobel Prize in physics. High school students would not be required to study chemistry. No one would know about Saturn's rings, and famous rock stars would not be spending millions of dollars trying to travel into outer space.

The realm of science might be seen as composed of two main elements: fact and theory. Facts are proven truths that have stood their ground, through the tests of time and the rigors of usage. Facts are things that are taken for granted to be true and unambiguous.

Most facts, though, do not start out as such, particularly in the world of science. In a field where innovation is part of the job, scientists are at times tasked with creating fact from scratch. Such creation does not come easily, nor is it handed to them on a silver platter. People are inquisitive and, by nature, have a tendency to question the environments and situations surrounding them. Sometimes things that are taken for granted as truth have to undergo rigorous examination and questioning by many, many people before they are finally accepted as fact.

Enter the theory. What exactly is a theory? It can be generally defined as a set of ideas that relate to each other in some way. Theories differ from facts in that they are unproven ideas; a theory is, by definition, speculative and not certain. Scientists, musicians, artists, philosophers, and people from just about every walk of life create theories every day. How? Simply by being alive and cognizant.

The Scientific Method

Einstein's ideas are called "theories" because they were initially unproven. They did not start out as facts; they were ideas that had to be tested. This aspect is, in and of itself, unremarkable. Most large-scale ideas that present new information, or suggest a reversal of old information, are going to be questioned by someone; as such, they will be considered theories until most people agree on their validity. This is what is called the "scientific method"—the method by which science tries to develop more and more accurate descriptions of the natural world around us.

The scientific method is the way in which scientists, over time, attempt to construct an accurate representation of the world around us. The foundation of the scientific method is experimental verification—any idea must be tested before it can be accepted.

Hypothesis

The scientific method is the basis of Einstein's work and of all other scientific research—in the past, present, and future. The scientific method begins with a hypothesis, which is a new thought or idea to explain some observation of the world around us. The hypothesis must be testable; this is the main difference between science and other fields such as religion or philosophy. In science, once a new idea or explanation is proposed, it must make specific claims or predictions that can be tested.

The scientific method consists of the following steps:

1. Observation of a particular phenomenon.
2. Formulation of a hypothesis to explain the observations.
3. Use of the hypothesis to make further predictions.
4. Performance of experiments to test the predictions made by the hypothesis.

Experimental Verification

The predictions are then tested by experiments performed by many independent scientists, not just the one or ones who initially made the hypothesis. If the predictions made by the hypothesis turn out to be correct, then the hypothesis has been proved accurate; it will eventually become elevated in stature to a theory or a law of nature. Even theories can be overturned. As you will see in the following chapters, Einstein's theories showed that Newton's laws of classical mechanics, the established theories of the previous century, did not hold up under certain conditions.

ALERT!

Only a scientific theory that has been subjected to experimental verification can truly be called a theory. An important example is the theory of evolution, which has made specific predictions that have proved correct. This theory can be compared to the idea of creationism, which can make no such predictions. Evolution is therefore a scientific theory, while creationism is not.

Revolutionary Theories

So what made Einstein's theories so special? One of the primary reasons Einstein stood out from his predecessors and contemporaries is that the theory of relativity (discussed in detail in Chapter 6 and Chapter 12) changed the way scientists fundamentally considered both space and time. Humankind's place in the universe was seen from a new perspective, and such a notion was both frightening and exciting. Other scientists had important theories; Einstein's were daring. Sometimes a little excitement goes a long way toward the creation of a legacy!

In fact, Einstein's ideas were so revolutionary that much of the scientific community initially rejected them as being too outlandish. Einstein won the Nobel Prize in physics, but for some much less controversial work he had done early in his career—not for relativity. It took many years for Einstein's ideas to become part of the scientific mainstream.

Einstein's Public Role

Theories do not stand alone, nor are they created by a faceless entity in a vacuum. Einstein himself was, of course, partly responsible for the success and popularity of his ideas. He was not the type of scientist to spend night and day isolated from the public. Quite the contrary; Einstein was involved in science, as well as humanitarian concerns, from a public and political viewpoint as well as research perspective. He was actively involved in many public organizations, including the League of Nations and the German League for Human Rights, and was able to promote both himself and his science on many levels.

Public Speaking

His interest in public speaking undoubtedly helped to provide awareness of his theories. He was in direct communication with world leaders, giving credence to his own research and to science in general. Being both a scientist and a figure of popular culture was enabling to members of the scientific community at large, as evidenced by the large number of radical and critical scientists who were Einstein's contemporaries.

Through being a public humanitarian, though, he was also able to gain public support for science. Bringing science to the people provided a popular base for Einstein's research. New scientific research and breakthroughs must be explained to the general public in order to really change the way we see the world, and Einstein's interest in public speaking provided an immense outlet for potential support and recognition.

Complex Ideas Made Simple

Did most people understand relativity when Einstein first presented his ideas in 1905 with a paper on the photoelectric effect? Probably not. Do most people understand these ideas today? Again, probably not, but lack of general comprehension didn't hurt Einstein's reputation. What was significant was the fact that other well-known and well-respected scientists did understand and give credence to Einstein, and the masses were more than willing to follow suit.

Those who wanted to understand Einstein, of course, could. Complex ideas can be broken down, and common terms can be used to decipher a maze of scientific lingo. Anyone who wants to can grasp Einstein's message.

Einstein's Science

So what was the gist of Einstein's work? While he made important contributions to many aspects of science, he is most famous for the theory or principle of special relativity. In a nutshell, special relativity is the idea that no difference can be detected between experiments taking place at rest, versus those taking place on an apparatus under constant motion. Things behave the same on a train moving at a constant speed, for example, as they would if they were just resting on the ground.

Strange Results from Relativity

However, not just objects obey this principle; light does as well. The invariance of the speed of light leads to all sorts of strange consequences, including variations in length and time depending on the speed at which something is traveling! Thus, lengths become shorter and time moves more slowly as one moves at speeds approaching the speed of light.

Einstein later expanded his theory of relativity to include gravity, and this second body of research became the theory known as general relativity. General relativity is based on the principle that acceleration and gravity are indistinguishable. From this relationship come all sorts of odd results, including black holes and the warping of space-time.

Einstein's main scientific contributions include his work on special and general relativity and his study of the photoelectric effect, which laid the groundwork for quantum mechanics. An application of his theory of general relativity led to the development of the field of cosmology, which is the study of the universe as a whole.

A Place in History

Einstein's work, of course, did not originate in thin air. His scientific predecessors created the basis from which his work could be conducted, and previous theories gave him the tools he would need to arrive at new theories. His new theories, in turn, laid the groundwork for many of the later scientific breakthroughs of the twentieth century, including quantum mechanics and cosmology. In particular, in an early paper, Einstein used general relativity to model an entire universe; he single-handedly started the new field of cosmology (the study of the universe as a whole).

The Search for a Theory of Everything

Einstein's reputation was unfairly tarnished later in his life by his being called the "father of the atomic bomb." In reality, neither his equations nor Einstein himself had anything to do with its development. His later life was spent mostly on a search for a "unified field" theory that would explain everything in a single, elegant theory. This theory was never realized, and many younger scientists thought that the aging Einstein had wasted the rest of his life on a fool's quest. However, his vision of a simple, coherent explanation for the way the world works in fact laid the groundwork for string theory, which is a modern attempt to find just such a grand unified theory.

Humanitarian Efforts

Einstein's search for a unified theory in physics ran parallel with his wish for global peace and a unified world government where people treated other people humanely and sensibly. He spent his life working toward both of these goals, the unity of science and of humanity. While he did not reach either, it can be argued that he made the world a better place on both fronts just through his efforts.

Einstein spent many years working for the fair treatment of people all over the world. His efforts led to the immigration of many Jewish refugees into the United States and later to the establishment of the nation of Israel. Einstein was even offered the presidency of Israel, but he regretfully declined! He continued to work for peace and justice until the end of his life.

Einstein's Legacy

Einstein's reputation has endured, and he is undoubtedly the best-known scientist of the twentieth century. $E=mc^2$ is probably the most recognized scientific equation among the general public. Einstein was even named Person of the Century in 2000 by *Time* magazine.

Einstein as Genius

Einstein became the prototype for a certain type of genius as portrayed in popular media and literature. With his wild white hair and lack of socks, Einstein certainly fits our mental picture of an eccentric scientific genius. Einstein has also invaded popular culture—he is commonly invoked as the face of genius, and his face adorns T-shirts, coffee mugs, and other commercial items. What would the modest patent clerk have thought of this kind of fame?

FACT

While Einstein's appearance later in his life certainly fits the "eccentric genius" stereotype, his appearance earlier in his life, such as when he produced his famous 1905 series of papers, was much more conventional. It was only later in his life that Einstein let his shock of white hair grow out! So perhaps our mental image of Einstein the genius should resemble the buttoned-down patent clerk more than the white-haired eccentric.

One of the main benefits of Einstein's personal fame is that it brought science into public view. Through the cult of his personality, Einstein was able to gain public recognition of some rather obscure breakthroughs in various areas of physics. Few other scientists have been able to get the public to listen to their theories at all, let alone have them enter popular discussions in ways such as "everything's relative."

Taking Advantage of Einstein's Status

Today, Einstein's name is present in society in ways both scientific and silly. The element einsteinium was named after him, in recognition of his many contributions to atomic science. A line of baby products, called "Baby Einstein," claims to be able to increase the intelligence of your infant. Capitalizing on the popular correlation of the name Einstein with genius, these products include videotapes, audio recordings, and other items—none of which have anything to do with Einstein! They attempt to provide an educational experience for your child that might help turn her into the next Einstein. Of course, none of this has been proven scientifically, but that doesn't stop legions of parents from purchasing them, eager to give their children any edge possible!

Why Do We Care about Einstein?

It is precisely Einstein's many contributions, in a wide variety of fields, that established him as the cultural icon he is today. If he had only created his early scientific theories, he would be remembered by the scientific community as an influential scientist; however, like most scientists, he would be largely unknown to the general public.

It is only because of Einstein's contributions to science, his humanitarian work, his public speaking, and his unique ability to explain detailed scientific theories that Einstein's place was firmly established in the realms of popular culture. The myth of Einstein, the Genius, also helped this positioning.

Einstein was a fully rounded person. He was never the kind of single-minded scientist who had no life outside the laboratory. Instead, Einstein had many interests, including music and sailing, in addition to his scientific pursuits. He was married twice, and there was much gossip throughout his life relating to the many women he spent time with. Einstein also had a deeply spiritual side, which was reflected in some of his scientific theories and pursuits.

For all these reasons, Albert Einstein is ultimately one of the most influential figures of modern times. The study of such an influential person, and his many contributions to the world, is as important as it is interesting; this study is the focus of this book. Ⓔ

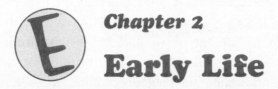

Chapter 2
Early Life

The first years of Einstein's life served as a canvas upon which the rest of his career, both personal and professional, would be painted. The basis was formed for his later approach to science, religion, and politics. All of the events that took place in these early years helped shape and create the figure that Einstein went on to become.

The Preschool Years

The life of Albert Einstein began in Ulm, Germany, on March 14, 1879. He was born into a middle-class German-Jewish family, parented by Hermann and Pauline. The small family moved to Munich in 1880. He had one sister, Maria (also called Maja), and a brother, Jakob.

Whether or not Einstein was actually a child genius is the subject of much discussion. Letters from his maternal grandmother suggest that he was already quite creative by the age of two and that his comprehension was quite advanced. When informed of the birth of his baby sister (when Einstein was about two and a half), he allegedly inquired as to the whereabouts of the wheels on his new toy; all toys should have wheels, Einstein deduced, and the squalling new plaything could optimistically be considered a toy. If true, these anecdotes would seem to suggest that Einstein's language was extraordinarily well developed for a young child.

Einstein: Retarded?

There are, however, the rumors that Einstein was "retarded," or slow, as a child. Einstein was slow to learn to talk, not speaking much until age three. His head was irregularly shaped, and some have speculated that this anomaly somehow delayed his language skills. A family maid noted that Albert often repeated his responses to questions. While it is probably true that Einstein didn't talk as much as some children, reluctance to speak and inability to do so are entirely different things. Family legend had it that Einstein actually just liked to think about what he said before he said it, and it's certainly hard to find fault with that as a character trait!

While reports of Einstein's development are often greatly exaggerated, the same may not be true for others. Any questions regarding a child's language or cognitive skills should always be directed toward the family pediatrician.

Even as a young child, Einstein's playing gravitated toward solving problems. He enjoyed puzzles and building blocks from a very young age. He was always interested in the construction of a project, not just the final result. He would later build elaborate houses of cards up to fourteen stories tall, showing incredible concentration and diligence for a child.

Albert's Antisocial Tendencies

Einstein was not the most social of children. Aside from his reluctance to speak at an early age, he did not enjoy playing with other children, and he generally kept to himself. While his later public career shows that he clearly got over this apparent shyness, it does show that he tended toward introversion and reflection. Such characteristics are almost unavoidable in a scientist like Einstein; he would go on to spend innumerable hours working alone in a laboratory, and to do so would seem to require that he enjoyed spending time alone.

First Science: The Compass

When Einstein was five years old, he came down with an illness that forced him to take bed rest. To help him pass the time, his father brought him a magnetic compass. As you may know, a compass is a device used to locate true north. Wherever you stand, anywhere on the planet, a magnetic compass will point north. Cool, huh? Einstein thought so too!

FACT

North is in fact not always north. Once every half-million years or so, the Earth's magnetic field reverses direction, and a compass's north end will switch and point south. The location of the magnetic North Pole has also wandered over time.

A compass of this sort is actually pretty simple in its construction. It consists of a magnet (called the "needle") balanced on a pivot point. Usually the end of the needle is marked with an N, to indicate which way north is. How does it work? Pretend that Earth has a gigantic bar magnet inside it, with its south end somewhere around the North Pole.

Opposites attract, especially when it comes to magnets, so the north end of the compass needle always points toward the south end of this imaginary bar magnet.

Compasses had been around long before Einstein came along. Greek and Chinese scientists knew about the Earth's magnetic fields, and some of the earliest surviving compasses come from the twelfth century. Einstein, the curious youth that he was, thought he could somehow trick the compass into pointing somewhere other than true north, but he was fascinated by the compass's refusal to play along. Even at this age, he recognized that there was a force invisible to the eye, untouchable with the hand, which guided the universe. This understanding surely influenced the path Einstein would take later in life.

Einstein the Musician

Music would play a large role throughout Einstein's life. He began piano lessons at age six, mostly due to the influence of his mother. She was herself an accomplished pianist and passed on a love of music to her children. Einstein would persist in both musical study and performance for years to come.

While continuing piano lessons throughout his childhood, Einstein also played the violin. He began private studies at age five. Although he threw a tantrum (and a chair) at his first teacher, luckily he was able to persist and become an accomplished musician. Not incredibly fond of the violin at first, he continued to play the stringed instrument throughout his life, and it became one of many things that made Einstein unique. Music and mathematics share many common elements, and Einstein undoubtedly found the same love in both. While he played largely for relaxation and not explicitly for study, it is no coincidence that music remained an important part of Einstein's life.

Some contend, in fact, that the theory of relativity would never have been arrived upon had it not been for Einstein's love of the violin. His intense desire to understand formula and theory transitioned from music to science. More than that, though, it's possible that using music as an outlet for his scientific exploration allowed Einstein to see science in an entirely new light, and this advantage may have given him insight that could have come from no other source.

Mathematics and music are inextricably linked. From the number of notes in an octave to the number of notes in a chord, math creates an order and definition for many aspects of musical theory and performance.

The Importance of Family

Einstein's family clearly played a large role in encouraging his curiosity and natural gifts, even from a young age. His immediate and extended families were reasonably well off, and were able to provide him with books and other objects that allowed him to advance his studies. While his father's income came and went, his grandparents and other relatives were able to help out enough that Einstein never had to suffer. This fact alone is significant in that Einstein had the luxury of being able to focus on intellectual pursuits as a child, rather than having to fight for mere survival.

His family was also emotionally supportive. Both his parents were educated, and they valued the education of their children. They provided a stimulating environment, one in which Einstein thrived. Homework never went unfinished. His parent's marriage was a happy one, and marital discontent doesn't appear to have been a distraction for Einstein either. Lack of major life issues probably gave Einstein much more freedom to develop intellectually than he might have had under different circumstances.

Both intelligence and aptitude for science ran in the family. His brother Jakob ran an engineering company, Einstein & Cie. His father was an electrician as well as an amateur electrical inventor. He actually established an electrotechnical factory in Munich soon after Albert was born, but he didn't have the best luck with business ventures. His mother was a homemaker and a musician.

Above all, Einstein the child was curious. He asked questions and sought answers. He was patient and determined, sticking with a problem until his curiosity was satisfied.

The School Years

When he reached school age, Einstein proved to be a gifted student. He first began public education at age six, in 1885, though he was given private tutoring a year earlier to help him get ready for school. German schools at the time were not geared toward a Jewish education or Jewish children, but Einstein excelled regardless, again showing his determination and ability to self-motivate. He did some amount of self-teaching as well; science and math classes were minimal in his early school years, but Einstein spent time outside of school teaching himself physics and math.

Einstein's Early Education

When he was nine years old, Einstein transferred to the Luitpold-Gymnasium, another school in Munich. His best subjects were said to be math and languages, particularly Latin. He was reputed to revel in his studies, but was less fond of the structure and apparently arbitrary discipline at this strict German school. He had difficulties in getting along with the form-master there, and he ended up never graduating. Einstein left the school in 1894 without a degree.

Incorporating Humanities into Einstein's Coursework

By the time he was eleven years old, Einstein was reading philosophy and religion, in addition to his regular school courses. Laying the foundation for later struggles, he was already starting to think about the dichotomy between science and religion, creationism versus evolution.

The religious atmosphere in the Einstein home also contributed to the ways in which Albert would come to formulate his theories later in life. His parents were nonobservant Jews, meaning they were Jewish but did not observe all the rituals and ceremonies of the religion. They did not keep a kosher household, nor did they attend synagogue services regularly. They did, however, respect Judaism, and they instilled that same respect for religion in their children.

First Breakthrough: Proving the Pythagorean Theorem

Also at age eleven, Einstein first read the Pythagorean theorem, the study of which would eventually influence Einstein's later work. Pythagoras was a Greek mathematician who lived between 569 and 475 B.C. He is sometimes called the "first mathematician," meaning he was one of the first scientists on record as having made important contributions to the field of mathematics. The child of merchants, Pythagoras spent much of his childhood traveling, and he was able to study from famous instructors in Syria and Italy, as well as his native Samos.

Background on Pythagoras

Pythagoras was a student of mathematics, learning from some of the most capable Greek teachers. He was more than just a mathematician, though—he also studied and worked with religion and philosophy. He was also a musician; he played the lyre, an instrument bearing notable similarity to the violin. His multiple areas of study may have piqued Einstein's interest and desire for emulation, since Einstein himself went on to become a student in many different areas.

Pythagoras founded a society whose purpose was to study mathematics; his group was called the Brotherhood of Pythagoreans. Composed largely of mathematicians, this school was also devoted to the studies of religion and philosophy. This group may have even inspired Einstein's later formation of his own discussion society.

The Theorem

The ancient Greek mathematician's best-known contribution was the Pythagorean theorem. What is this theorem exactly? It's the idea that the sum of the squares of the sides of a right triangle is equal to the square of the hypotenuse. Although this concept had been known since Chinese and Egyptian times, Pythagoras was one of the first to prove it.

FACT

Einstein became obsessed with the Pythagorean theorem and was able to arrive at a proof after several weeks of work. Pretty amazing for a college student, let alone an eleven-year-old boy! His determination in this endeavor was matched solely by his innate abilities with math and logic.

Pythagoras was one of the first scientists to study acoustics, or the science of the transmission and reflection of sound waves. Pythagoras used stretched strings to describe sound waves in terms of what would come to be musical terminology. He created stretched strings with movable bridges, the basis for the modern-day violin, and showed how the sound would change when the string was plucked at different points along the string. Einstein's lifelong connection with the violin may have been influenced by Pythagoras in that, from a very young age, he saw the connection between science and music.

The Impact of Euclid

Einstein's second formal introduction to mathematics came at age twelve, when he first marveled at Euclidian geometry. Euclid was a mathematician who lived between 325 and 265 B.C., some 250 years after Pythagoras. He wrote a treatise on mathematics called *The Elements,* and the fact that this work is still known today suggests that Euclid was one of the Greek world's most famous math teachers.

Background on Euclid

Euclid's main practical contribution to the field of mathematics came from the basic definitions he created in the course of his work. "Euclidian geometry" is the study or theory of points, lines, and angles that lie on or in a flat surface. Such geometry is, in a nutshell, flat. Any elements along a curved surface are considered "non-Euclidian."

The Elements both defined mathematical terms and created what have come to be known as the Five Postulates. What is a postulate? It's something that is claimed to be true. In this case, Euclid's postulates can be considered as ground rules for understanding math. The first postulate states that a straight line can be drawn between any two points. The second postulate purports that any straight line can be extended indefinitely. The third postulate says that any straight line can be used as the radius for a circle. The fourth postulate states that all right angles are congruent.

The Parallel Postulate

The parallel, or fifth, postulate says that for every line and point that is not on that line, there is another, unique, nonintersecting line that passes through that point. Euclidian geometry is in a language of straight (flat) lines, so it satisfies this postulate. While this idea may seem obvious, it is important to note that Euclid was, in a way, honest in his thinking and work. He formulated a sound basis for individual, small-scale ideas from which larger postulates and theories would later grow. This aspect of Euclid's stylistic approach to mathematics surely influenced Einstein's later approach to his own work.

What impressed Einstein most about Euclidian geometry was that it was possible to use lines and angles to prove concepts that were not immediately apparent; this aspect of mathematics laid the foundation for Einstein. All of a sudden, he understood that it was possible to come up with an idea that had not yet been proven and to create a system whereby that idea could become fact. Rules and games could be created by the same player; truly innovative scientific thought was possible.

Euclid was perhaps a role model for Einstein in other ways as well. He was a teacher, which may have influenced Einstein's later forays into education. He was a brilliant scientist who was not shy of sharing his ideas and thoughts with those around him, and this aspect of Euclid's personality may have subtly helped Einstein overcome some of his earlier shyness. Euclid put forth his ideas for discussion even when he was not entirely convinced of their merit; his fifth postulate, for example, could never be proven as a theorem, but Euclid included it in his book nonetheless. Einstein may have learned by example that taking a chance, being a bit daring, was perhaps the best way to draw attention and commentary.

Einstein's Study of Philosophy

When he was thirteen, Einstein spent much time and energy with philosophy, particularly the works of Immanuel Kant. Kant was a philosopher who lived from 1724 to 1804. He was born in Konigsberg, East Prussia, which today is part of Russia.

Unlike Einstein, Kant was raised and schooled with the religious tenets of Pietism, an offshoot of Christianity with heavy evangelical roots. Studying the Bible and attending devotionals were important aspects of this religion. Kant's father was a saddle maker and his mother was unemployed, so Kant was the first in his immediate family to attend university.

Kant spent all of his life cloistered in his small town. He never left the city, let alone the country. He never married, and left his house only to go to his university and take a daily walk. Like most of Einstein's intellectual mentors, Kant was a teacher; he taught a range of courses in both mathematics and logic at the University at Konigsberg.

Key Elements of Kant's Theories

Kant published his first work, *Thoughts on the True Estimation of Living Forces,* at the age of twenty-two. One of Kant's main theories was that the basic, underlying foundations for mathematics and science could be known "a priori"—by intuition, not experience. Reason was, for Kant, insufficient in establishing the laws upon which the universe rested. A certain amount of trust or faith in human intuition was mandatory. People, then, were at least as important as fact in interpreting the world everyone inhabits. Kant's ideas were consistent with the European Enlightenment, a movement that was going on during Kant's lifetime throughout Europe.

These aspects of Kant's philosophy were shown by another of his most important beliefs. He wrote about how representation made the existence of an object possible; it was not, for Kant, that the object itself made representation possible. For example, an apple wouldn't exist if there were no way to see or describe it. This view differed from that of other philosophers in that Kant's contemporaries might have said that it was the apple itself that made seeing or describing it possible. Kant's basic philosophy focused on the idea that human contribution was essential to understanding.

The Categorical Imperative

Another of Kant's major contributions to philosophy came in the area of ethics. He had a theory known as the categorical imperative, an idea that morality depended on one single command (an imperative is a command). In other words, morality was absolute. This maxim can be interpreted as saying, act as if everything you do comes from and creates a universal truth. Kant's view is opposite to a contemporary notion called the hypothetical imperative, which stated that morality is conditional. "If your foot hurts when you kick the wall, stop kicking the wall" is an example of a hypothetical imperative.

QUESTION?

What's the difference between the categorical and hypothetical imperatives?
The categorical imperative refers to an absolute state (something is either good, or it isn't), whereas a hypothetical imperative is not absolute (there's a condition according to which something is either good, or it isn't).

Kant published one of his best-known works, *The Critique of Pure Reason*, in 1781. In this work he describes the notion of "a priori" knowledge that doesn't come from experience. He also explores how philosophy should use science and math to try and figure out how much knowledge can come from intuition alone, and how much requires experience.

Einstein studied *The Critique of Pure Reason* extensively. So how might Kant's ideas have influenced Einstein's early thinking? Much of Kant's philosophy is based on its relationship with mathematics and physics, subjects of clear interest to Einstein. However, Kant's theories of intuition implied, to some extent, that much of the world was just an illusion, and not something proven by hard scientific fact. The world only existed, for Kant, because living creatures were there to represent it. Einstein would take issue with much of this aspect of Kant's philosophy.

Kant adamantly declared that the universe was infinite. Einstein, on the other hand, would prove just the opposite—that the universe is finite. In fact, Einstein's theory of relativity would overthrow much of Kant's theory about the extent and creation of the universe.

Einstein's Childhood Legacy

Concerning Einstein's early childhood, the question remains: Was he a child genius, or "merely" a prodigy? It seems clear that he was an exceptional child, performing tasks far beyond his age. His interests went beyond his years as well, and he was always looking for the next goal. His determination and patience let him achieve things that wouldn't have been possible for someone without these characteristics. Curiosity and patience are a great combination, and they certainly served him well.

Einstein himself, however, said that he hadn't been born with any special gift. He was intelligent and determined, and those two qualities certainly allowed him to achieve remarkable goals. There is no way to know if his natural abilities alone would have merited a genius tag, but given what he accomplished, does it matter? Einstein's life work determines the basis for his legacy, not a label, and what he accomplished with his research far exceeds what any title could ever provide.

Chapter 3

Scientific and Cultural Background of Einstein's Time

In order to fully digest Einstein's theories and research, it's useful to have a basic understanding of the general state of science during the time leading up to Einstein's seminal papers. Many key scientists played a role in setting the stage for Einstein. Their work created a basis from which Einstein and relativity would build.

General Nineteenth-Century Views of Science

The period before Einstein began his work, the mid- to late-1800s, was ripe with scientific invention and discovery. Medicine, mechanics, chemistry, biology, and a range of other fields all benefited from a series of "firsts." What a century of discovery!

Some of the many advances of the mid-nineteenth century include the first anesthetized surgery in 1846; Henry Bessemer's 1854 invention of the first process for mass-producing steel; and Charles Darwin's theory of evolution in 1859. The law of chemical equilibrium was established in 1864; the first "modern" telephone was invented around 1877; and photographic film was produced in 1885. By 1895, the first moving picture had been created.

Major scientists, both before and during the nineteenth century, were of paramount importance in determining how twentieth-century science would be established. Einstein relied heavily on the advances made by his predecessors, and Chapter 9 details the influence his contemporaries had on his research. Some of the most important scientific research of this period was developed by Isaac Newton, Michael Faraday, James Maxwell, and Ernst Mach.

Newton's Laws of Mechanics

Isaac Newton (1642–1727) is best known for his three laws of motion. These principles would create the primary background for later work in physics and mechanics, and they certainly gave Einstein the starting point he needed to conceptualize relativity. So what were these laws, and what did they mean?

Newton's laws stated:

- **Newton's first law**—an object in motion tends to stay in motion.
- **Newton's second law**—the force applied to an object is equal to the object's mass multiplied by its acceleration.
- **Newton's third law**—every action has an equal and opposite reaction.

Newton's First Law

Newton's first law states that if an object is traveling at a constant speed in a straight line, it will continue to do so unless it's acted upon—pushed, pulled, or otherwise influenced. Suppose someone rolled a ball down the street. Does that mean that the ball should keep rolling forever? No, of course not—experience tells us that the ball will run into sticks, rocks, gravel or other impediments that will make it stray from its course. Suppose the ball is instead rolled down a smooth surface, like a bowling alley—would it keep rolling forever? Again, the answer would be no—any force, no matter how undetectable by a human observer, will slow the ball down. These forces would include friction from the floor (even a smooth floor would offer some friction) and air resistance.

So when would this part of Newton's first law apply? It's a theoretical proof, meaning it is true in theory. If the ball were in a vacuum with no outside forces, once set into motion it would keep going forever. This idea also suggests the converse—if an object is at rest, it will stay at rest unless it's acted upon by a force. A ball outside that's not rolling (just lying still) would eventually be moved by wind, or perhaps a slight slant to the road. In "perfect" conditions, though, the ball would remain motionless until something happened to change its condition.

FACT

Newton's main body of work was published in his *Philosophiae naturalis principia mathematica* of 1867, often called the *Principia*. This work showed Newton's idea of motion and gravitation applied to both objects on Earth and to the celestial bodies.

Newton's Second Law

Newton's second law of motion says that when an object is acted upon by a force, the object will accelerate in the direction of that force. If a ball is kicked, it will tend to travel in the direction that it was kicked. Seems obvious, doesn't it? Such ideas are known by children worldwide, but Newton was the first to codify them in terms of mathematical relationships between objects and forces.

Newton also stated in his second law that the amount an object accelerates is directly proportional to the force exerted on it. The harder someone kicks a ball, the faster it will travel. A corollary of this theory is that the acceleration of an object is inversely proportional to the object's mass. This idea means that a heavy ball would need to be kicked much harder than a light ball if they were to travel at the same speed. Again, these ideas all make intuitive sense. Someone would have to work much harder to kick a basketball, for example, than a beach ball, because, although the objects are roughly the same size, the basketball is much heavier.

Newton's Third Law

Newton's third law states that for every force, there is an equal and opposite force. Under this logic, everything offers a resistance. When someone kicks a ball, does that mean the ball kicks back? Not exactly. The ball is not a willing participant in being kicked—it would rather just stay still, according to Newton's first law. However, the ball does offer some resistance to being kicked—which is why someone has to work in the first place in order to kick the ball!

Classical Physics

Newton's laws, together with his theory of gravity and other ideas about space and time (discussed in more detail in Chapters 6 and 10), provided the foundation for what would come to be a classical description of physics and mechanics. Newton liked to sum up the world as definitive, and his laws of motion were a tribute to defining the complexity of the universe in absolute terms. However, as the means to measure and quantify became more and more developed in the nineteenth century, Newton's theories of space and time started to seem increasingly inconsistent. Einstein and relativity would eventually wreak havoc with Newton's conceptual framework.

The history of science is one where a series of giants stand on each other's shoulders to achieve greatness. Newton formulated the basics of motion and gravity; Coulomb's work with electromagnetism preceded Faraday, whose work let Maxwell arrive at his conclusions. Einstein then built off Maxwell's ideas to formulate relativity. Talk about a chain of intelligence!

Early Studies of Electricity

The history of electricity is a long one. Greek scientists discovered around 600 B.C. that certain materials, such as amber, could produce strange effects when rubbed together. Experiments in electricity and magnetism were made over the years, and electric properties started to be formally codified around A.D. 1600. The seventeenth century held many advances in electricity, one of the most significant coming from Charles Du Fay—he was the first to distinguish between positive and negative charges.

Burgeoning Changes

Eighteenth-century advances in electricity were enormous. The year 1729 marked Stephen Gray's discovery of electrical conduction. Forces between charges were studied, and advances were made by Joseph Priestley and Charles Augustin de Coulomb. Toward the end of the century, Alessandro Volta created the first electric battery.

Charles Coulomb (1736–1806) was a French physicist who came up with a system for allowing electric fields to be calculated. His formula, which describes how much electrical force is due to positive and negative charges, would later be codified as Coulomb's law.

Nineteenth-Century Research

In the nineteenth century, some of the most significant advances in electricity were made by Michael Faraday (1791–1867). As a child, Faraday began experimenting with electricity; he also studied chemistry and other sciences. In 1821, he discovered what would become the field of electromagnetism—as the name suggests, this is the theory of how electricity relates to magnetism. Part of the theory of electromagnetism proved that visible light belonged to a much larger spectrum of electromagnetic (EM) radiation. This spectrum included all types of waves, including radio waves and X rays.

QUESTION?

Where do X rays fall on the electromagnetic spectrum?
Electromagnetic radiation includes visible light, waves that are longer (such as microwaves and radio waves), and waves with shorter wavelengths, such as ultraviolet, X rays, and gamma rays. X rays are shorter than visible light, but longer than gamma rays.

Faraday built the first electric motor during this period. His device involved a coiled wire, which carried an electrical current, wrapped around a magnetic pole. He was able to produce motion using this scheme. The 1830s marked the period in which Faraday would unveil the means by which electromagnetic induction worked. Electric current could be induced through the motion of the magnet; this new method for generating electricity would change the way power stations worldwide operated. Faraday's research set the backdrop for James Maxwell, whose work Einstein would later refute.

James Maxwell and His Equations

James Maxwell (1831–1879) was a Scottish physicist and mathematician. He was rumored to have been an inquisitive child, always looking for the causes of natural wonders. He was generating mathematical equations for geometric shapes by the time he was fourteen, and he studied the writings of Newton extensively.

Maxwell continued Faraday's work in the definition of electromagnetism. In 1856, he actually published a paper entitled "On Faraday's Lines of Force." In this paper he applied mathematics (never Faraday's strong suit) to some of Faraday's theories. Maxwell's major contribution to Faraday's work was the idea that at the core of electromagnetism is the concept of the electromagnetic field.

There were, Maxwell posited, two main types of electromagnetic fields: stationary and changing. A static field was one where the field itself remained bound to its origin; an example would be the type of magnetic field generated around a wire conducting electrical current. The other type of electromagnetic field would be a changing field, where the field takes on a wave motion as it propagates. Radio waves, gamma rays, X rays, and microwaves are all examples of changing electromagnetic fields, whose waves travel at the speed of light.

One of Maxwell's most significant contributions to science was the idea that light, electricity, and magnetism were fundamentally just different manifestations of related concepts. Maxwell codified his thinking with "Maxwell's equations," four major ways of describing the way electricity and magnetism relate to each other. These equations are actually partial differential equations, and they describe the complex interdependencies between charges, density, and the electric field. These equations are inherently very complex and difficult to understand; the important part, though, is knowing that they are what describe electromagnetism.

Maxwell's equations are as follows (expressed in macroscopic, differential form, standard MKS units):

- Charge density and the electric field: $\nabla \cdot D = \rho$
- Structure of the magnetic field: $\nabla \cdot B = 0$
- A changing magnetic field and the electric field: $\nabla \times E = -\partial B / \partial t$
- Source of the magnetic field: $\nabla \times H = J + \partial D / \partial t$

H = magnetic field strength	B = magnetic flux
J = current density	t = time
ρ = electrical charge density	∇ = del (a mathematical function
D = electric displacement field	made up of partial derivatives)
E = electrical field	

Inconsistencies in Maxwell's equations led to the eventual formation of Einstein's theories. By all accounts, electromagnetism as defined by Maxwell would become a precursor to relativity. However, there were some fundamental aspects of Maxwell's theory with which Einstein later took issue. One of the major issues was that Maxwell, in his description of light as a wave, ended up with a precise speed at which light traveled. Absolute numbers were certainly appealing, especially in a new field that was constantly being questioned! Einstein would raise the important issue of how this speed was being defined (that is, with respect to what?), and his concept of relativity would spring from this basic discrepancy.

Ernst Mach (1838–1916)

Another essential contributor to the general state of nineteenth-century science was Ernst Mach. His philosophy and science laid important groundwork in providing Einstein a framework within which relativity could be created. Mach was an Austrian scientist who belonged to the school of positivism, a philosophy that posited the idea that objects could be understood by their sensation as well as their physicality.

This idea impacted Einstein greatly. It implied that time and space were not absolute notions, and in this sense Mach went directly against the going ideas at the time. Mach's rejection of Newtonian concepts of time and space gave a background for Einstein's later suggestion that space and time were not absolute.

FACT

Mach is also known for the Mach number (*Ma*), which is given as the ratio of an object's speed (μ) to the speed of sound (μ_s). So, $Ma = \mu/\mu_s$. This principle helped Mach study shock waves.

Mach also worked extensively in the area of wave dynamics and optics. His early research particularly contributed to the growing field of acoustics. He combined these areas of interest by studying the Doppler effect. This was a concept first solidified in 1845 by Christian Doppler.

It is the idea that, to a stationary observer, waves appear to change in frequency (or wavelength) if they are emitted by something moving. This phenomenon is best explained by the way a train whistle, for example, will appear to change in pitch as the train approaches, then rushes past someone standing still. Mach was always interested in the senses, both in terms of physics and perception. He also studied what would be more futuristic principles, such as supersonic speed!

Another part of Mach's research involved the creation of a theory of inertia. The basic idea behind inertia followed Newtonian principles; bodies at rest tend to stay at rest unless they are acted upon by a discrete force. Mach contributed a different view of inertia in which only relative motion, rather than absolute motion, was important. Einstein would later coin an expression, "Mach's principle," that referred to Mach's idea that the inertia of one body was related to all other bodies in the universe. These ideas came into play in a major way for Einstein and his study of relativity, especially in his development of relative frames of reference with no absolute rest frame.

ALERT!

The history of science, unlike some of Newton's theories, never takes place in a vacuum. New inventions in one area might influence the development of other technologies or ideas in completely different fields. Even seemingly unrelated ideas often have more to do with each other than one might think.

New Forms of Transportation

The first part of the twentieth century was filled with invention, and not just in science. Many aspects of modern society were being formed, and the period was ripe with creation and innovation. The twentieth century was a grand time to be an inventor, in no small part because advances in science and technology provided for the existence of innovation in other areas. Some of the major innovations of this period (which would be relevant to everyone of the time, including Einstein) included the automobile, the airplane, the radio and phonograph, and jazz music.

The Automobile

The history of the automobile is more complicated than one might expect. Contrary to popular belief, Henry Ford didn't invent the automobile. In fact, Renaissance artists such as Leonardo da Vinci came up with designs for motorized vehicles, although such designs would not be executed for hundreds of years. The first steam-powered vehicle was developed by Nicolas Cugnot in 1769; it had to stop to build up power every few minutes, though, and as such was not very efficient.

The first gas-powered cars came about toward the end of the nineteenth century. In 1885, Gottlieb Daimler invented the precursor to the modern gasoline engine. Scientific developments led to the refinement of the internal combustion engine, which became the primary force behind the creation of the modern motorcar. The first patent for a gasoline-powered automobile was given to Karl Benz in 1886. While a variety of attempts at the automobile were constructed as one-off ventures, it was the assembly line that truly allowed for mass production of cars.

QUESTION?

Where did the word "automobile" come from?
The word actually came from a fourteenth-century artist, Martini, who developed a design for a man-powered vehicle. The word comes from the Latin roots *auto* (meaning "self") and *mobils* (meaning "movement").

What was the big deal about mass production? Everything! Mass production was incredibly important for the automobile to take off as a viable invention for two main reasons. It meant cars were suddenly available to many more people, and increased efficiency in automobile production would bring the cost down considerably (making them accessible financially). The curved dash Oldsmobile was the first car to be mass-produced using an assembly line in 1901, although Henry Ford dramatically improved the concept of the assembly line in 1913. Ford's Model T of 1909, while not the first automobile, was one of the first to be successfully mass-produced. These innovations in automobile design and production were roughly contemporary with Einstein's development of the theory of special relativity.

The Airplane

When people had to travel across the ocean prior to the twentieth century, such excursions were done by boat. It was either that, or swim. However, late-nineteenth-century innovation would lead to the development of an entirely new way to travel—the airplane. The late 1890s was a period in which a number of inventors were trying their hand at developing flying machines. Otto Lilienthal's hang glider experiments, for example, served as a major predecessor to the airplane.

The first major successful airplane innovation, though, would come at the hands of two Americans, the Wright brothers. Orville and Wilbur Wright were the developers of the first manned airplane. They were actually trained as bicycle builders, and they owned a bicycle repair shop before turning to aviation. After years of study and testing, in 1903, they successfully flew their first heavier-than-air craft in Kitty Hawk, North Carolina. They didn't start out building complete airplanes, of course—first they built a kite, followed by several gliders. The momentous flight in Kitty Hawk was the first of its kind—it was sustained, powered, and controlled. Wilbur Wright would go on to make several public exhibition flights in France in 1908.

The development of the airplane represented a complete turning point, historically. Not only could people suddenly travel to places that had been previously unreachable, they could do so relatively quickly. Commerce enjoyed entirely new boundaries as well, making it possible to sell goods in places previously unthinkable. The airplane would also have political ramifications; it would change the way wars were fought. The bombing of Hiroshima, for example (in which Einstein had a minimal role, see Chapter 15 for more information) couldn't have been conceived, let along carried out, if not for the advent of air travel.

Innovation in Sound

The invention of the radio closely paralleled the technology that made possible other new inventions, such as the telephone and telegraph. James Maxwell actually predicted that the transmission of radio waves would be forthcoming—and how right he was! An Italian inventor named

Guglielmo Marconi sent and received the first radio signals in 1895, and the first transatlantic radiotelegraph message was sent in 1902.

The Radio

Technically speaking, of course, Marconi did not invent the radio wave. What he created was a means to manipulate and transmit radio frequencies. He was not the first person to work with radio waves, either. Faraday's theory of electrical inductance was actually the beginning of the research that would eventually allow radio waves to be directly manipulated. Heinrich Hertz demonstrated electromagnetic waves of energy in 1887. In 1892, Edouard Branley developed the first electromagnetic wave receiver. Marconi followed this invention in 1895 with the first complete wireless system.

Many different inventors claimed to have invented the radio. Nikolai Tesla invented the theoretical model that would become the basis for most future inventions in this area. Guglielmo Marconi received an English patent for his design, but it was J.C. Bose, an Indian scientist, who obtained the first U.S. radio patent in 1904.

Radio would transform the way people received information. The Russo-Japanese war of 1905 was the first whose news was reported via wireless radio transmissions, and by 1906 weather reports were being sent via radio. News could be transmitted more immediately now than ever before, and decisions could be made with unprecedented timeliness. Lines of radio transmission between America and Europe were opened in 1910. Radio would prove to be an especially useful communications tool during World War I and World War II. This new media world, of course, also became very important in propagating news of the latest scientific breakthroughs, such as those belonging to Einstein and others.

The Phonograph

The development of the first system to record and replay sounds represented another scientific breakthrough. In 1859, Leon Scott developed a device in which sound waves were recorded onto a rotating cylinder. Thomas Edison designed and built a more sophisticated device in 1877 that recorded sounds and played them back onto plates consisting of rotating foil. In 1893 Emile Berliner developed the gramophone, a machine that used hard rubber disks instead of cylinders.

Companies were starting to sprout up around the burgeoning phonograph business, providing another example of technology spurring commerce. In 1901, Eldridge Johnson founded the Victor Talking Machine Company. Virtually all early phonographs displayed a large, somewhat unsightly horn that emitted the audio. Later versions, such as the company's signature Victrola model, let the horn fold down into a cabinet case and provide increased convenience. Many new and lower-priced models became available in the coming years, and technological advances continued up to and during the years of World War I.

Jazz

In addition to a myriad of technological and scientific inventions, the turn of the century also gave rise to what would become one of the world's most popular music styles—jazz. Born in New Orleans around 1895, jazz combined elements from previously established musical styles, including blues and ragtime. Jazz broke from the previous Western musical traditions in that it was largely improvisational; strict scripts weren't always adhered to, and the individual musician played a big part in performing jazz. Some of the most famous jazz musicians included Joe "King" Oliver, Jelly Roll Morton, and Louis Armstrong.

Scientific invention also played a role in jazz! The development of the phonograph, along with the entire recording industry, actually contributed greatly to the rapid rise to fame of jazz music. The first jazz album was recorded in 1917, allowing the music to be propagated throughout the country (and eventually the world). It was a symbiotic relationship. Recording spurred the music, and the music in turn carried the recording industry to new heights and innovation. Jazz music gained popularity in other cities like St. Louis and Chicago, and recordings that could be heard and imitated around the country sparked a revolution.

All of these technological and scientific inventions combined to form the backdrop for Einstein's work. These years were full of innovation in virtually every field. The twentieth century was coming to light, and Einstein's work was much celebrated as part of this coming-of-age of the modern world. Ⓔ

Chapter 4

Education and Later Life

The early period of Einstein's life provides a fascinating insight into what factors helped shape Einstein's later career. The next period, the years beginning with his university experience, are equally important. Einstein matured both intellectually and personally in this period. Though he faced many challenging experiences, this time of his life was critical in forming the basis for his future ideas and research.

The Move to Italy

After leaving the Munich Luitpold-Gymnasium in 1894 without having finished his degree, Einstein moved to Milan, Italy, and joined his family there. His father's business in Germany had failed in 1890, and he was offered the chance to set up a factory in Pavia (a town near Milan). At this point, in 1890, the rest of his family moved to Italy, but Einstein initially remained behind in Germany to finish his schooling for several more years.

Dissatisfaction with the German Educational System

Since the family house had been sold, Einstein moved in with relatives for the duration of his stay in Germany, but he was apparently unhappy about his prospects there. He became depressed and got along even worse with his school instructors than he had before. The German educational system was strict, and Einstein was forced to stay within the German organization at that time. In addition, participation in the German military was required at this time, making it all the more difficult for Einstein to attempt to leave the country.

Even at this age, Einstein was already showing an independence of both body and spirit. He wanted to move to Italy with the rest of his family, so it's rumored that he pretended to throw "fits" to have himself declared of ill health. He got a certificate from his family doctor stating that he was officially unhealthy and shouldn't return to school until he improved. He was thus permitted to travel on to Italy to be with the rest of his family.

Einstein was bright and cunning enough to have himself declared unfit to return to school. He would later use these same skills to his advantage, when he used the same tactic to avoid military service.

ETH: First Attempt

Einstein thought that he might be interested in a career in electrical engineering, like his father and brother. Despite his not having finished the German equivalent of high school, he decided to take the entrance exams to the prestigious Eidgenössische Technische Hochschule (abbreviated ETH; also known as the Swiss Federal Polytechnic Institute) in 1895 in Zurich, Switzerland. This was the most famous school of its kind, and to Einstein it represented the best in academia. However, he wasn't accepted due to poor performance on some parts of the admission exam. While he did fine on the technical and science section, he actually failed the arts and French sections! Though his French entrance essay was supposedly quite good, it was apparently not up to the standards of the Swiss instructors.

FACT

It's somewhat ironic that Einstein failed the French part of his ETH entrance exam. An essay he wrote for a French class in 1895 described what would come to be his future as a scientific researcher!

The ETH earned its reputation quickly. It was founded by the Swiss government in 1854 as a polytechnical school, accepting its first class of incoming students in 1855. The school was (and still is) divided between teaching and research; faculty members do both, and students had access to research facilities on campus. The ETH was definitely a one-of-a-kind institution. It actually remained the only national university in Switzerland until the 1960s. Today, the university is expanded and consists of two campuses—one in Zurich and one in Lausanne.

After failing to get in the first time, Einstein decided to attend an intermediary secondary school in Aarau, Switzerland, instead. He worked on the areas in which he'd done the poorest and was determined to gain admission to the ETH. He earned a diploma in Aarau after a year, and decided to try again for his prestigious school.

ETH: Second (Successful) Attempt

He reapplied to the ETH and, this time, was admitted in 1896. At that time, he studied to be a physics and math teacher. He graduated in 1900 at the age of twenty-one with degrees in both his primary areas of interest. Einstein loved physics and mathematics, but he was starting to realize that he would never be an outstanding overall student because he liked spending so much time in the lab. He preferred hands-on research to studying in the library, a characteristic that would stay with him throughout his life.

Achieving His Educational Goals

Einstein's years at the ETH were critical to his academic development. He was finally challenged at a high enough level that he pushed his own thinking beyond what he'd thought possible. Resources were plentiful, and, probably for the first time, he could engage in intellectual discussion with other scientists at or above his own level. It was here that Einstein first began to study the effects of bodies in motion. These studies and experiments would eventually lead him to the theory of relativity. Although he was still far from reaching his ultimate goal, his years at the ETH gave him the tools to begin down the path.

It was also during these years that Einstein studied Maxwell's theories. James Maxwell (1831–1879) was a mathematician best known for developing the kinetic theory of gases and the electromagnetic theory of light. Maxwell also created four partial differential equations, known as Maxwell's equations. They basically describe electricity, magnetism, and light in terms of the same fundamental rules that govern much of real-world math and physics. These equations, discussed in more detail in Chapter 3, were first published in *Electricity and Magnetism* in 1873, and would eventually form the basis for much physics research that came later.

The Impact of Michele Besso

While studying at the ETH, a classmate named Michele Besso presented Einstein with the writings of Ernst Mach (1838–1916). Mach was an Austrian philosopher and physicist who worked in the areas of optics, wave dynamics, and mechanics. Mach was a proponent of the school of positivism, a major philosophical idea in Europe during his lifetime. The theory basically said that knowledge was sensation—all objects were understood by their sensations.

His influence on Einstein was that Mach's theories got to the very root of all the assumptions on which physics was based. In as much as his theory relied on sensation, Mach rejected the notion that space and time were absolute. In a way, he helped pave the path for Einstein's theory of relativity. Mach developed theories of inertia—that a body at rest tends to stay at rest unless otherwise disturbed, and a body in motion tends to stay in motion—and Einstein credited these ideas as one of the primary sources of inspiration for relativity.

Perhaps even more important than the general knowledge Einstein acquired at the ETH, his polytechnical schooling gave Einstein the ability to come up with ideas about electrodynamics and then to design experiments that would prove his theories. An unproven idea doesn't carry the same weight that a proven theory does, and Einstein recognized this fact. At the ETH he learned how to substantiate his own research, an incredibly important skill for a scientist. The work he began at the ETH in electrodynamics would stay with him through his first papers on relativity, and it's probably fair to say that the course of his life wouldn't have been the same without this education.

Think the best students are the ones who go to class every single day? Think again! Einstein routinely skipped classes, although he caught up using a friend's notes.

Because of his interest in laboratory science, though, Einstein didn't attend all his classes. He relied on friends for assistance with class notes, particularly before exams. One of his good friends was a young man named Marcel Grossmann. Grossmann would come to play an important role in Einstein's life. He would later help Einstein with some of the mathematical theory behind relativity, and Grossmann's father actually helped Einstein get his first job.

First Renouncement of German Citizenship

In 1896, Einstein gave up his German citizenship; in 1901 he became a Swiss citizen. It was customary for Swiss male citizens to join the military and provide service, but Einstein was able to avoid this requirement. He claimed he had both flat feet and varicose veins, and he never had to serve in the army. Since he was no longer officially a German citizen, he didn't have to serve in their army either. Einstein's intelligence paid off in more ways than one. Pacifism was a hallmark of Einstein's later life, and some of its roots are seen in this earlier period.

Einstein in Love

The year 1898 marked the first time that Einstein succumbed to something other than science—love. He met and was enchanted by a Hungarian classmate at the ETH named Mileva Maric (1875–1948).

To some extent, it was sheer fortune that allowed Einstein and Mileva to meet. While women were admitted into the ETH, they were still second-class citizens in many regards—they were not even allowed to vote at this time. Had Einstein attended another school, or had the ETH been less liberal in its dealings with women, this union might never have happened. Even with this relatively newfound liberalism, Mileva was the only woman in her class at the ETH, so her meeting with Einstein was, to some extent, unavoidable. In fact, Mileva was the only female student in physics during Einstein's entire time at the ETH.

FACT

Einstein's first wife, Mileva Maric, was the first female student in the physics department at the ETH. Not only the first—she was the only female student there! Today, the ETH actively tries to promote the role of women in science and technology.

A Relationship of Understanding

It seems natural that Einstein would fall for a scientist—someone with whom he could exchange intellectual ideas. More important, perhaps, was that Mileva was someone who understood Einstein because they shared the same interests, academically and otherwise. She was one of the brightest students at the ETH, considered by many to be a brilliant physicist. She kept pace with Einstein throughout their school years, taking most of the same courses as he.

Shortly after meeting, Einstein and Mileva moved in together. Legend has it that they shared everything, including class notes and textbooks. They were supposedly quite compatible in most aspects of life. Mileva took on some of the stereotypical female roles of a wife even from this early period, performing most of the cooking and cleaning. She did the laundry for the couple, dealt with the finances, and often had to remind Einstein to stop working and eat a meal.

Religiously, at least, she had a different background than Einstein. She was raised in the Eastern Orthodox Christian tradition, while Einstein had been raised in an admittedly unobservant Jewish household. She was four years older than Einstein, walked with a limp, and was not known for her beauty. "Bookish" is a term generally used to describe Mileva Maric.

Undergoing Changes

The year 1902 was seminal for Einstein in several respects. It was the year his father, Hermann, died. Einstein would later describe his father's passing as one of the greatest shocks in his life to date. He threw himself into his work, and this renewed energy probably contributed to his major works of 1905. In 1902, he had a paper published in "Annalen der Physik." Publishing papers in major journals is an accomplishment for any scientist, let alone one who had undergone such personal trauma in the same year.

Facing the Odds: Children and Parents

Einstein and Mileva also had their first child in 1902. His parents vehemently opposed the marriage at this time, so their daughter (to be named Lieserl) was considered illegitimate. While no one knows exactly what happened to her, it is generally thought that she was put up for adoption, probably in Serbia.

Very little is known about Lieserl Einstein because she was born out of wedlock at a time when such children were subject to a lifetime of prejudice. While some think she lived to adulthood, most think she either died at birth, or within a few years thereafter.

A Union Facing Opposition

Einstein's parents, particularly his mother, were opposed to their union from the beginning. Perhaps Mileva's Serbian nationality played some role in Einstein's parents' dislike of her. More likely, though, his mother felt threatened by this new woman. Mileva was modern, smart, and Einstein was clearly taken by her. His mother probably felt challenged, as if she were no longer the primary woman in her son's life.

Einstein tried to mollify the situation by spending vacations with his mother and showing her his devotion. Although this tactic may have worked to some extent, it probably didn't help his relationship with Mileva. Einstein and Mileva often spent vacations apart because he would return home to his family, where Mileva was not welcome. This division in the family may have been cause for strife. Einstein had to try to convince Mileva that she was, in fact, the most important woman in his life, but there isn't much evidence for how successful he was.

Einstein's First Marriage

Albert and Mileva were married in 1903. Einstein's mother continued to object strongly to their union, but the couple ultimately could not be deterred. Their first legitimate child was born in 1904, a boy they named Hans. Einstein celebrated the birth of his son, but he was never completely overtaken by fatherly duties.

Supposedly, Einstein was not against the idea of being a father, but he didn't understand children all that well. He thought it would be interesting to have a child and didn't have many options when Mileva became pregnant again. However, especially when his children were infants, Einstein was not a role model for stay-at-home dads. He would often research, write, and discuss science with friends while he was supposed to be taking care of the children, acts which irritated Mileva. On the other hand, sometimes he would set his work aside for hours to play with the children; he seems to have been able to keep personal and professional careers in an acceptable balance, at least at this point in time. Their second child, Eduard, was born in 1910.

The Science of Relationships

Einstein and Mileva's relationship was undoubtedly one of both science and love. While they probably discussed their intellectual goals extensively, they do not appear to have been true partners in research. What seems more likely is that Einstein discussed his developing theories and ideas with Mileva, and her contributions, while perhaps not recognized, surely contributed to Einstein's eventual successes. Not much is known about their professional relationship with each other; her role in Einstein's professional life is generally said to be small, but significant. Mileva certainly was brilliant. The fact that a woman was able in 1900 to gain admission into the ETH at all indicates the extent of her capabilities.

Many love letters between the couple survive, though, indicating that Einstein had a romantic side. Indeed, Einstein showed evidence of an interest in romance even before Mileva. A letter to his mother, written when he was eighteen, indicated that he was frustrated with thwarted love, and that he planned to use science and other intellectual pursuits to lead him through the turmoil of love. Because he wasn't successful with love, he pushed himself even harder with his studies than he might have otherwise. So, in a sense, the world is lucky that Einstein's first girlfriend dumped him.

Intellectual Equals

Love and science had to come together for Einstein. He probably wasn't even capable of loving someone with whom he couldn't hold an intellectual conversation. Einstein often described Mileva as someone who was his equal, both personally and academically. The respect for women that Einstein's mother raised him with probably allowed him to consider his wife as an equal, rather than a possession, a view that would not have been uncommon in Germany of the 1900s. Einstein's mother provided a strong female role model with her musical and artistic abilities, and he was not raised to denigrate or look down upon women.

Their union, while allowing Einstein to prosper intellectually, unfortunately did not do the same for Mileva. She never graduated from the ETH, failing to pass her final exams. This inelegant exit from the ETH undoubtedly did not help her professional career. To her credit, though, women were prejudiced against at the school, and that factor may have played a role in her failure to graduate. In addition, she was eight months pregnant with their second child at the time of her exams. Her Serbian descent might have played a role in failing her exams as well—the teachers at the ETH were no more exempt from prejudice than anyone else at the time, and looming problems in Europe created tensions between countries. Mileva eventually applied for a teaching certificate after they were married, but she never passed the exam and appears to have allowed Einstein's career to dominate hers after this point.

Life Beyond the ETH

Einstein graduated from the ETH in 1900, although with the lowest grade point average in the class. Following graduation, he eventually became a teacher for a brief period, between 1901 and 1902. He applied to become a teacher at the ETH along with several of his classmates (including Marcel Grossmann), but wasn't successful. He eventually got a job teaching math and physics at the Technical High School in Winterthur, and there served as an Aushilfslehrer (assistant lecturer).

First Jobs

He never was able to become a full-time teacher there, though. Part-time work didn't pay well enough, so he had to look for other work as well. He also obtained a temporary teaching job at a school in Schaffhausen. Between these jobs and giving private tutoring sessions,

Einstein was able to earn a living in this way for the next year.

He moved to Bern, Switzerland and formed the "Akademie Olympia" with Conrad Habicht and Maurice Solovine. Solovine was a philosopher. One of the reasons he joined the group was to learn more about physics and other hard sciences. Who better to ask than Einstein? Habicht was a mathematician, and his interests in joining the group were probably similar. Discussions of mathematics, science, and philosophy helped provide Einstein with an early forum for formulating and discussing the ideas that would later become the basis for his theories.

A Little Help from His Friends

Einstein tried to find other jobs but had a difficult time. His university professors knew he skipped many classes, and they refused to write him the recommendations he needed to get a job. In 1902, Einstein was determined to obtain different work. Eventually, his friend Marcel Grossmann's father recommended him to the Swiss patent office, located in Bern, and he was hired as a technical expert, third class. Working as a civil servant may not have been the most exciting career choice, but it paid the bills and left Einstein with plenty of time to do his own research on the side. Einstein did well at this job, and four years later in 1906 was promoted to technical expert, second class. He worked at the patent office from 1902 to 1909, and he actually did some of his most significant early research during these years.

ALERT!

An education from a prestigious university does not always provide a free ticket to a great job. Even Einstein had to start at the bottom and work his way up to where he was respected and trusted, by scholars and the public alike.

In 1905, Einstein finally received his doctorate degree from the University of Zurich. His thesis was called "On a New Determination of Molecular Dimensions." The stage was set for what would come to be some of Einstein's most influential and revolutionary work: the writing of his three major papers in the period beginning in 1905.

Chapter 5

The Photoelectric Effect

The year 1905 is what some historians have called Einstein's *annus mirabilis,* his miracle year. The cliché of the Swiss patent clerk revolutionizing physics is true—while working in the patent office, Einstein published three papers that shook up the scientific community. The first of these three papers was on the photoelectric effect, and this work would eventually earn him the Nobel Prize.

The Photoelectric Effect

Scientists in the nineteenth century knew that when a metal was exposed to light, the surface of the metal absorbed some of the light. The energy of the light, when absorbed by the surface, causes some of the electrons in the metal to become excited. Some of these electrons absorbed enough energy that they were ejected completely from the metal, flying off the surface. This process was called the photoelectric effect.

QUESTION?

What is the photoelectric effect?
The photoelectric effect is the emission of electrons from a metal that is exposed to light. The surface of the metal absorbs enough energy from light that some electrons are freed from their atoms, and they fly off the surface.

Hertz Looks for Waves of Light

Many scientists in the nineteenth century studied the photoelectric effect, including Heinrich Hertz (1857–1894) and Philipp Lenard (1862–1947). Maxwell's theory of electromagnetism, published in 1865, suggested for the first time that light itself was a type of electromagnetic wave. Following this theory, a number of scientists set out to try to detect these electromagnetic waves. In 1886, Heinrich Hertz performed the first successful experiment that both produced and detected electromagnetic radiation using an electrical device. In the process, he accidentally stumbled upon the photoelectric effect.

Hertz's Experiment

Hertz caused electromagnetic radiation to be emitted from two conducting pieces of brass connected to an induction coil. A spark would form in the gap between the two conductors, creating a conducting path when it connected the two. Then, charges would oscillate back and forth between the two conductors, emitting electromagnetic radiation in the process. This radiation could then be detected with a receiver, made simply from a piece of copper wire with a point on one end and a sphere on the other end, bent into a circle about the size of the palm of a hand.

If the receiver and transmitter were designed correctly (so that the current generated by the transmitter had a period close to that of the receiver), then electromagnetic radiation could be detected in the form of a tiny spark in the gap between the point and the sphere in the receiver. This spark was very small, since the gap between the point and the sphere was typically a few hundredths of a millimeter. Using this setup, Hertz was able to detect electromagnetic radiation up to fifty feet away from the transmitter. Maxwell's theory of electromagnetic waves was thus confirmed. However, in trying to improve his setup, Hertz stumbled on a surprising effect.

A Surprising Result

Since the spark in the receiver was very small and faint, Hertz tried putting the receiver in a darkened box so that he could see it better. But something strange happened—instead of making the spark more visible, the spark actually got much smaller when it was inside a box or case! He did a thorough investigation to figure out what was causing this phenomenon.

Light can be broken up into a full spectrum of colors based on its wavelength. The waves of red light are longer than the waves of violet light. Light with waves shorter than violet is called ultraviolet, and light with waves longer than red is called infrared. The electromagnetic spectrum spans a much larger range than just visible light, stretching from long radio waves to microwaves, then to visible light, then to shorter waves such as X rays and gamma rays.

Hertz determined that the receiver spark was only diminished when it was shielded from the transmitter spark. A sheet of glass shielded the spark as well as a piece of casing, ruling out some kind of electromagnetic effect. However, when Hertz tried to shield the spark with a piece of quartz, he found that the shielding effect did not take place. He also determined that the wavelength of light that caused the little spark to be amplified was in the ultraviolet range, beyond the visible spectrum of light. Hertz published his observations in 1887, but he had no explanation for them.

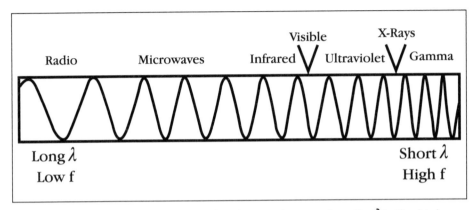

▲ The electromagnetic spectrum: The shorter the wavelength (λ), the higher the frequency (f).

The Electron

The photoelectric effect remained a mystery until the discovery of electrons in 1897. Earlier, in 1888, Wilhelm Hallwachs (1859–1922) devised a simpler method to reproduce Hertz's results, showing that a negatively charged plate lost its charge very quickly when exposed to an ultraviolet light, but that a positively charged plate did not exhibit the same effect. Still, however, Hallwachs had no explanation for the effect.

J. J. Thomson (1856–1940), studying mysterious cathode rays in 1897, showed that they were made up of negatively charged particles. When he devised a method to measure the ratio of the mass of these new particles to the charge they carried, the result was amazing. Either these new particles were incredibly tiny, a thousand times smaller than a hydrogen atom, or they carried an immense charge. Later, experiments by Philip Lenard and others showed that indeed these new particles were incredibly small.

Particles Smaller Than an Atom?

This was the first time it had been suggested that there could be something smaller than an atom. Before 1897, it was thought that atoms were indivisible, the smallest possible piece of matter. Now, with these new results, Thomson and others had showed that there were indeed particles smaller than an atom, and that atoms were made up of these constituents.

The tiny negatively charged particles were called electrons. Later experiments by Thomson's student, Ernest Rutherford, showed that atoms were in fact made up of a large, positively charged nucleus. The nucleus was later showed to be composed of protons and neutrons, orbited by a few negatively charged electrons.

Emission of Electrons

Returning to the photoelectric effect, in 1899 Thomson showed that when ultraviolet light was applied to a metal surface, it caused electrons to be emitted from that surface. These were the same particles that were found in cathode rays. Once electrons were understood to be the particles emitted from a metal surface in the photoelectric effect, the changes that occurred with changing intensity and frequency of the light could be studied.

FACT

The photoelectric effect is behind the operation of solar panels, which produce electricity when sunlight falls on their surfaces. Solar panels can use photovoltaic cells, ones that convert sunlight to electricity using a silicon panel embedded in glass.

Lenard's Experiments

Philipp Lenard, following up on some work by Hertz, began working in 1902 to study the photoelectric effect in more detail. As the process was understood at the time, electrons bound to the atoms at the surface of a metal were caused to vibrate by shining light or other electromagnetic radiation on the surface. When the vibration was sufficient, some electrons could actually be shaken loose from the surface of the metal, and they were then emitted.

The number of electrons shaken loose by this process, and the energy with which they were ejected from the surface, were observed to vary with the brightness and color of the light. Bright light, with a high intensity, has more energy than a dimmer light. Scientists therefore expected that electrons emitted due to a high-intensity light would have a higher average speed due to the higher energy of the source light, and that there would also be more electrons emitted overall due to the increased vibration.

Similarly, the color of the incident light is important. Color is related to the frequency (or wavelength) of the light. Higher-frequency light, toward the violet end of the visible spectrum or beyond, would shake the electrons faster. Again, it might be expected to cause more electrons to be emitted, as well as produce a higher average energy.

"Wavelength" is the length of one wave of light or other electro-magnetic radiation, measured in distance from peak to peak. Frequency is the number of waves or other oscillations per time, measured in waves per second (called "hertz"). The wavelength is proportional to the inverse of the frequency—light with a shorter wavelength has a higher frequency.

Changes in Intensity and Color

Lenard began a series of experiments to measure the effects of the changing intensity of light on the electrons that were emitted. He found that there was a minimum amount of light required to emit any electrons at all—if the light was too faint, nothing was emitted from the surface of the metal. However, when he began increasing the intensity of the light, he found that while the number of electrons emitted also increased, the average energy of the electrons did not. For example, if he doubled the intensity of the light, he got twice as many electrons emitted, but their average, and maximum, energy was be the same as before.

of different colors of light. He

of the light, it affected the energies

d higher-frequency, shorter-wavelength

nd of the spectrum, the electrons

es.

ake any sense, given the wave model

ature of light was firmly accepted in the

revious scientists had suggested that light

es, in 1803 the British scientist Thomas

double-slit experiment that showed the wave

rimental setup included a sheet of metal with

ain separation between them. Light shone

np far away from the metal sheet.

of particles, then one would just expect to see

slits and form their outline on a screen placed

r, Young showed that this experiment actually

tern, similar to how sound waves can cancel

laces in the pattern on the screen, the light

er, producing a bright band; in other places,

out, producing a dark region. There was no

way to produce the interference patterns observed by Young using traditional optics, which assumed that light is composed of particles. Once Young's experiment was confirmed, the wave nature of light seemed firmly established.

Lenard's Contradictions

If light were indeed composed of waves, as was assumed at the time, there was no explanation for Lenard's results. The energy contained in a wave depends only on its amplitude, or intensity, and not on its frequency, or its wavelength. In the wave model, light of different colors (frequencies) should not change the electrons emitted in the photo-electric effect—only the intensity, or brightness, of the light should produce a different result.

A beam of red light and a beam of violet light, with the same intensity, would be expected to produce the same number of electrons with the same average (and maximum) energy, under the wave model. However, remember that Lenard had found that light of different colors produced different energy electrons—shorter-wavelength, higher-frequency light like violet or ultraviolet light produced electrons with higher average energies than lower-frequency light.

Similarly, under the wave model, increasing the intensity of the light should have increased both the number of electrons emitted and their average (and maximum) energy. But again, Lenard's observations contradicted this idea, showing only an increase in number, with no change in energy, with increasing intensity.

There was, simply put, no way to explain Lenard's results given the wave model of light. This contradiction puzzled Lenard (who won the Nobel Prize in physics in 1905 for other work with cathode rays), and it was not explained until Einstein's first paper in 1905, for which he won the Nobel Prize. Even though it was Einstein who solved the paradox, Lenard never forgave the young scientist for stealing his thunder.

Black Body Radiation

Einstein's first major paper, submitted in March of 1905, solved the paradox of the photoelectric effect by showing that light could act like particles as well as waves. His work built on the research conducted by Max Planck, who was able to explain black body radiation.

Heat and Color

In 1900, one of the many puzzles that physicists were trying to explain was black body radiation. When an object is heated, it gives off radiation. Experimental physicists studied the radiation given off in an effort to relate this amount of radiation and its wavelength. The phrase "black body" refers to a dark-colored object that absorbs almost all of the light that hits it. While light-colored objects reflect most of the light that hits them, and stay cooler, dark-colored objects absorb most of the light and become hotter. For this reason, people generally feel hotter when wearing a dark-colored shirt on a hot summer day; this phenomenon also explains why it can be hotter inside a dark-painted car than a white one.

The "albedo" of an object is a measure of the fraction of light hitting the surface that is reflected back. A bright white object has an albedo of 1, and a dark black one has an albedo of 0.

When a dark material absorbs sunlight, it is absorbing electromagnetic radiation that makes the atoms in the material vibrate more rapidly. These vibrations give energy to the electrons, and the excess kinetic energy is radiated away from the material in the form of heat. Scientists studied the heat given off by a radiating system by heating an oven to a certain temperature, T, and then measuring how much radiant energy (heat) was given off at a variety of wavelengths or frequencies. They found experimentally that the amount of energy radiated per area, measured as a power P, was proportional to the fourth power of the temperature.

An example of black body radiation can be seen in the heavens. The whole sky radiates at an equivalent temperature of 3 degrees Kelvin. This radiation is left over from the Big Bang, the event that led to the formation of the universe.

The Ultraviolet Catastrophe

The intensity of the heat given off also has a peak at a certain wavelength, or color, of light. This peak is dependent on temperature. A hotter oven will give off radiant energy with a peak at a shorter (bluer) wavelength than a cooler oven. This effect can be seen by looking at a candle flame—the parts of the flame closest to the wick, which are the hottest, look blue or purple, while the outer, cooler parts of the flame are more yellow or orange in color.

The amount of energy radiated by the oven is related to the number of degrees of freedom in the electromagnetic waves inside the oven. Classical wave theory said that the number of degrees of freedom increases with higher frequency, and so the oven should be radiating much more energy at higher frequencies (shorter wavelengths, that is, toward the ultraviolet).

But the experimental results showed that the radiated heat peaked at a certain wavelength, and then fell off after this peak. This conflict was called the "ultraviolet catastrophe"—classical physics could not explain why the amount of radiant energy given off by a heated body didn't keep increasing up toward infinity at ultraviolet wavelengths.

Planck's Quanta

Max Planck (1858–1947), in 1900, proposed a solution to the puzzle of black body radiation. He suggested that rather than allowing the oscillating particles in the heated oven to radiate energy continuously, as a wave would, perhaps they were constrained to radiate energy only in discrete packets. He called these packets "quanta." The size of the packet of radiation emitted was related to the frequency, so at higher frequencies (shorter wavelengths), energy could only be emitted in large doses.

ALERT!

The word *quanta* (singular, *quantum*) comes from the Latin word *quantus*, meaning "how much." The root is the same for the word *quantity*, for example. Contrary to popular usage, a "quantum leap" is actually the smallest possible leap!

This theory explained why the energy emitted peaked and then decreased at higher frequencies. Since it could only be emitted in very large chunks at these high frequencies, the probability that any individual particle would have enough energy to emit an entire chunk was very low.

Planck found that the size of the energy quantum was linearly related to the frequency: $E = hf$, where h was a new constant now called "Planck's constant."

Initially, Planck did not have any justification for his new theory, except that it fit the experimental results perfectly. Other scientists were also dubious, and Planck's formula was initially disregarded. Not only was there no theoretical justification for the theory, it also completely contradicted Maxwell's equations of electromagnetism. Energy was not supposed to be quantized; the wave theory of electromagnetic radiation required a smooth continuum of radiation.

Einstein's Solution

In 1905, in his first major paper, Einstein suggested a simple and elegant solution to the paradox of the photoelectric effect. Building on the work of Planck, Einstein suggested that the photoelectric effect could easily be understood if the incoming radiation absorbed by a metallic surface was quantized.

Although Planck's work was clearly elegant and fit the experimental data well, few scientists initially believed it because it had no theoretical basis. Einstein was one of the few scientists to take Planck's work seriously at first.

In this case, rather than being able to absorb any continuous amount of radiation, the radiation would be rationed out to the electrons on the surface in particular doses called quanta. These quanta had a particular energy that was proportional to the frequency of the radiation: $E = hf$. This expression was Planck's relationship, as he had determined in studying black body radiation.

In Einstein's theory, when an electron at the surface of a metal is hit by light, it absorbs one individual quantum of radiation. If there is enough energy to free the electron from the atom it was bound to, the electron is emitted. Unless the electron started out right at the surface of the metal, it must use some of its energy to escape from the metal. Then, once it leaves the surface, it has a kinetic energy equal to whatever is left over of the energy it absorbed from the light.

A Solution to Lenard's Problems

Einstein suggested that the relationship between the energy of the quanta and the frequency of the radiation could explain the contradictions that Lenard had found in studying the photoelectric effect. Remember that Lenard had found two puzzling effects.

First, he had observed that when the intensity of the light was doubled, the number of electrons emitted from the surface of the metal doubled, but the average kinetic energy of the electrons did not change. This observation made no sense in the wave view of light. However, in Einstein's new quantized view, it is possible to understand why this phenomenon occurs.

When the intensity of light is doubled, twice as much radiation hits the surface of the metal as before. There is therefore twice as much radiation for the electrons in the metal to absorb, and twice as many electrons can be emitted. However, since the energy of the quanta absorbed by the electrons is proportional to the frequency (or color) of light, doubling the brightness of the light does not affect the energy of the electrons emitted! The quantum absorbed by each individual electron stays the same, so their average kinetic energy once they're emitted stays the same as well.

Einstein's solution also explained Lenard's other contradictory observation. Remember that he had tried using different colors of light on the surface of the metal. In this case, when light with a higher frequency (shorter wavelength) was used, electrons were emitted from the surface of the metal with more energy. Since the energy of the quanta is related to frequency, higher-frequency light has higher-energy quanta, so the electrons are able to absorb more energy. The average kinetic energy of the electrons that are emitted is actually higher.

The Photon

Not only did Einstein's new theory explain the photoelectric effect, it also revolutionized physics. Einstein's proposal of a quantum of light showed that light did not in fact behave like a wave—it had the characteristics of a discrete particle as well. These new particles of light were called photons. One photon was equal to one quantum of light (or electromagnetic radiation).

Einstein's new theory of the photoelectric effect not only explained this puzzle and revolutionized physics, but it also provided a new way to measure "h," Planck's constant. However, not everyone was pleased with Einstein's work. Lenard, for example, was always bitter that Einstein had one-upped him by explaining his puzzling experimental results.

Robert Millikan (1868–1953), an American physicist, was also disturbed by Einstein's new quantized view of light. The view of light as discrete photons, rather than continuous waves, contradicted Maxwell's equations as well as much of nineteenth-century physics. Millikan spent ten years, until 1916, trying to disprove Einstein's work on the photoelectric effect. He developed new experimental techniques, and reproduced Lenard's experiments with much higher accuracy. Nevertheless, his efforts proved unsuccessful, and he was unable to prove Einstein wrong. The photon, and the quantized view of light as particles rather than waves, were here to stay.

FACT

Although he was unable to prove Einstein's theories wrong, Millikan's experiments at least had some reward. As a sort of consolation prize, Millikan received the Nobel Prize for his efforts in 1923.

The Nobel Prize

Einstein's solution to the problem of the photoelectric effect, and the establishment of the quantized nature of light, won him the Nobel Prize in physics in 1921. It is interesting to note that he won the prize for his first major scientific result, and that it was for the relatively more mundane (though nonetheless revolutionary) photoelectric effect rather than for his work on relativity. Though Einstein is better known for his work on both special and general relativity today, in 1921 these discoveries were still deemed too controversial to be eligible for the Nobel Prize.

The citation for Einstein's 1921 Nobel Prize read: "For his services to Theoretical Physics, and especially for his discovery of the law of the photoelectric effect." Clearly, Einstein's breakthrough discovery, which paved the way for the development of quantum physics, was recognized by scientists worldwide. Ⓔ

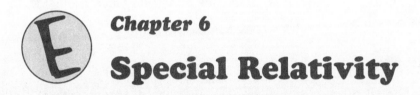

Chapter 6

Special Relativity

The second of Einstein's trio of ground-breaking 1905 papers was called "The Electrodynamics of Moving Bodies." The paper was originally intended to discuss some inconsistencies in Maxwell's theory of electromagnetic radiation. In fact, as it turned out, Einstein's discoveries would yet again shake the laws of physics, this time disrupting Newton's orderly view of the universe with a completely new conception of space and time.

Classical Physics

Physics, at the beginning of the twentieth century, was an orderly subject as developed over the previous centuries. The views of space and time in physics were based primarily on work done by Galileo and Newton, and this work was disrupted by Einstein's new revelations. Almost in passing, Einstein also proved the nonexistence of an odd facet of nineteenth-century science, the "ether."

The Ether

Einstein's work on relativity disrupted the prevailing nineteenth-century view of the medium through which light, and other electromagnetic radiation, traveled. Scientists had known for some time that sound waves were compressional waves, which can only travel through a medium such as air, water, wood, or some other material. This material is what does the "waving"—the vibration of the material, causing it to contract and expand as the energy of the sound wave moves through it, is what transmits the wave.

ALERT!

Contrary to what's seen in most science fiction movies, since space is a vacuum, no sound is transmitted in space! Starships don't make a "whooshing" sound as they go by. The movie *2001: A Space Odyssey* was one of the few movies to accurately depict the silence of space.

Since sound waves required a medium to travel in, scientists of the nineteenth century assumed that light required such a medium as well. It was known that light could travel through a vacuum; therefore, scientists proposed that light traveled in an undetectable medium called the "ether." In fact, different ethers were proposed as the means of travel for a variety of waves, including light, heat, electricity, and magnetism.

Since the light from the stars is observable, the ether was required to stretch throughout space as a medium to carry the light back to observers on Earth. As light travels very fast, the theory required the ether to be a very stiff medium. (A softer, springy medium would slow down the light waves too much, just like sound waves travel faster through a stiff medium that is harder to compress.) But the ether couldn't have too much drag, or it would slow down the orbits of the planets around the sun too much! Solid bodies had to be able to pass through the ether without slowing down. This mysterious substance was imagined to be something very odd, like a "ghostly wind."

FACT

"Ethernet" was originally the name for a local area network developed by the Xerox Corporation, but it is now a standard networking type. The name actually comes from the type of cable used in the original Ethernet, but it evokes the idea that data move magically between computers on the network, as if carried by the mysterious "ether."

Attempts to Find the Ether

Once Maxwell had developed his theory relating electricity and magnetism, and had established that light itself was an electromagnetic phenomenon, scientists attempted to detect the ether. Scientists assumed that Earth moved through the ether on its travels around the sun. In the 1880s, Albert Michelson (1852–1931) began a series of experiments meant to detect the ether by finding its drag on the speed of light. He was later joined in these experiments by a contemporary scientist, Edward Morley (1838–1923). Their experiment set up two beams of light, one parallel to the direction of Earth's travel around the sun, and one perpendicular to Earth's motion.

If there really was such a thing as ether, the Michelson-Morley experiments should have been able to detect it. They measured the speed of light that was going in the same direction as the ether, and that therefore would be assisted by its motion (like to a tailwind for an airplane), then compared that data to the speed of light going across the ether, which did not have this assistance. However, they observed no difference in the speeds of either type of light. The speed of light, c, was measured as a constant value (about 186,300 miles per second), no matter whether it was going along with or perpendicular to the ether.

Michelson spent many years perfecting and redoing his experiments, and he was never satisfied with the results. He thought that his experiment just wasn't precise enough to detect the ether. However, there was another alternative; that ether, in fact, did not exist at all.

The Speed of Light

As we learned in the previous section, another puzzle in the late nineteenth century was the fact that the speed of light seemed to be fixed. Maxwell's new view of light as an electromagnetic wave in fact predicted that it should have a speed of about 186,300 miles per second, which was experimentally verified. However, a big question of the time was what that speed was relative to.

If light were a wave similar to a sound wave, then there would be an obvious answer. Sound waves propagate in air or another medium, so the speed of sound is measured relative to the speed of the air. If the air were moving toward you from the source of a sound, for example, you would hear that sound sooner than you would if the wind were blowing away from you.

If light were similar to sound waves, then the ether would take the place of air, and the speed of light would be measured relative to the ether. However, the Michelson-Morley experiments had shown that the speed of light was independent of the direction of its travel through the ether, and therefore that it seemed to be independent of the speed of the ether altogether! Another possibility was that the speed of light was fixed in relation to the object emitting the light, but this was also disproved.

Early Relativity

Now that the stage has been set to represent the state of classical physics at the turn of the twentieth century, we can consider Einstein's contribution in his understanding of special relativity. But first, we should study where the idea of relativity first came from. Einstein did not invent the idea; he did, however, refine and extend the idea, both physically and mathematically.

Ancient Views of Space and Time

We can begin with the views of space and time in the pre-Renaissance period, especially in ancient Greece and Rome. The view of this time was that there was a natural reference frame for viewing and measuring objects. This frame of reference was simple: It was a state of rest, that is, the state of not moving. In this view of the world, there was an absolute reference frame, called "absolute rest," and all observers would agree that this reference frame was at rest. The absolute reference frame also had an absolute time, from which all other times could be measured.

FACT

One Greek philosopher and scientist was Aristotle, who lived from 384 to 322 B.C. Aristotle wrote many works on logic, philosophy, physical science, natural history, and metaphysics. He also wrote extensively on ethics and politics. In his varied writings, he set the course for much of Western intellectual development, which would follow his philosophical and scientific system of logic.

Galileo's View of Relativity

Changes to the pre-Renaissance views of space and time came with work by Galileo Galilei in the mid-seventeenth century. Galileo first described the "principle of relativity." This new idea came about when Galileo considered what the laws of physics would look like to an observer on a ship moving at a constant speed, as compared to a stationary observer on the ground. Galileo noted that as long as the ship was moving at a constant speed, in one direction, on calm seas without waves or other disturbances, that an observer inside the ship would not be able to do any experiment to prove that the ship was moving (except, of course, looking out the window)!

Galileo's principle of relativity stated that the results of all experiments performed by an observer on the ship would be the same as the results of experiments performed by an observer on the ground. A ball would roll the same way, and would fall to the ground in the same time, for instance. His principle can be stated more concisely by saying that the mechanical laws of physics are the same for any inertial observer.

What does inertial mean?
In this case, an inertial observer (or reference frame) is one that is either fixed or moving at a constant speed in a constant direction. An observer who is accelerating (changing speed) or not moving in a straight line is not an inertial observer.

Galileo's New World-View

Galileo's results were different from the pre-Renaissance views of Aristotle and others. In Galileo's new description, there was no absolute stationary reference frame. An observer at rest and an observer moving in an inertial reference frame would not be able to agree on which one of them was moving and which one of them was not. Also in Galileo's view, there was no absolute reference "at rest" frame that all observers would agree on.

One can understand Galileo's world-view by thinking about an observer on the ground and an observer on an airplane. The observers synchronize their watches beforehand, and at a particular time the observer on the plane sits in her seat. At this time, both observers agree on her position. Then, she walks up a few rows to visit a friend for a few minutes, and then walks back to her seat. The observer on the plane would think that she has returned to the same place she was located a few minutes before.

FACT

Galileo is perhaps better known for his work in developing the telescope as an astronomical instrument (though he did not invent it). He observed four moons orbiting the planet Jupiter, the first confirmation of celestial bodies orbiting a body other than Earth. This work eventually disrupted the geocentric, Earth-centered, view of the solar system, in favor of the sun-centered, or heliocentric, view.

However, the observer on the ground would think differently, because the airplane is of course moving at a speed of hundreds of miles per hour with respect to the ground! In the reference frame of the plane, the observer on the plane returned to the same place when she went back to her seat. However, in the reference frame on the ground, the location of her seat has moved a few hundred miles from when she was first in it to when she returned after talking to her friend.

Newton

The laws of classical physics were first described by Sir Isaac Newton (1643–1727) in the late seventeenth century. In Newton's 1687 work, *Philosophiae naturalis principia mathematica* (called the *Principia*), he analyzed the motion of objects under a variety of forces. His application of his theories all around the solar system led to his law of universal gravitation, which described how all material attracts other material with a force related to the two masses and the distance that separates them. Two masses will attract each other with a greater gravitational force if one or both of them are very large—like the attraction between a planet and the sun—or if they are located close together.

Newton's new theories allowed him to describe the motions of planets and comets, the tides, the moon, and other natural phenomena. His theories were groundbreaking, and they changed the earlier view of forces as only being able to act on contact, rather than at a distance. Newton's laws of motion took into account Galileo's principle of relativity, and a key element of Newton's theories was the idea that a particle in an inertial (nonaccelerating) reference frame will move in a fixed direction at a fixed speed. Newton also assumed that time in various reference frames could be measured with respect to an absolute time, one which was unchanging.

Problems with Newton's and Maxwell's Views of the Universe

At the end of the nineteenth century, both Maxwell's elegant, orderly formulations of electromagnetism and Newton's classical mechanics were showing some problems. A few seemingly small inconsistencies had been noted, and try as they might, scientists were unable to explain them satisfactorily. These inconsistencies included the fact that the orbit of the planet Mercury around the sun was slightly different from the predictions made by scientists studying orbits. Also, there were problems with Maxwell's equations, the ether, and moving reference frames. Scientists were puzzling over issues that had been taken for granted before, such as whether the speed of light was actually fixed or not.

Maxwell's equations, which unified the study of electricity, magnetism, and optics (by including light as an electromagnetic wave), showed that the speed of light was a fixed constant. However, the presence of a fixed velocity for light is not compatible with the views of Galileo and Newton, who stated that speed varies depending on the observer. If an observer in motion measures the speed of light, it should be different from the speed measured by an observer who is at rest. However, Maxwell's equations required a fixed speed of light which does not vary, no matter who is observing it! Sound confusing? It is, and Einstein came along at just the right time to provide some clarity.

Einstein's Solution

In his 1905 paper, Einstein proposed a solution to the problem of the speed of light. In this paper, Einstein first strengthened Galileo's original principle of relativity. Galileo's view of relativity had only applied to mechanical laws of physics. Einstein, however, broadened the initial statement to include all laws of physics. Einstein's new statement of relativity was that all the laws of physics are the same for an inertial observer.

Einstein's Postulates of Special Relativity

Einstein's new statement meant that not only was there no mechanical experiment that an observer could do to prove whether or not she was moving (at a constant velocity), but also there was no electromagnetic or optical experiment that she could do! Einstein stated that the speed of light is the same for all inertial observers, and does not vary or depend on the motion of the source. Observers can't even use the speed of light to tell whether or not they, or the source of the light, are moving.

Einstein's two postulates of special relativity are as follows:

1. The laws of physics are the same for any inertial reference frame.
2. In an inertial reference frame, the speed of light (c) is the same whether it's emitted by a source that's moving (uniform motion, not accelerating) or stationary.

Space-Time

Remember that Galileo's views of relativity made us get rid of the idea of fixed locations in space. In the example of the airplane, when the observer on the plane returned to her seat, she thought she was going back to the same location in space. However, to an observer on the ground, she did not return to the same place. Instead, she was in an entirely new location because of the motion of the airplane with respect to the ground. This example shows that the two observers do not agree on location—location depends on each person's individual frame of reference.

Einstein's new view of relativity took this one step further. It not only removed the idea of fixed locations in space, but removed the idea of fixed time as well! Events that occur at the same time are simultaneous. Einstein showed that simultaneity is not fixed across reference frames—events that appear to be simultaneous to one observer can occur at different times for a different observer.

In a way, Einstein's scientific theory of relativity set the stage for advances in philosophical thinking as well. If motion, time, and simultaneity were relative, the individual took on much more importance than if all motion obeyed fixed, static laws. This new idea of perception would go on to affect many other disciplines; the effect of Einstein's theory cannot be underestimated.

These results made time another variable of location in "space-time." With the help of the German mathematician Hermann Minkowski (1864–1909), Einstein showed that events could be thought of as occurring at a particular four-dimensional coordinate: three dimensions for the typical spatial location (such as latitude, longitude, and elevation), plus a fourth dimension for time. And just as the three spatial positions can vary according to the reference frame (as in the airplane example), the fourth dimension, time, can also vary.

The Relative Train

Einstein suggested a thought-experiment to help understand how one observer could think that two events were simultaneous, and another observer think they were not. Imagine a train, with an observer on a car in the middle of the train and another observer on the ground. At some particular time, the two observers are directly opposite each other, and synchronize their watches as they wave to each other in passing.

Then, two bolts of lightning hit, one leaving marks at the front end of the train and on the ground at that same point, and one leaving marks at the back of the train and at the same point on the ground. The two observers record the events.

The observer on the ground receives the light from both lightning strikes at the same time. He measures the distance between the two marks on the ground, and finds that he was standing exactly halfway between the two points. Since he knows that the speed of light is a constant, he can conclude that the two lightning strikes occurred at the same time, that is, simultaneously, since the light traveled the same distance to him from each mark and the two signals reached him at the same time.

The observer on the train, however, comes to a different conclusion. She is standing in the middle of the train, and so she knows that the distance from the mark left by the lightning at the front of the train is the same as the distance from the mark left by the lightning at the back of the train. However, she receives the light emitted by the lightning strike at the front of the train before the light emitted from the lightning strike at the back of the train. Since she knows the speed of light is a constant, and the distance from each mark is the same, she concludes that the lightning strike at the front of the train happened before the lightning strike at the back of the train.

How is this possible? The two events were simultaneous for the observer on the ground, but they are not simultaneous for the observer on the train. We can understand how this happened by looking at the motion of the observer on the train. During the time that it took for the light to get to her from the front and back of the train, she was moving along with the rest of the train. The direction of her motion was toward the front of the train. So as compared to the distance on the ground, the light from the front of the train had to travel a smaller distance to get to the observer, while light from the back of the train had to travel a greater distance. This difference in travel time explains why the observer on the train concluded that the light from the two events was not simultaneous.

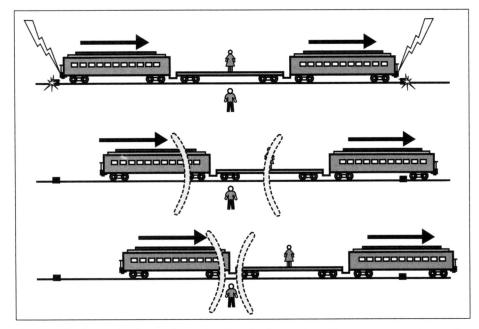

▲ The relative train shows how the fourth dimension, time, can vary depending on the observer.

Thus, Einstein's initial work on relativity showed that neither space nor time is absolute. The perception of each depends on the observer and her reference frame. However, Einstein did replace these notions with a new, more fundamental absolute. In his new theory of space and time, the one absolute was light. The speed of light is absolute, independent of reference frame. So while two observers will never agree on which of them is in motion, or whether events are simultaneous or not, they will both always agree on the speed of light. As odd as this theory sounds, Einstein's new view of relativity actually made a number of predictions that have been tested and found to be true. Einstein's view of the universe seems to be correct.

No More Ether

In formulating his initial work on relativity, Einstein also showed (almost as a by-product) that there is no ether. Since he had shown that there was no measurement that could be taken in a particular inertial reference frame to show whether an object was moving or at rest (including measuring the speed of light in the reference frame), the idea of a natural resting reference frame, which was not moving, made no sense. It could never be proven that a particular reference frame was at rest with respect to all others.

However, the experiments performed by Michelson and Morley had attempted to detect the speed of light with respect to the ether, which they assumed was a natural rest frame. If there were such a natural reference frame, then the speed of light would be measured relative to this frame, and it would vary in different reference frames. Since the speed of light is a constant, there is no natural reference frame. The ether cannot exist. The speed of light is a constant as measured with respect to the observer, and if an observer sets up an inertial reference frame and measures the speed of light, she will always find it to be the same value (which we use the shorthand variable c to denote).

So what about the need for an ether as a medium for light to move through? What is doing the "waving"? It turns out that light waves are not compression waves like sound waves; they are transverse waves. This type of wave does not require a medium, and can easily travel through space or a vacuum. Thus, electromagnetic radiation, including light, can travel through either air or the vacuum of space without requiring an ether or any other medium to be present.

The removal of the ether from scientists' conception of the universe certainly required hard facts and evidence, but it was also a leap of faith. For the first time, the world was considered complete without this mystical medium. Scientists, philosophers, and everyone else would have to grapple with the idea that there was no single medium binding everything together. Questioning the basics would become a fundamental part of early twentieth-century life. This might have made many people uncomfortable, but it also set the stage for the incredible wave of innovation that would follow Einstein's discovery.

Some Puzzles of Special Relativity

In addition to the strange results mentioned previously, where events are no longer simultaneous if measured from different reference frames, special relativity also results in some very strange behaviors when velocities approach the speed of light. Exploring some of these strange consequences, which are all consistent with Einstein's view of the universe, led to the many exciting ideas that influenced the path science would take.

Time Dilation

First, let's start with another of Einstein's famous thought-experiments. In this case, imagine two clocks, one which is moving with an observer on a train and one that is stationary on the ground. Imagine that these are light clocks, in which time is measured by having a pulse of light bounce from one mirror to another, as detected by a light detector. If the observer on the ground looks at his clock, he will see the light pulse bounce back and forth from one mirror to the other in a straight line, measuring time. Similarly, the observer on the train will see the same thing if she looks at her clock, which is moving on the train with her.

FACT

Trains were the major form of transportation of Einstein's time. This is probably why so many of his famous thought-experiments involve trains, rather than other means of transportation. Also, it is easy to imagine a train running on a long, straight track, which is a perfect inertial reference frame.

However, suppose that the observer on the ground decides to check the time using the clock that's moving on the train. He watches one pulse of light bounce off one mirror, then bounce off the second. But in the time the light took to travel from one mirror to the other, the whole clock moved some distance down the track on the train. So the path that the light takes from one mirror to the other will look like a zigzag pattern to the observer on the ground.

The observer on the ground can compute the distance traveled by the light pulse, and he knows that the speed at which it is traveling is c, the fixed speed of light. Since speed multiplied by time gives distance, he can see how much time it took the pulse to bounce off the two mirrors. That amount can be used to compare the time on the moving clock to the time on his fixed clock.

But when he compares the two clocks, he is in for a surprise. Even though the two observers carefully synchronized their clocks at the start of the experiment, when the observer on the ground compares the time on his clock to the time on the moving clock, the moving clock is running slower than his stationary clock! This effect is called "time dilation."

Time dilation works for any moving clock, not just a special light clock. (The observers could easily have used the light clocks to set their own watches or other clocks in their reference frames.) It is a consequence of the fixed speed of light. Since the speed of light is the same in all reference frames, when the moving clock is observed by the fixed observer, it seems like the light pulses travel a longer distance. Because they travel that distance at the same speed (the fixed speed of light), they therefore must take longer to do it. For this reason, time runs slower in the moving reference frame.

This scenario also applies in reverse. If the observer on the train looks at the clock on the ground, she thinks that she is stationary and the ground is moving backward. So to her, the clock on the ground is the moving clock, and she will measure the same time dilation. To her, the clock on the ground is running slow!

Time dilation is the fact that moving clocks run more slowly than stationary clocks. A moving observer will therefore age more slowly than a stationary observer! If people stayed in constant motion, would they cease to age at all?

Of course, if the train is moving at a typical train speed of about 50 or 60 miles per hour, the change in time on the moving clock will be very small. However, if the train were able to move at a sizable fraction of the speed of light (remember that the speed of light is 186,300 miles per second, so it would have to be an imaginary rocket-train), then the time dilation effect would be much more sizable. In fact, not only clocks run slow in the moving reference frame—everything does, including the body of the observer on the train. So because of time dilation, she will even age more slowly than the observer on the ground.

The effects of time dilation have been measured experimentally. One such experiment was done by synchronizing two identical clocks, and then flying one around the world on an airplane while the other stayed at rest on the ground. When the two clocks were compared after the plane flight, the one that had been in motion on the plane showed that less time had elapsed than the one on the ground. What seems like futuristic science has actually been around for decades.

Length Contraction

A related effect of moving versus stationary reference frames is length contraction. Suppose that the train moving over the tracks left marks on the track every second, as measured on the train. If the train were moving at 10 feet per second, then the observer on the train would measure that the marks on the track were located every 10 feet.

However, if the observer on the ground measures the distance between the marks, he will measure something different. To him, the train's clock is running slow. According to his clock, then, the marks were left at intervals greater than one second, and therefore are located at a distance greater than 10 feet apart.

This effect is called "length contraction." Length contraction means that to a moving observer, distances look shorter than they do to a stationary observer. In fact, to a moving observer, all distances seem to get squished up in the direction of motion.

Length contraction is another strange side effect of special relativity. At speeds close to the speed of light, lengths seem to get shortened in the direction that the observer is moving.

The Twin "Paradox"

Perhaps the most famous thought-experiment related to special relativity is the so-called twin paradox. Actually, it is not a paradox at all, but a problem that can be explained consistently with the principles of relativity as Einstein defined them.

In this story, consider a pair of twins. One, the sister, sets off in a spaceship for the nearest star, Alpha Centauri, which is four light-years away. When she gets there, she turns around right away and comes back to Earth, where her brother is waiting for her. If her spaceship travels at a speed of 0.6 c (0.6 times the speed of light), then according to her brother on Earth, the trip took 160 months (thirteen and a third years). However, remember that since she is in motion, her clock appears to run slow to her brother on Earth (who is not moving; remember the example of time dilation on the moving train). So to the sister on the spaceship, the total time it took her to get to Alpha Centauri and back was only 128 months (ten and two-thirds years). She has aged two and two-thirds years less than her brother!

However, remember that to the sister in the spaceship, if she looks at her brother back on Earth, to her it looks like the Earth is moving backward away from her at the same speed, 0.6 c. So to her, it would seem like her brother's clock is running more slowly, and he should age less over the trip than she.

When her rocket ship arrives back on Earth, the paradox goes, who is older? The answer is that the brother is older. The sister, who traveled in the rocket ship to Alpha Centauri and back, experienced accelerations on her trip to Alpha Centauri—the rocket ship had to accelerate when it left Earth, slow down as it reached the star, turn around, and then re-accelerate on its trip back to Earth and brake when it got back to Earth. Because of this, the sister's reference frame is no longer an inertial reference frame.

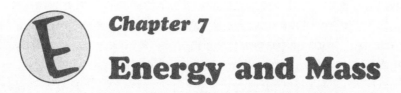

Chapter 7

Energy and Mass

In September of 1905, Einstein published a short but important paper that used his concept of special relativity to look at the relationship between matter and energy. This relationship led to the development of his famous equation, $E=mc^2$, perhaps one of the best-known scientific equations of all time.

Momentum and Work

In September of 1905, Einstein published a brief paper that described an important consequence of his work on special relativity. This paper described the equivalence of mass and energy. Einstein realized that special relativity required him to re-evaluate the Newtonian ideas of momentum, work, and energy. Special relativity also had important consequences for dynamics, the study of moving bodies and their interactions. Before discussing the consequences, one must first consider a few definitions for momentum, work, and energy.

Mass is the amount of matter in an object, and it is measured in kilograms. Mass is different from weight—weight, measured in pounds, can only be measured under acceleration such as a gravity field. A 1-kilogram mass weighs about 2.2 pounds on the surface of Earth, but weighs only 0.8 pounds on the surface of Mars.

Momentum

Momentum was first described by the French philosopher René Descartes (1596–1650). Momentum means "amount of motion," and is defined as the mass of a body multiplied by its velocity. A large body moving slowly can have as much momentum as a small body moving quickly. Momentum can be transferred from one object to another—think of a moving billiard ball bumping into a stationary one. If they hit directly, the first ball will stop, and the second will move off at about the same speed. Thus the total amount of momentum, or net motion, stays the same.

Momentum can also be canceled out, instead of being transferred, if the two objects are moving in opposite directions. If two balls coming from opposite sides of a billiard table bump into each other, one can be thought of as having negative momentum and one positive momentum, since their velocities are in opposite directions. When they bump into each other, the momentum cancels out and both balls stop.

Momentum is conserved in any collision between two objects—provided, of course, that no third object gets in the way. This "third object" includes friction from the surface they are moving over, so theoretical physics usually assumes they are moving on an imaginary "frictionless" surface. Momentum conservation works no matter what the sizes and speeds of the objects are, or if they bounce off each other or stick together after the collision (as long as they don't break up into multiple pieces). While Descartes deduced that momentum should be conserved, it was Newton who formalized the conservation of momentum as part of his laws of motion.

QUESTION?

What is the difference between speed and velocity?
Speed is just how fast you are going. Velocity is a "vector" quantity, meaning that it involves both how fast you are going and the direction in which you are traveling. Technically, speed is called a "scalar" quantity because it does not involve a direction.

Work

The physics definition of work means that a force has been exerted to move a particular object over some distance. Work is defined as force multiplied by distance, where the distance counts only in the direction of the force. Since gravity pulls all objects downward on the surface of the Earth, picking up an object off the floor involves work. A force is defined as mass multiplied by acceleration, where acceleration is the change in velocity of an object. From this relationship comes Newton's famous equation, $F = ma$, where F is a force, m is a mass, and a is the acceleration.

Energy

The definition of energy is "the ability to do work." There are different types of energy: kinetic energy is the energy that comes from motion, while potential energy is the energy that comes from position. A baseball has kinetic energy, and can smash a window if it hits one; an apple hanging from a branch in a tree has potential energy, which is converted to kinetic energy when it falls.

If we pick up an apple from the ground and put it on a tree branch, ready to fall on the head of some unsuspecting passerby, we do work in lifting the apple from the ground to the height of the branch. This same amount of work will be done by gravity as the apple falls back to the ground. So the energy that the apple has when sitting on a tree branch is stored work, or potential energy.

The kinetic energy of an object is related to the mass of an object and the velocity at which it is traveling. An object with more mass, or traveling at a higher velocity, will have more kinetic energy than a slower or lighter object. The actual relationship between kinetic energy, mass, and velocity can be expressed as $E = \frac{1}{2}mv^2$, where E is kinetic energy, m is the mass of the object, and v is its velocity.

Relativistic Addition of Velocities

Returning to the world of special relativity, another point to consider is how the speeds of two objects add together when one is moving at close to the speed of light. At low speeds, we can use our common sense to deduce that if a train is moving at 50 miles per hour, and a person walks toward the front of the train at 5 miles per hour, then her speed with respect to an observer standing on the ground is 55 miles per hour.

However, this common-sense addition of velocities doesn't work if one of the velocities is close to the speed of light. As seen in the previous chapter, if a pulse of light travels from the back of a train to the front, the speed of the pulse of light is the same if measured by an observer on the train or by an observer on the ground. The speed of light is constant, and it does not increase by 50 miles per hour as measured by the person on the ground.

In fact, due to time dilation and length contraction, the sum of the two velocities must be divided by a factor that is proportional to one plus the product of the two velocities divided by the speed of light. If the two velocities are called u and v, we can write their relativistic sum as:

$$\frac{u + v}{1 + \dfrac{uv}{c^2}}$$

Here, c is the speed of light. So if the two velocities are both much smaller than the speed of light, then the expression simplifies to just the sum of the two velocities. If one of the velocities is equal to the speed of light, then the sum of the velocities is just the speed of light. Therefore, the speed of light is the maximum speed that any object can go.

Conserving Momentum

Remember that momentum is defined as the mass of an object multiplied by its velocity. Since velocity is a vector, this definition implies that momentum has a direction as well as a magnitude. Conservation of momentum is a simple, elegant idea, since it does not depend on the details of the collision or the bodies involved in it. The elegance of momentum conservation in part led Einstein to work toward finding a way to preserve momentum conservation in his new system of dynamics, which included the new ideas of space and time that are part of special relativity.

FACT

Einstein's new momentum conservation law stated that momentum should be conserved in a collision in any inertial reference frame. This statement is another one of those obvious postulates that, like much of special relativity, turns out to have some interesting ramifications.

Momentum and Special Relativity

Remember that for objects moving at speeds close to the speed of light, both time dilation and length contraction become important. Think of two racecars moving toward each other from opposite directions down a long straight road at speeds comparable to the speed of light. We can imagine that they are offset from each other just a little; when they meet, they bump into each other, and bounce off at a slight angle to the road they were just traveling on.

Momentum will be conserved in this collision, and because they bounced off each other at a slight angle, both racecars are no longer traveling directly along the road, but are traveling at a slight angle to the road. Because of this angle, they not only have a velocity that is along the road, but also a slight velocity when measured away from the road.

Time Dilation and Length Contraction

To an observer standing on the ground, the two racecars will seem to be moving away from the road at the same rate, and the whole picture will look symmetrical. However, if one of the racecar drivers looks at the other car and tries to figure out how fast it is moving away from the road, she will get a puzzling result. Since both cars are moving at speeds close to the speed of light, time dilation comes into play.

However, because length contraction only contracts lengths along the direction of motion, the distance to the road (which is perpendicular to the direction of motion) is not length contracted. Therefore, the system no longer seems symmetric when the driver of one car views the other car. It appears that the two cars are traveling away from the road at different velocities, and total momentum would no longer seem to be conserved.

Einstein's Solution

Einstein was worried by this seemingly inconsistent result, and once again he found a simple and elegant way to avoid it. Also as usual for Einstein's solutions, the simple and elegant solution went against almost everyone's common sense and intuition, but was found to be correct based on future experimental results.

In this case, Einstein proposed that the way to ensure the conservation of momentum was to make the mass of an object dependent on its velocity. As strange as it seems, this proposal is the only way to cancel out the seemingly mismatched velocities in the previous racecar thought-experiment, which resulted from time dilation with no accompanying length contraction.

Einstein proposed that the only way to ensure conservation of momentum for objects moving at velocities close to the speed of light was if the mass of an object was dependent on its velocity!

Rest Mass

The mass of an object that's not moving is called the "rest mass," and the mass of a moving object increases as the velocity increases by a factor related to the velocity of the object squared divided by the speed of light squared. So when an object is moving slowly, the mass increase is very small, but when an object is moving at speeds comparable to the speed of light, the mass increase can be very large. In fact, for an object moving at the speed of light, the mass becomes infinite.

The actual relationship between the mass of an object and its velocity can be expressed as follows. If an object has a mass M at rest, then its mass when it is moving at a velocity v will be

$$\frac{M}{\sqrt{1 - \frac{v^2}{c^2}}} \quad \text{where } c \text{ is the speed of light.}$$

Experimental Confirmation

As odd as it may sound for an object's mass to increase if its velocity increases, it was confirmed by experiments soon after Einstein proposed it. As early as 1908, a measurement was made of the mass of electrons moving quickly in a vacuum tube, and it was found that their masses were increased by the expected amount.

Since the mass of particles increases dramatically as particles approach the speed of light, the speed of light can be seen as a natural "speed limit" for matter. It is impossible (or so we think) for material to become infinite in mass, and therefore it is impossible for material to travel the speed of light. This speed limit has stymied those who hope for faster-than-light space travel, and so far no solution has been found for *Star Trek*–like "warp speeds."

Kinetic Energy of Relativistic Particles

Remember the previous discussion of the kinetic energy of a particle as related to the particle's mass and its velocity in the equation $E = \frac{1}{2}mv^2$?

This model works just fine for particles moving at slow, everyday speeds, but things become a bit strange when the speeds approach the speed of light. At speeds close to the speed of light, as energy is increased slightly, the mass increases along with the increase in velocity.

When speeds get very near the speed of light, they can't increase any more. Once particles hit this point, any increase in energy goes directly to an increase in mass of the particle! If we have a particle moving at a speed close to the speed of light, and we apply a force to it for a time interval of one second, the energy and therefore the mass of the particle will increase slightly, by an amount we can call m. Since the force is equal to the rate of change of mass, multiplied by the velocity, this gives us the equation F=mc (where F is the force, m is the slight increase in mass, and c is the speed of light, as usual).

Increase in Kinetic Energy

So what is the increase in kinetic energy of the particle as a result of applying this force for one second? Remember that energy is the ability to do work, so the increase in energy is the work done during one second. The work done by the force is equal to the force multiplied by the distance. If the particle is traveling at the speed of light c, 186,300 miles per second, then in one second the particle travels 186,300 miles, or c miles. Therefore, the increase in kinetic energy of the particle is equal to the force multiplied by c miles.

So what is the end result? F=mc, and E=Fc. So we can combine them to show that $E = mc * c = mc^2$! Does this look familiar? We have just shown where Einstein's famous equation $E=mc^2$ comes from. It allows us to compare the increase in the mass of a particle moving at a speed close to the speed of light with its increase in kinetic energy.

Slow Particles

Particles moving at speeds close to the speed of light increase in mass as compared to their resting masses. What about particles moving at more mundane, everyday speeds? It turns out that mass increases also take place for particles moving at much slower speeds. In fact, over the whole span of speeds from very slow to near the speed of light, particles experience a mass increase that's related to their increase in kinetic energy by the equation $E=mc^2$.

So why don't we notice this effect in our everyday life? Does your mass increase when you are running as opposed to when you are standing still? Even though it may feel like it does, the increase, while real, is so tiny it is very difficult to measure. This is true even at speeds that are significant but still much less than the speed of light. For example, the mass increase of a typical airplane flying at 2,000 miles per hour would only be about half a milligram as compared to its mass while at rest on the ground! This amount is almost undetectable.

Nuclear Physics

The equation $E=mc^2$ generalizes to more than just kinetic energy. Any increase in energy, including potential energy, also increases the mass of a particle by the amount indicated by the equation. In most instances, the increase in mass is very small at speeds obtainable on Earth.

Nuclear Fission

However, there is one case in which the increase in mass becomes important. Consider the nucleus of a helium atom. It has two protons and two neutrons. These particles are attracted together in the stable nucleus by a very strong force called the nuclear force. However, if enough energy is supplied from outside the nucleus, it can break apart into two separate pieces, each of which has a proton and a neutron. These pieces are similar to hydrogen nuclei.

Nuclear *fusion* is the combining of smaller nuclei into one large nucleus, while nuclear *fission* is the breaking up of a large nucleus into smaller nuclei.

Since the attraction inside the original helium nucleus is so strong, it takes a lot of energy to get it to separate into two pieces. When this experiment is done and the mass of the two final pieces is compared to the mass of the initial helium nucleus, the mass has increased by about half a percent. This mass increase is equal to the amount of energy that was required to break apart the helium nucleus, multiplied by c^2. Einstein's equation works again!

Nuclear Fusion

This experiment has an even more important result when it is run in reverse. If the two hydrogen nuclei created by the previous experiment are allowed to crash into each other with sufficient energy, they will combine back together to form a helium nucleus again. They require a significant velocity to perform this combination because, since each nucleus is negatively charged, they will repel each other unless they are going fast enough to bump into each other. Therefore, when the two pieces are set to collide, they have a significant amount of kinetic energy.

When the two hydrogen nuclei collide and recombine into a helium nucleus again, they not only liberate the kinetic energy they needed to get close together, but they also give off the same amount of energy that they had originally required to split in two. This energy was stored in the mass increases of the two particles, and is emitted when they combine back into a single helium nucleus.

FACT

If mass can be converted into energy, then energy can be converted into mass. This idea was proved in 1933 by Irène Joliot-Curie (1897–1956, the daughter of Marie Curie) and Frédéric Joliot (1900–1958, her husband), who took a picture showing the conversion of one photon (light energy) into two particles.

This nuclear reaction is the basis of nuclear fusion and fission. Fusion is how the sun generates the heat and light that supports life on Earth, and it is also the system by which hydrogen bombs work. As is the case for so many of Einstein's results, the equation $E=mc^2$ has important and far-reaching consequences, both for the existence of life here on Earth, and for the potential of its destruction.

Chapter 8

Other Major Early Papers

In addition to his three main papers of 1905, Einstein also published thirty-two scientific papers during his years in Bern, from 1902 to 1909. These include a paper on Brownian motion, which pioneered kinetic and atomic theory, and a paper that showed how to calculate both the size of molecules and the number of molecules in a given amount of gas.

Discovery of Brownian Motion

Brownian motion was first described in an 1828 paper by the British botanist Robert Brown (1773–1858) as the random motion of grains of pollen or dust in water. Actually, the same process had been described in 1785 by Dutch scientist Jan Ingenhousz, who observed the random flickering of coal particles on the surface of alcohol. However, it was Brown's work that received more attention.

The motion of particles in a liquid can be described as a "random walk." This is a series of steps of the same length, each of which is in a different, random direction. Over time, such motions build up to a long, zigzag path between any two points.

FACT

A random walk is an odd mathematical function. Its definition leads to the fact that there is a random walk possible between any two points, but the path itself consists of an infinite number of segments! This method is not the best way to get where you are going.

Brown's Observations

Robert Brown was a gifted botanist who was one of the first Westerners to describe many new species while on a trip to Australia. He was a very skilled observer with a microscope, and he documented the microscopic structure of many different plants. He first noticed the odd motion that was called "Brownian Movement" (later Brownian motion) when observing grains of pollen suspended in water.

Brown had originally intended to study the minute structure of the grains of pollen, but instead noticed an odd phenomenon. The tiny particles would not stay still under his microscope lens for long enough for him to observe them! Instead, they were in constant motion.

Life in Motion?

Given the scientific theories of the time, an obvious explanation would have been that Brown was observing life in motion. The grains of pollen were, after all, the seeds from which new life would arise, so was it not likely that they could be capable of motion on their own?

Brown, however, was not so easily persuaded that he was watching motion due to a living organism. His many studies of various plants led him to believe that an alternate explanation must be more likely. Brown carried out a series of careful experiments to determine the source of the motion. He was able to rule out currents in the fluid and gradual evaporation of the liquid as causes of motion.

Next, Brown attempted to see if it was the living essence of the plant pollen that provided the motion. First, he performed observations of plant pollen that had been suspended in an alcohol solution for eleven months. These observations showed the same motion, suggesting that it was not only fresh, living pollen grains that exhibited this behavior.

Inorganic Motion

Brown then attempted to replicate the behavior by suspending fine particles ground from rocks and other inorganic substances. Indeed, particles of rock behaved the same as grains of pollen, exhibiting random motions under a microscope. This behavior ruled out the possibility that some living phenomenon was responsible for the motion.

Having ruled out the motion's being caused by some property of living material, Brown was left with a puzzle. He was unable to come up with an explanation for the motion of inert, microscopic particles of material suspended in solution. It wasn't until another of Einstein's groundbreaking 1905 papers was published, seventy-five years later, that the mystery was finally solved.

Atomic and Kinetic Theory

In 1905, Einstein published a paper entitled "On the Movement of Small Particles Suspended in Stationary Liquids Required by the Molecular-Kinetic Theory of Heat." In summary, Einstein used this paper to show how a new theory of the creation of heat (by tiny moving molecules) could result in the motion of particles visible through a microscope.

This research provided an explanation for Brownian motion, almost as an unintended consequence of the work.

Atomic Theory of Matter

To understand where Einstein's work came from, we must first consider the atomic theory of matter. It had long been thought that all materials could consist of a multitude of tiny particles, invisible to the naked eye. This theory was even considered in ancient Rome, as it is mentioned in the writings of the Roman philosopher and poet Lucretius (99–55 B.C.). However, Aristotle did not believe in this view of the natural world, and so it was discredited for many centuries.

In modern times, Daniel Bernoulli (1700–1782) was the first person to describe the composition of a gas as a multitude of tiny particles that move about rapidly. He began researching this problem in 1738. Bernoulli believed that it was this motion that allowed gases to exert pressure, such as the pressure that keeps a balloon inflated. However, most other scientists did not agree with Bernoulli's description, instead believing that gases were made up of motionless particles that were held in their places by the ether.

Kinetic Theory of Heat

It was not until 1859, when James C. Maxwell studied the problem, that a new understanding of the atomic view of matter began to form. Maxwell also formulated a new approach to the kinetic theory of heat. He realized that while Bernoulli's view (that of the atoms in a gas as tiny particles bouncing off each other elastically) had merit, there were far too many collisions to study them all using Newton's simple laws of mechanics.

Instead, Maxwell described the particles of gas in a closed container as being evenly distributed, with a certain distribution of velocities. For a typical distribution of velocities, there must be a single average velocity with fewer and fewer particles moving at speeds both much faster and much slower than average. The temperature of a gas was just related to the distribution of velocities.

Thermodynamics

Ludwig Boltzmann (1844–1906) was able to generalize Maxwell's distribution of velocities to large systems. Boltzmann also related the thermodynamics of systems, in particular the entropy (a measure of the order of a system), to the statistical nature of the velocity distribution. In the process, he created the field of statistical mechanics. He also calculated the probability of being in any particular energy state for a system in thermodynamic equilibrium at a particular temperature.

Entropy is a measure of the degree of order, or disorder, in a system. Entropy is increasing with time in the universe as a whole, as the system goes from a state of more order (lower entropy) to a state that is more uniform and less orderly (higher entropy).

A main element of Boltzmann's work was the relationship between tiny atoms and the everyday world of matter. His theories showed how the microscopic behavior of atoms and molecules produced effects visible on a macroscopic scale.

An important side consequence of Boltzmann's theories concerned reversibility. In the world of Newtonian mechanics, all actions are reversible in time. However, in his studies of microscopic behavior and entropy, Boltzmann showed that this was not necessarily the case. While it is theoretically possible that a system could move from a simple, uniformly distributed state to a more organized one, in practice the probability that this could happen is so small that it is effectively zero.

FACT

Boltzmann's theories were not believed by everyone at the time. He encountered resistance from Wilhelm Ostwald, a well-known chemist, who did not believe in atoms. The lack of acceptance of Boltzmann's theories could have led to his suicide in 1906, although he also suffered from a mental illness.

We can understand the improbability of such a situation by considering the air in a room. While it is certainly possible that all the molecules in the room will spontaneously gather on one side, leaving the room's occupants in a vacuum, the probability of such a thing happening is so small that it is basically zero. Thus, given the laws of probability, entropy is always increasing with time, so time appears to be irreversible.

Einstein's Solution

In his 1905 paper, Einstein used the molecular kinetic view of heat to explain the motions of microscopic particles suspended in a liquid, that is, of Brownian motion. Einstein's explanation was different from other attempts to understand this motion. He showed that it was the movement of tiny molecules, not visible under the microscopes of the day, that resulted in the motion of the larger, microscopic particles.

The theory that Einstein came up with depended on the kinetic theory of gases as studied by Maxwell and Boltzmann. Einstein concluded that the thermal motions of the molecules in a gas caused the tiny molecules to continually collide with the larger particles visible in a microscope. Even though the molecules in a gas (or in water) were not visible themselves under a microscope, their presence could be detected through the study of their effects on the visible, larger particles that they impacted. It was these impacts that caused the continual, random motion of particles that had so puzzled Brown and those after him.

Displacement

Einstein's approach was important because rather than attempting to use Newtonian mechanics to follow the motion of individual particles, as previous scientists had tried, he instead considered the system as a whole. Previous approaches had tried to track and record the motion of various individual particles, recording their velocities and directions. The problem with this method was that particle paths become very complicated very quickly. Since the scientists of the time were recording observations by hand using simple microscopes, it quickly became impossible to continue following a particular particle.

What is the difference between microscopic and macroscopic?
Microscopic means objects or particles that are only visible with the aid of a microscope. *Macroscopic* refers to things that are visible to the naked eye. In fact, in the case of atoms, microscopic doesn't even describe them properly, because they are so small they are only visible with special electron microscopes and not with a conventional optical microscope.

Since the velocities of the particles varied tremendously during their journeys, and the paths themselves were incredibly complex, Einstein decided not to base his equations on either. Instead, he defined the displacement as the straight-line distance between the beginning and end points of a path taken by an individual particle. Clearly, if the motion were more active, then the average displacement of the particles would be greater (although the individual displacement of any particular particle could be smaller, since the paths involved random motion and could double back on themselves).

Mean Free Path

Einstein then observed that the average displacement of particles increased with time. In fact, if the time was increased four times, the average displacement increased two times, and so on. With this line of reasoning, Einstein showed that he could calculate the mean free path for such particles. This path is the average distance that a particle could travel between collisions, as a function of time.

In his work on Brownian motion, Einstein boldly combined ideas that came from very different parts of physics, including kinetic theory, atomic theory, and hydrodynamics. His work also provided a firm theoretical support for the theory that matter consisted of tiny atoms and molecules. He showed that these tiny particles, even though they were invisible, could have an effect that was observable and possible to study.

Einstein's work on Brownian motion and kinetic theory spurred Jean Baptiste Perrin (1870–1942) to perform experiments to confirm Einstein's theoretical predictions. In performing these experiments, Perrin also proved that matter was made up of discontinuous atoms and molecules, and for this work he received the Nobel Prize in 1926.

Diffusion

Einstein's work on Brownian motion also introduced a new way to study the idea of diffusion. Diffusion is a process by which particles tend to separate and move from regions of higher concentration to regions of lower concentration. It can be seen in action by adding a drop of ink to a glass of water. At first, the ink remains clustered together; over time, even without stirring, the ink will gradually disperse until it is evenly distributed in the water.

Einstein suggested that Brownian motion was basically the same process as diffusion. He also calculated a way of finding the diffusion coefficient of a particular substance (the rate at which a given material will diffuse within another material), based on the radius of the particles doing the diffusing and a number of other material properties. This work was published in a 1906 paper entitled "On the Theory of Brownian Movement."

Molecular Dimensions

The last of Einstein's influential 1905 papers was in fact his doctoral dissertation, submitted for publication in April of 1905. This paper was entitled "A New Determination of Molecular Dimensions." In this work, Einstein showed how to calculate the sizes of molecules and Avogadro's number. This turned out to be one of Einstein's papers that has been referenced the most by other scientists over the years.

In this paper, Einstein used some experimental results on the diffusion of sugar dissolved in water to calculate the size of sugar molecules. These results suggested that sugar molecules were only about 1 nanometer in diameter (equivalent to 1 billionth of a meter). Einstein's new results also showed that when sugar was dissolved in water, some of the sugar molecules actually attached themselves to the water molecules. This result was a new one, and it caused the scientific community to take notice.

Einstein's doctoral dissertation, "A New Determination of Molecular Dimensions," was only seventeen pages long. It was originally rejected for being too short, but Einstein added one sentence and resubmitted it, and it was accepted by his thesis advisor and the ETH. Bigger isn't always better!

Avogadro's Number

In his paper, Einstein found expressions for the viscosity and the diffusion coefficient for a hard sphere in a continuous medium. Using these expressions and some experimental data based on diluted solutions of sugar in water, he obtained a value for Avogadro's number that was very close to the currently accepted value.

Einstein had an error in one of his equations in the 1905 paper on molecular dimensions, and it was not until he revised his work five years later that he calculated the correct value of Avogadro's number. Even Einstein didn't always get it right the first time! In fact, Einstein had to get help from one of his students to find the error in his original work.

Avogadro's number is defined as the number of molecules in a gram mole of a particular elemental substance. Avogadro's number is named after the chemist Amedeo Avogadro (1776–1856), who first suggested the idea that elements had particular weights. Avogadro did not actually calculate the value of the number, which has been honorarily named after him. In fact, the term "Avogadro's number" was first used by Jean

Baptiste Perrin in 1909 in his paper that followed Einstein's theoretical result and calculated the size of molecules.

So what is Avogadro's number good for? Avogadro's original theory, in 1811, suggested that a particular volume of any gas, at the same temperature and pressure, contained the same number of molecules no matter what gas it was. Experiments were done, and eventually it was concluded that one cubic centimeter of gas contained Avogadro's number of gas molecules, or about 6×10^{23} molecules.

The current value of Avogadro's number is 6.022×10^{23}, as determined by experiments using X ray diffraction. Avogadro's number is very difficult to determine, and many experiments over the years have refined this current value.

FACT

Avogadro's number is a very, very big number. It's so big that it is hard to comprehend. In fact, Avogadro's number of pennies placed next to each other in a line would be more than a million light years long.

The Mole

Avogadro's number is also used to define the mole. A mole, in addition to a small furry mammal, is defined in chemistry as the amount of a substance that contains Avogadro's number of molecules (or other units). A mole of oxygen contains 6.022×10^{23} oxygen molecules. A mole of sandwiches contains 6.022×10^{23} sandwiches. That's a lot of peanut butter and jelly!

Avogadro's number can also be used to convert between number and mass. Chemists defined the "atomic mass unit (amu)" as a relative measurement of mass. Since atoms and molecules are difficult to see even with the best microscope, it is nearly impossible to measure the mass of an individual atom. So scientists defined the atomic mass unit as $1/12$ of the mass of an atom of the element carbon-12.

ALERT!

The definition of Avogadro's number can seem confusing, but just think of it as another special name for a certain number of items. For example, a dozen contains twelve items. A gross contains 144 items. Avogadro's number of items contains 6.022×10^{23} items.

Molecular Masses

The atomic weights of elements, in atomic mass units, are used to line them up sequentially in the periodic table. The atomic mass of carbon-12, for example, is 12 amu, while the atomic mass of oxygen is 16 amu. Due to how atomic masses are defined, then, 12 grams of carbon-12 will contain the same number of atoms as 16 grams of oxygen.

But remember the definition of the mole as 6.022×10^{23} units. A mole of carbon, for example, will contain 6.022×10^{23} atoms of carbon, which will weigh 12 grams! The conversion from moles to grams depends on the molecular mass of the substance in question. To convert from moles to grams, just multiply by the molecular mass in grams per mole.

Einstein's Role

In coming up with a theoretical way to calculate Avogadro's number, Einstein provided essential support to the atomic theory of matter, which was still in question at the time that Einstein wrote his paper. Einstein's theoretical result spurred Perrin to measure Avogadro's number experimentally, thus providing solid experimental proof for the existence of atoms and molecules.

Other Early Science

In addition to the results described, Einstein also published a number of other early papers. These included a 1906 paper entitled "Planck's Theory of Radiation and the Theory of Specific Heat," which laid some of the groundwork for the quantum theory of solids. In 1910, Einstein published a paper on mixtures and light scattering, called "Theory of Opalescence of Homogeneous Liquids and Liquid Mixtures in the Neighborhood of Critical Conditions."

In 1908 Einstein submitted his habilitation thesis, which was an extra thesis that was required of scholars before they could become lecturers in the German university system. Einstein's habilitation thesis was entitled "Consequences for the Constitution of Radiation Following from the Energy Distribution Law of Black Bodies." It followed up on some of his previous work on the photoelectric effect and the quantum nature of electromagnetic radiation.

During this time, Einstein also published a number of other early papers that laid the groundwork for quantum mechanics; these ideas are discussed in Chapter 13. Einstein also began to work on his theory of general relativity during this time, and this topic is discussed in depth in Chapter 12. In the first decade of the century, therefore, Einstein managed to sow the seeds for his life's work and to begin the revolution in physics that would continue throughout his lifetime.

Chapter 9

Einstein's Contemporaries

The impact of Einstein's seminal papers cannot be underestimated. Scientists and laypeople alike of the early to mid-twentieth century knew his name. So what were other scientists around the world doing at this time? How was their work connected to Einstein's, if at all, and what reaction did they have toward Einstein?

Atmosphere in the Early Twentieth Century

The primary focus of the world's attention during the early to mid-twentieth century was, of course, World War I. It occupied virtually everyone's attention between 1914 and 1918. However, the war didn't stop science and technology. On the contrary, in fact—these years constituted a period of increased activity and development. Funding lay in war-oriented research, but scientists continued developing ideas and researching new theories.

Both scientists and inventors in this period were highly respected. Their creations had public appeal, especially when it became clear that the underlying technology would trickle down to the rest of society—as was the case with the invention of the radio and the television. Some scientists relished the attention the world paid to them, and celebrated in their lofty realms of academia; others, like Einstein, were less infatuated with their celebrity status. Einstein's political career would later thrust him more into the public eye, but in this early period he preferred working rather than merely garnering attention.

Einstein's research, though widely known, was somewhat resisted both during this initial period and to some extent later on. He was breaking with a well-established tradition, after all. Relativity was a new idea, one that was based on uncertainty rather than absolutism. In a time of political and social turmoil, Einstein contributed to these feelings by presenting a theory that denied the role of absolute time. It shook people's comfort level, changing both scientific expectations and the intuitive understanding of the surrounding world. However, the sheer genius of Einstein's work was irrefutable, and even the most questioning scientists of the day recognized the importance of his discoveries.

Einstein's work was considered controversial enough that, despite his genius, he eventually won a Nobel Prize not for his work in relativity, but rather for the photoelectric effect.

Louis de Broglie (1892–1987)

Louis de Broglie was a French physicist who won the Nobel Prize in physics in 1929. He actually studied history first, earning a degree in 1910, then went on to earn a science degree in 1913. He served in World War I, specializing in wireless technology. De Broglie is responsible for developing what would become the modern science of wave dynamics.

De Broglie Wavelength

His contributions were significant enough that de Broglie had a physics term named after him! The "de Broglie wavelength" defines a wavelength in terms of its motion by the equation $\lambda = h/p$. In this equation, λ is wavelength, h is Planck's constant, and p is relative momentum. This equation can be used to discover the wavelength of solid matter—de Broglie showed that a wavelength could be defined even for a solid object like a person. Einstein offered vocal support of this new theory, actually aiding de Broglie in receiving his degree from the University of Paris in 1924. Einstein championed de Broglie and his research, and the favor would be returned years later.

Between 1930 and 1950, de Broglie was active as a teacher, taking a great interest in his students' work. He was always interested in finding ways to bring science to the general public, and he explained things in ways that anyone could understand. In fact, in 1952 UNESCO (the United Nations Educational, Scientific and Cultural Organization) awarded him the Kalinga Prize for his explanation of physics using common terminology. Creating an international scientific community was one of de Broglie's life-long goals, and he worked hard at trying to expand the boundaries of science beyond the existing geographical barriers.

FACT

UNESCO, the United Nations Educational, Scientific and Cultural Organization, was founded in 1945 to promote collaboration between different countries. It sets standards, provides a forum for exchanging ideas, and researches future concepts of science and society.

Wave Mechanics

De Broglie spent much of his own professional career studying various aspects of wave mechanics. The theory of particle spins, new theories of light, and nuclear physics as relating to wave mechanics are just a few of the areas in which de Broglie had influence. Albert Einstein's work had a profound effect on de Broglie in this arena. Einstein uncovered the photoelectric effect, which purported that light was actually dual in nature. De Broglie would use this information to theorize that matter, not just light, is also dualistic; it could behave as both a particle and a wave.

If waves can exhibit particle-like behavior, particles can also act like waves. This idea would come to be known as "wave-particle duality," and set the stage for future research in this area (see Chapter 13 for more information).

Niels Bohr (1885–1962)

Niels Bohr was a physicist from Copenhagen, Denmark. Both of his parents were highly educated and intelligent individuals, so it's safe to say that he established his interest in science from a very young age. He received a master's degree in physics from Copenhagen University in 1911, following that with a doctorate in 1913. He worked largely in theory; research interested him far more than practical application.

Atomic Studies

Expanding on the research from Max Planck, Bohr formulated a theory about the atomic structure of elements, describing their chemical and physical properties. Defining the structure of the atom is what Bohr is most well known for; in fact, he received the Nobel Prize in physics for this work in 1922.

The subject of what made up the nucleus of the atom took precedence in Bohr's research after 1930. His work in quantum mechanics was summarized by his "concept of complementarity," which described the paradox of the wave-particle duality that was also being researched by de Broglie. He formulated the "liquid droplet theory" as a means to explain the atomic nucleus. Bohr described the nucleus as analogous to a drop of liquid, and this comparison would pave the way for research into nuclear fission. Fission is the process whereby a large atom is split into smaller ones, and a massive amount of energy is released.

Bohr left Copenhagen in 1943 to get away from the Nazi threat, and he spent the next few years in England and America. His research on nuclear science made him an important figure in the Manhattan Project, which would go on to create the nuclear bomb that was used in World War II. He actually worked in Los Alamos for a period. Like Einstein, however, he devoted the later part of his life toward lobbying for nuclear physics to be used for peaceful applications, and he was a huge proponent of international cooperation in controlling nuclear proliferation.

Bohr Versus Einstein

While Bohr and Einstein agreed on some things, they certainly didn't agree on everything! They differed substantially in their views of quantum mechanics. Bohr championed the "Copenhagen interpretation," which basically suggested that observation of the world was fundamental to constructing its reality. In Bohr's estimation, things didn't exist until they were observed. Einstein, on the other hand, posited that objects existed irrespective of observation; observation alone did not create reality. The two physicists would have many debates on this subject. See Chapter 13 for more information on their differences.

Max Karl Ernst Ludwig Planck (1858–1947)

In addition to de Broglie and Bohr, Max Karl Ernst Ludwig Planck was a scientist of fundamental importance during this period. A German-born physicist, Max Planck was the child of a law professor. He earned his doctorate in 1879, and after years of academic accomplishment, he became a full professor at Berlin University in 1889. Research in his early years focused on entropy, thermodynamics, and radiation. One of his most important breakthroughs was in the study of what was called "black body radiation," or the radiation emitted by solid bodies once they'd been heated. The current physics model couldn't explain his results, so in the true spirit of the burgeoning twentieth century, Planck changed the model. See Chapter 5 for more information on black body radiation.

Planck's Constant

The main puzzle of black body radiation, as considered by Planck, was related to the amount of heat that was given off by a heated body at various wavelengths. He was able to explain the odd experimental results if he assumed that radiation was quantized, and that it could only be given off in certain predetermined amounts. His seminal work in this area was codified by a relationship he developed between the frequency and energy of radiation around 1900. Planck required a multiplier, or a constant value, to make the relationship hold true. He described this relationship in terms of a universal constant, which is commonly called h, or Planck's constant.

Planck contributed to the philosophy of science (as did most physicists of the time!). He developed Planck's principle, which stated that scientific facts became recognized as such not through brute force, but by acceptance through the generations. He thought that once people had grown up with a series of ideas, they'd come to accept them as fact.

Planck would be remembered throughout history for his work in this area. It fundamentally changed the way physics was conceived of, overturning the views of Maxwell and others who had considered radiation as a continuum process, one which could take on any arbitrary value. Although his ideas were so new as to be frighteningly disruptive to the status quo, years of proof would give Planck approval and validity. Einstein's work with the photoelectric effect would rely greatly on Planck's research, as would Niels Bohr for his research with the atom. Planck won the Nobel Prize in physics in 1918.

Planck Versus Einstein

Einstein's work and Planck's would overlap on all levels. Planck showed that energy could be quantized, or referred to in terms of discrete units of energy, and that the size of these quanta depended on the frequency (or color) of light. This revelation would prove to be of primary importance in Einstein's work as well. The wave-particle duality would impact both their research, as would further developments in the study of electromagnetic radiation. Planck and Einstein together are commonly attributed with redefining physics in the twentieth century.

On a personal level, Planck was torn by the influence of the Nazi regime in Germany. He was philosophically against the terror Nazis imposed on the Jews, but he also felt an obligation to remain loyal to his country. He differed substantially in this regard from Einstein and other European scientists of the time. However, he did share other personal elements with Einstein, such as his love of music.

Marie Curie (1867–1934)

Marie Sklodowska Curie was born in Poland in 1867. She was the daughter of a teacher and was exposed to scientific training in her early school years. She moved to Paris in 1891, studying mathematics and physics there. She received a doctorate degree in 1903, and became a professor of general physics at the Sorbonne in 1906—she was their first female professor. She married Professor Pierre Curie, a physics professor, in 1895, but he unfortunately died in 1906.

The Curies performed research together up until Pierre Curie's death. Their path was paved, in a way, by the late-nineteenth-century discoveries of Henri Becquerel in the area of X rays and radioactive properties. One of the Curies' most significant contributions was the isolation of two new substances—radium and polonium. The nuclear generation would rely greatly on these discoveries.

Curie worked primarily with separating out the radioactive parts of a substance in order to study how radioactive material could be used. She was especially interested in using it for medical healing purposes, and she worked extensively in this area throughout World War I. She helped provide mobile X ray vans for use during the war, training the technicians herself. She was at the fore of nascent cancer research, convinced that radium "burns" could actually be used to treat malignant tumors, such a cancer.

FACT

Interestingly, Marie Curie initially didn't file a patent application for radium or polonium because she believed that radioactivity should be explored by as many people as possible. Would greed, or a desire for fame, have changed the path that her research took?

Marie Curie won two Nobel Prizes during her lifetime. One, the prize in physics, was shared with her husband in 1903. The second was in chemistry (for her work with radioactivity), which she won in 1911. These awards were in spite of the odds against her personally—being both a foreigner and a woman worked to her disadvantage. However, she persisted. In 1914, the Curie Laboratory was established at the Radium Institute, part of the University of Paris. She later established a radioactivity lab in Poland, and President Hoover donated a substantial amount of money to her work in 1929.

Einstein met Marie Curie at the first Solvay Conference. This physics meeting was held in Belgium in 1911, and some of the greatest minds of the time were in attendance. The 1927 conference, for example, would allow Curie, Einstein, Planck, Bohr, and many other physicists to meet and discuss ideas. While their research was carried out largely independently, these scientists who were defining history were very much aware of each other's ideas and work. Albert Einstein had great regard for Marie Curie, calling her one of the only people he knew who had not been corrupted by fame.

ALERT!

Yes, radiation is as dangerous as you think it is! Although the Curies and their technicians took some precautions, they didn't know exactly how much radiation they were being exposed to. Marie Curie actually died of leukemia, cancer that could have been caused by radiation exposure.

Leo Szilard (1898–1964)

One of Einstein's close friends and future colleagues, Leo Szilard, was a Hungarian physicist who was born into an engineering family. His areas of future research would focus on nuclear physics, nuclear engineering, mechanics, and biology. Szilard first studied engineering at Budapest Technical University in 1916, then joined the Austro-Hungarian army in 1917. He moved to Berlin in 1920, studying physics at the University of Berlin. Perhaps as a precursor of things to come, he actually took classes from both Albert Einstein and Max Planck.

With the impending Nazi regime and its worldwide influence, Leo Szilard left Hungary and traveled to England in 1933. His research in the 1930s led Szilard to arrive at the concept of the chain reaction, the idea that events could trigger other, related events. His research into nuclear science, coupled with the idea of a chain reaction, led him to become one of the foremost scientists of the nuclear age.

In the late 1930s, Szilard moved to the United States. The more he realized the potential for nuclear technology, the more fearful he became that the Germans were also developing these ideas. Szilard collaborated with other scientists working in the same field, especially Einstein and Enrico Fermi. Szilard and Fermi would, in 1942, create the first controlled nuclear chain reaction. Like Einstein, Szilard recognized the potential of atomic technology were it to be used to create a bomb. Also like Einstein, Szilard didn't favor using such technology to create instruments of war, but if someone were to build a bomb, he didn't want it to be the Nazis.

Szilard was involved to varying extents with the United States and the Manhattan Project. He was one of the signers of Einstein's famous letter to President Roosevelt, in which they warned of the dangers of the impending nuclear age (discussed in more detail in Chapter 15). By 1946, Einstein and Szilard had cofounded the Emergency Committee of Atomic Scientists. In 1955, Szilard and collaborator Fermi were awarded a patent for their design for the nuclear fission reactor. In 1957, Szilard helped create the Salk Institute for Biological Studies, located in La Jolla, California.

Einstein and Szilard clearly shared many common goals and ideas. While their research interests had different foundations, they had the same convictions about the use of nuclear technology. Szilard was active in encouraging countries such as the Soviet Union to disarm militarily, and in 1962 he went on to found the Council for Abolishing War.

FACT

Beginning in 1926, Szilard worked with Einstein on several inventions, including the development of a home refrigerator pump. This invention, discussed in detail in Chapter 20, would be known as the Einstein-Szilard pump.

Literature and Philosophy of the Period

Many other aspects of society and culture were profoundly changed by the advent of the twentieth century. Philosophy, religion, and literature are just a few examples of fields in which leaders emerged, creating new styles and policies. Although Einstein was firmly enshrined in the scientific community, he was influenced as well by changes in other areas. Particularly in his later years, Einstein turned his focus to politics; how did psychology and literature, for example, provide a counterpoint to some of his other interests?

Sigmund Freud (1856–1939)

Born Jewish but proclaiming atheism later, Freud was born in Austro-Hungary. He moved to Vienna as a child, staying there until the Nazi occupation in the late 1930s. He studied medicine in school, although pure science was much more interesting to him. He decided to obtain a specialty in neurology and go into private practice.

Freud learned about hypnotism from a physician named Josef Breuer; this method would become known as the "talking cure." Although he tried this method himself, he found patients responded much better to relaxing on a couch and being asked to talk about whatever came into their minds. This method would be called "free association," and was one of the hallmarks of Freud's therapy.

He was interested in uncovering past trauma as the root of people's current suffering. Freud published his ideas in 1900 in *The Interpretation of Dreams.* Freud was one of the first to promote the idea of the unconscious mind, one that would retain information but allow it to resurface in different forms. This psychological research, which many take for granted today, was new to the turn of the century. Freud had a very significant impact on the burgeoning field of psychology—he was a prolific writer, and his name soon became a household word.

Einstein and Freud had direct communication. While Einstein would have been considered a "hard" scientist (meaning one who studied physics, chemistry, and so on), he had tremendous respect for Freud's work on the unconscious. Einstein recognized that factors other than genetics contributed to what a person would become, and he encouraged Freud's exploration of this relatively new field. Einstein included Freud when organizing a meeting of worldwide intellectual leaders, showing how greatly he admired Freud's research.

The two corresponded on a variety of subjects. At one point, Einstein wrote to Freud concerning war. He was curious to know what someone who studied the human psyche thought about the concept of war—the question he raised was why world leaders persisted in initiating conflict, despite the terrible aftereffects. It was during this period that Einstein was developing his idea for a world government; he saw a global governing body as the only means by which to avoid individual nations going to war with each other. It's very interesting that Einstein respected a "soft" scientist such as Freud enough to use him as a sounding board for developing his ideas!

Great Authors

Literature was another field in which many great minds appear to have surfaced around the turn of the century. James Joyce (1882–1941), for example, was an Irish writer and poet who would have enormous influence over twentieth-century writing. His early major works included *Dubliners* from 1914 and *A Portrait of the Artist as a Young Man* from 1916. He introduced (actually reintroduced, from antiquity) the concept of the epic novel. In 1922 he published *Ulysses,* a novel that was based on Homer's *Odyssey.*

Despite the differences in subject matter, there are similarities between the work of Joyce and Einstein. Both were innovators, at a time when invention was both welcome and necessary. Joyce's style of writing was experimental and groundbreaking; it showed that there were new ways in which novels could be written and understood.

Critics at the time even compared Joyce to Einstein. Their masterpieces were contemporary; each strove to define new ideas through his own medium. Einstein's theory of relativity may have even provided Joyce with the tools to develop his writing style. Relativity provided a framework in which multiple truths could exist; the old way of doing things wasn't necessarily the only way, and perhaps Joyce absorbed this idea in the process of creating the style of the epic novel.

T. S. Eliot (1885–1965) was another author whose work impacted Einstein, and vice versa. Born in Missouri and educated at Harvard, Eliot moved to England, becoming a British citizen in 1927. He believed that poetry should represent reality. The English language was a very complex one, and he tried to show that complexity through his writing. Eliot is probably best known for *The Waste Land*, completed in 1922. He was one of the most innovative poets of the twentieth century, and he actually won a Nobel Prize in literature in 1948.

One of the most important innovations of twentieth-century poets like Eliot was the rampant use of the pronoun "I" in their writing. It brought about an affirmation of relativity, in a way, with the author taking a central role. Relativity, to authors such as Eliot, represented just this kind of radical switch in the way they were used to thinking; they took Einstein's scientific studies and applied them to their own work and lives.

Eliot had a connection to Einstein, as well as James Joyce. In his 1923 "Ulysses, Order and Myth," an essay in which Eliot ponders about using myth to convey meaning, he connects Joyce to Einstein directly. He describes how, as Einstein made scientific invention and discovery, Joyce did the same for mythology and writing. Great minds truly do think alike, despite belonging to different fields of study and different geographical locales. Ⓔ

Chapter 10

Background on the General Theory of Relativity

After the success of special relativity in uniting space and time, Einstein began working on a more general theory of relativity, which eventually united relativity with gravity. Einstein's work was an extension of the theory of gravity, as originally developed by Galileo and Newton.

Special Versus General Relativity

Einstein's theory of special relativity, as described in Chapter 6, revolutionized the way scientists viewed space and time. It combined them into a new theory of space-time in which both time and distance were variable instead of fixed. The only fixed quantity in Einstein's special relativity was the speed of light. However, special relativity was restricted to inertial reference frames—those that did not accelerate or change direction.

Einstein began working almost immediately to generalize his theory of relativity. He wanted a theory that would explain what happened not only in inertial reference frames, but in any frame—moving, accelerating, or changing direction. As it turned out, there was another problem with special relativity: It was incompatible with Newton's law of gravity. In working to unite gravity with relativity, Einstein eventually came up with his theory of general relativity.

Einstein's theory of general relativity can also be called "Einstein's Law of Gravitation," and was based on the work done by Galileo and Newton on gravitational attraction. Beginning in 1907, Einstein began his attempts to use gravity as an invariant in a more general theory of relativity, just as the fixed speed of light was the invariable quantity in his theory of special relativity.

To read Einstein's own words about special and general relativity, check out this free online version of a book written by him in 1920. The title is *Relativity: The Special and General Theory,* and it provides an interesting insight into Einstein's easy-to-understand writing style (and very few equations!). You will find it at ✐*www.bartleby.com/173/.*

Galileo's Principle

The first mathematical codification of gravity was performed by Galileo Galilei (1564–1642). Galileo, while perhaps best known for his observations with the telescope, also developed the first formulaic description of gravity. In studying gravity, Galileo determined that all objects will fall with the same acceleration, no matter what their mass. The motion of a falling body depends on two things: the way in which the body was released, and its initial velocity. Thus, heavy objects fall as fast as lighter objects.

How did Galileo come to these conclusions? Gravity was known from ancient times as an attractive force. However, from the time of the first Greek scientists until the Renaissance, it was thought of as a force that only acted when two objects were touching each other.

Galileo refined this idea by thinking of gravity as a force that attracts any two masses to each other. He did a series of experiments to test his ideas, which involved rolling balls down ramps and dropping objects off of towers.

Since accurate clocks were not yet available in Galileo's time, he used a water clock to measure time intervals. In this type of clock, water dripped through a small hole in the bottom of a tank. Time could be measured by measuring the amount of water that had poured out of the tank, since the small hole resulted in a fairly constant flow rate.

Experiments with Projectiles

In Galileo's ramp experiments, he rolled balls down a series of ramps that ended above the ground. He then measured the trajectory of the balls after they left the ramp, recording the height at which they were released at the top of the ramp, and the distance they traveled from the bottom of the ramp before hitting the ground.

Galileo also did experiments by dropping objects from a tower. He showed that if he dropped a heavy cannonball and a lighter ball at the same time, they hit the ground at the same time. These experiments showed that the acceleration of gravity is independent of the mass of an object.

ALERT!

Although legend has it that Galileo performed a famous experiment by dropping objects off the Leaning Tower of Pisa to compare how fast they reached the ground, there is no solid historical evidence that he ever used the tower for such a purpose!

Air Resistance

Of course, if Galileo had chosen to drop two objects of different shape, such as a feather and a cannonball, they would not have reached the ground at the same time. Why? The answer is air resistance, or drag, which is proportional to the surface area of an object. Two objects with the same shape, but different masses, will reach the ground at the same time. However, since a feather has more surface area than a ball, the feather will take more time to reach the ground than a compact object of the same mass. If two objects are dropped in a vacuum, however, they will reach the ground at the same time, independent of surface area, because there is no drag.

FACT

Apollo astronauts actually demonstrated this principle on the surface of the moon, where there is basically no atmosphere. Apollo 15 astronaut David Scott dropped a feather and a hammer on live television and, sure enough, they reached the ground at the same time. You can see a movie of this experiment at this Web address: ✑ *http://nssdc.gsfc.nasa.gov/planetary/image/feather drop_sound.mov.*

Galileo's experiments showed that the acceleration of gravity was the same for all falling objects and that any two objects would hit the ground at the same time if they were not subject to drag. This overturned previous notions, such as those of Aristotle, which assumed that heavier objects fell faster than lighter ones. Galileo's results, however, were purely experimental. He did not provide an explanation for how gravity worked, or any mathematical basis for his theories.

Galileo's principle of gravity states that heavy objects fall as fast as lighter ones, in the absence of other forces like air resistance. A body's motion depends only on how it was released and its initial velocity.

Newton's Discoveries

Following Galileo, the next major breakthrough in the study of gravity was by Isaac Newton (1642–1727). Newton is perhaps most famous for his laws of motion, in which he defined a force as $F = ma$, where F is a force, m is a mass, and a is an acceleration. Newton was also responsible for a mathematical theory of gravity, called Newton's law of universal gravitation.

Kepler's Laws of Planetary Motion

Newton's study of gravity was initially prompted by a desire to explain the laws of planetary motion that had been described in the early 1600s by Johannes Kepler (1571–1630). Kepler was an astronomer as well as a mathematician, and he spent many years analyzing the painstaking observations of planetary positions that had been made by his teacher, Tycho Brahe (1546–1601).

Using Brahe's observations, Kepler was able to determine the motions of the planets around the sun, with respect to time. These observations also helped support the heliocentric view of the solar system, in which the planets orbited around the sun rather than around the Earth. Kepler was able to describe the motion of the planets with three laws of planetary motion:

1. Planets move in paths around the sun, which are shaped like ellipses, with the sun at one focus.
2. A line from the sun to a planet will sweep out equal areas in equal times. What this idea means is that when the planet is close to the sun, it moves faster than when it is farther from the sun.
3. The squares of the periods of planets are proportional to the cubes of their average distances from the sun.

While Kepler's laws have proven to be accurate even today, Kepler provided no explanation for why planetary motion followed his laws. He could only suggest that there was some sort of interaction between the planet and the sun that guided its path, but he did not know what form that interaction took.

Newton's Apple

Newton was puzzled by Kepler's laws, and he set out to determine an explanation for their form. He was also intrigued by the motion of the moon around the Earth, which he knew to follow a circular path. Because of the elliptical and circular motion of these bodies, Newton inferred that there must be some sort of central force at work. Without a central force, motion would just follow a straight line. Since the planets and moon both followed closed loop-like orbits, they had to be subject to some sort of central force to keep them from leaving the system.

ALERT!

Legend has it that Newton developed his theory of gravity when he was hit on the head by a falling apple at age twenty-four. However, there is no historical proof that this event ever took place—Newton never mentions it in his own writings, for example.

Whether or not the legend of Newton getting hit by an apple is true, he did have a breakthrough in relating the motion of falling objects on Earth to the motion of the moon and planets in the sky, and this insight led to his law of universal gravitation. Newton initially studied the motion of projectiles such as cannonballs, which are launched with a certain trajectory and speed.

Cannonballs

Newton performed a thought-experiment, in which he considered a cannonball launched horizontally from the top of a tall mountain (without any air resistance to change the results). If there were no gravity, a cannonball would just travel along a long, straight path after its launch. However, since there is a gravitational force acting on the cannonball, this force will make it fall down below its horizontal path and eventually hit the surface of the Earth.

Newton realized that the shape of the cannonball's path curved like a piece of a circle! He then imagined firing the cannonball with an even greater velocity, still horizontally. In this case, the cannonball would travel a longer distance before falling to Earth. In fact, if the cannonball in Newton's thought-experiment were fired with enough initial velocity, it would travel all around the Earth in a circular path and return to the mountain it had started from (assuming it didn't hit any other mountains along the way, of course).

The Moon

Newton then realized that if the initial mountain could get out of the way, the cannonball (or other projectile) would continue on its circular path around the Earth, becoming a satellite of the Earth in much the same way as the moon orbits the Earth! His thought-experiment had related the force of gravity, which makes objects fall to Earth, with the force that keeps objects in orbit.

There was still a problem with Newton's theory that gravity was responsible for the orbits of the moon and planets. Scientists in Newton's day measured the acceleration that the force of gravity produced on falling objects. They also measured the acceleration of the moon. However, the two forces were not the same! The gravitational acceleration of falling objects at the surface of the Earth was much greater than the value for the acceleration of the moon. If both motions were due to the gravitational attraction of the Earth, then how could their values be so different?

The Inverse Square Law

Newton decided that the force of gravity must depend on distance. In comparing the acceleration of the moon to the acceleration of a falling object on the surface of the Earth, he discovered that the value of acceleration decreased as the square of the distance increased. The distance in this equation is the distance from an object to the center of the Earth.

For example, the distance for an object falling at the surface of the Earth (such as an apple falling from a tree) is one Earth radius. The distance from the center of the Earth to the moon is about 60 Earth radii. Since the force of gravity decreases with the square of the distance, the gravitational force felt by the moon must be about $1/60^2$ times the gravitational force felt by an apple on the surface of the Earth. Sure enough, when Newton compared the accelerations measured for falling objects on the surface of the Earth to the acceleration of the moon, the moon's acceleration was about $1/3600$ times as much.

Newton's Law of Universal Gravitation

Putting together all the pieces of the puzzle, Newton was finally able to describe a universal law of gravitation that applied both to falling objects on Earth and to the moon and planets orbiting in the solar system. Remember from Newton's laws of motion that a force is equal to a mass multiplied by an acceleration: F=ma. Newton knew from this equation that it was not only the distance between two objects that determined the force with which they attracted each other. Since force is proportional to mass, from this he surmised that the gravitational force was also dependent on the masses of the two objects.

Newton's law of universal gravitation can be summarized as follows:

$$F = \frac{Gm_1m_2}{r^2}$$

Here, F is the gravitational force, G is a constant of proportionality, m_1 and m_2 are the two masses that are attracting each other, and r is the distance between them.

The reason that Newton's discovery is called "universal" is that it applies to all objects. Everything with mass attracts everything else with mass, with a force that is proportional to the masses of the two objects and the distance between them. This theory applies to all matter in the universe, from the smallest atom to the largest galaxy.

QUESTION?

If all matter attracts all other matter, why don't we feel a gravitational attraction from a person standing next to us?
There is in fact a gravitational force, but it is very small. Gravity is a relatively weak force, and it can be felt only when objects become very large and massive. For this reason, the gravitational force of the Earth pulls you down much more strongly than the gravitational force of a person pulls you toward her.

Cavendish Measures G

The constant G in Newton's law of universal gravitation was not measured precisely until a century after Newton's time. The primary scientist responsible for these measurements was Henry Cavendish (1731–1810). Cavendish used an experimental device called a torsion balance to perform a very delicate experiment. He had a rod with a large mass on each end, balanced in the center by another rod. If the masses rotated, the suspension rod twisted and the amount of twist could then be measured very precisely. Once the experimental setup was in place, Cavendish brought two very large masses near the ones attached to the rod, causing them to be attracted slightly and to twist the suspension rod.

Cavendish used this experiment to measure the amount of gravitational attraction very precisely. Using his measurements, he determined a value of G that is very close to today's value of $6.67259 \times 10^{-11} \mathrm{Nm}^2/\mathrm{kg}^2$. This is a very small number, an observation that makes sense because the attraction of gravity is a very small force. The small value of G helps us understand why gravitational forces are only felt from very large objects like the Earth, and not from smaller ones like people.

Refinements to Gravitational Theory

Newton's ideas of gravity held up very well until the advent of the twentieth century. Around this time, a number of scientists began to investigate problems and extensions of the study of gravity. The major problem with Newton's theory of gravity was that while his theory held up elegantly in explaining how masses reacted to the presence of other masses, it could not explain how one mass knew that another was present to interact with.

Maxwell's Suggestion

In 1864, James Clerk Maxwell (of electromagnetic fame) made a few comments relating electromagnetic interactions to gravitational interactions. Since electromagnetic interactions also decreased with the square of the distance, Maxwell suggested that there might be a similar cause for both phenomena due to the action of the medium surrounding the charges or masses.

Gravitational Waves

In 1900, Hendrik Lorentz (1853–1928) suggested that gravitational interactions could be caused by the propagation of some sort of information that traveled at the speed of light. Later, Jules Henri Poincaré (1854–1912) published a paper in 1905, just before Einstein's theory of special relativity. This paper suggested that such information could be in the form of gravity waves, which traveled at the speed of light. Einstein would extend these theories as he developed his own theory of gravity.

Newton's theory of gravitation was highly successful for a number of centuries after its publication. However, the main problem with Newton's ideas was that no one was able to suggest how each of the two bodies gravitationally attracting each other knew that the other was there!

Einstein Searches for a More General Theory

So where do all these experiments on gravity fit in with relativity? Recall that special relativity, as developed initially by Einstein in 1905, did not include gravity. It was only valid in inertial reference frames, those that were not accelerating or changing direction. Einstein wanted to generalize his theory to all possible reference frames, including those that were changing direction or speed.

There was also a problem with special relativity in that it was incompatible with Newton's law of gravity. According to Newton, if a gravity field is reconfigured, there is an instantaneous response that is felt by all objects affected by the gravitational field as they adjust to the new configuration. However, according to the theory of special relativity, nothing can travel faster than the speed of light—including information! There can be no instantaneous response to changing conditions. Such a response would also require a universal time, another quantity that was inconsistent with special relativity.

To solve these problems, Einstein began work on a new theory of general relativity, one that included gravity as its new invariable quantity. He was first aware of the problem in 1907, soon after the publication of his first paper on special relativity, and began work on the problem in earnest around 1911. His work would finally be completed in the theory of general relativity, discussed in depth in Chapter 12.

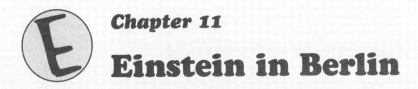

Chapter 11

Einstein in Berlin

The years between 1905 and 1910 were some of the most critical in Einstein's early career. The three seminal papers he produced influenced the path the rest of his life would follow. His personal and professional lives would take a variety of interesting twists and turns in the "middle period," from about 1905 until the early 1930s.

Chapter 4 left off with Einstein having taken a job with the Swiss Patent Office in 1902. While this job was certainly not what he'd been looking for in terms of a teaching or research position, it paid the bills. It also sharpened some of his nonscientific skills. He had to be careful and precise, and he learned about researching things quickly and thoroughly.

First University Appointment

In 1908, Einstein was appointed Privatdozent, or lecturer, at the University of Bern. This step was important for Einstein in that he was getting more of the recognition he deserved. Why was he able to get a teaching job now, when he wasn't able to before? Part of the reason is that he submitted his "habilitation" thesis in this year.

In order to become a lecturer at a German university, scientists were required to submit this extra thesis, which was to be completed after their doctoral theses. Einstein's habilitation was entitled "Consequences for the Constitution of Radiation Following from the Energy Distribution Law of Black Bodies." When he submitted this work, the administration at the University of Bern took notice, and Einstein was able to teach at a university.

Working at the Patent Office

1909 would find Einstein still working at the Swiss Patent Office in Bern. Later that year, he would finally resign. His resignation came about for several reasons. He'd taken the job because he needed to earn a living, and the job had a schedule so that he had plenty of time for his own work. One of the great advantages of working at the patent office was undoubtedly just this—that Einstein had time to work on his own projects and research, but it was still a day job. He had responsibilities there that took time and energy, and they would eventually take a toll on his research time.

When Einstein's main papers on relativity were presented, the outpouring of support was comparatively enormous. The idea of making a living as a scientist was becoming more and more real. He was starting to become recognized as one of Europe's premiere scientific thinkers and researchers. It was during this year that Einstein finally was able to devote his professional life more fully to science and research. In 1909, Einstein earned an associate professorship at the University of Zurich, and he was able to make a clean break with the patent office. He also resigned from his lectureship at the University of Bern.

FACT

Einstein's stint at the patent office certainly wasn't without benefits. He walked home from the patent office each day with Michele Besso, an Italian Swiss friend with whom he collaborated on scientific writings in 1913 concerning the motion of Mercury's perihelion. Einstein collaborated with other scientist friends as well, including Marcel Grossmann.

Major Life Changes

After the isolation of his early years in science, Einstein's professional career began to pick up once his work on relativity was recognized internationally. A number of other events also took place at this stage of his career.

The Birth of Einstein's Second Son

Einstein's personal life took a turn in 1910 with the arrival of his second son, Eduard. His approach to parenting two children seems to have been similar to when Hans was Albert's only child. Family was important and to be cherished, and love was in abundance, despite Einstein's obsession with his work. Einstein was reputed to have been able to work despite a baby's crying, or despite just about any other interruption.

The Move to Prague

In 1911, Einstein finally earned a full-time teaching position in Prague. He was appointed a full professor of theoretical physics at the Karl-Ferdinand University. It was here that Einstein began developing his theory of gravity—that there was a relationship between acceleration and the Earth's gravitational field. The family, however, was less than pleased with the move to Prague. Mileva never liked it there. In addition, their second child took a toll on Mileva. She now had two small children to care for, and Einstein himself required much care in terms of daily life. She was finding herself more and more exhausted, and this additional stress put a damper on her relationship with Einstein. Both Albert and Mileva were frustrated with the situation, and they came to associate Prague with this discontent. Anti-Semitism was rampant in Prague at this time, another factor that contributed to the Einstein family's dislike of their current situation.

Einstein's research took a turn in 1911. He was able to make predictions about how a ray of light from a far-off star that passed close to the sun would appear to be bent toward the sun. Proofs of this idea were very important because they provided actual, hard evidence that supported Einstein's theory.

Reacquaintance with a Long-Lost Cousin

In 1912, after a long absence, Einstein became reacquainted with a cousin named Elsa Lowenthal. The cousins had gotten together many times during Einstein's youth, when his family still owned a large villa in Munich. By the time they met up in 1912, Elsa had been married and had two daughters of her own. It seems to have been love at first sight for Albert and Elsa. She was from a cultural and economic background similar to his, and there was a familiarity between them that didn't exist with Mileva. They enjoyed the same foods and appreciated the same ideals of simple living. Being related, of course, probably contributed to that sense of the familiar. Albert and Elsa began writing letters back and forth, and this communication would remain strong.

The Glorious Return to the ETH

1912 was the year in which old ghosts were absolved. Einstein was invited back to the Eidgenössische Technische Hochschule—from which he'd barely graduated—only this time as a professor. He was able to reunite with Marcel Grossmann, and the two continued their personal and professional relationships. Einstein was also chosen for membership in the elite Prussian Academy of Science in Berlin in 1913, showing how much respect he was starting to garner in the international community.

At this time, Einstein met Friedrich Adler. Adler was a famous Austrian whom Einstein met during his time at university. Adler was a pacifist, who was vehemently opposed to the impending war. His antiwar ideas rubbed off on Einstein, and they would continue to influence him for years to come. Adler would later become more notorious than famous. He actually assassinated the prime minister of Austria in 1916! Einstein certainly had some important friends.

There was a bit of competition between the two men, as well. Adler was offered a teaching position at the University of Zurich in 1908, the same position Einstein applied for (and was first rejected for). Adler declined the offer, saying that the university was ridiculous for rejecting Einstein. Adler was also responsible for introducing Einstein to the Second International, a political group consisting of socialist/democratic Europeans. While Einstein solidified some of his growing pacifistic ideas here, the group was always divided amongst itself and never gained widespread popularity. Though Einstein and Adler met through science, they discovered much other common ground, and respect appears to have been paramount throughout their relationship.

World War I

The outbreak of World War I was, without question, the most significant event in Einstein's middle years. The war had a tremendous impact on not just Einstein's research, but on the scientific community in general. To understand how the war affected Einstein, it's necessary to understand the war itself, especially how the fighting between countries affected Einstein's places of residence. World War I fundamentally changed the way Einstein interacted with his family and his colleagues, as it did for many other European citizens of the time.

Background

To understand the history of World War I, it's a good idea to look at the overall alignment of European countries. Politically, early-twentieth-century Europe was a system of alliances. Countries were grouped by how they saw each other—friend or foe—and these relationships weren't always strictly geographical. People were not always free to simply travel from country to country, and these political boundaries created conflict and complication.

FACT

There were two main factions in Europe at this time—the Central Powers and the Allied Forces. The Central Powers consisted of Germany, Austria-Hungary, and Italy, while the Allied Forces were comprised of Russia, France, and Britain. The war itself, then, was bounded politically as well as geographically.

World War I officially began on June 28, 1914. A Slav citizen named Gavrilo Princip assassinated Archduke Francis Ferdinand, who was to become king of the Austro-Hungarian empire. Ferdinand's supporters immediately blamed Serbia for the attack, and thus began the war. Britain officially entered the war on August 4, 1914, when Germany invaded Belgium (a neutral country, although one the British had sworn to protect). Trenches were dug and machine guns were set up; the land war proceeded throughout this part of Europe.

However, the war was not limited to the mainland continent of Europe. Japan soon allied itself with the Allied Forces, and the Ottoman Empire with the Central Forces. Other countries and nations joined in, hence the name World War I. It truly became a worldwide affair, one that affected just about everyone.

During the period in 1915, the United States made loans to Britain. Since most European men of working age had been drafted or voluntarily joined the service, women were taking over traditional men's roles back home in their communities. Bulgaria joined the Central Forces, and Italy switched sides to fight with the Allied Forces. Also in 1915, German Zeppelin airships dropped bombs over Britain. Submarine warfare was also an element, making this war truly a "world war" found on land, in the sea, and in the air. The United States declared war on Germany in 1917 and, to make a very long story short, in 1918 an armistice was signed between Germany and the Allied Forces.

Impact on Einstein

So how did World War I affect Einstein? For one thing, it brought out the pacifism in him that had been somewhat latent in previous years. Einstein had always had pacifist tendencies, and had successfully avoided serving in either the German or Swiss military during his youth. The breadth of the war, and the influence it had on just about every aspect of European life, made Einstein realize how little he wanted to be involved with the fighting.

The war also brought about a change in priorities for Einstein. He had, up until this point, been obsessed largely with science and research. Family provided a happy diversion, as did his day job at the patent office, but science was first and foremost upon his mind. The devastating and far-reaching impact of World War I made Einstein much more aware of the importance of politics. His political consciousness was born in this period. Politics occupied more and more of Einstein's time, particularly in the middle years of the war.

A Commitment to Pacifism

His discontent with the war did not earn him new friends in the academic community. Einstein was horrified by what he saw as the "civilized" nations of Europe engaging in down-and-dirty, primal battle. However, many of Einstein's colleagues were either of a military background, or otherwise pro-war. Still a Swiss citizen, Einstein was in no danger of having to fight for Germany, but his political views were definitely solidified during this period.

At the start of the war, a coalition of German scientists and other intellectuals signed a manifesto in support of Germany's position in the war. Einstein, on the other hand, signed antiwar petitions. His pacifism probably offended some of his contemporaries and contributed to a growing personal alienation Einstein felt, both in his marriage and in his professional life.

The Move to Berlin

1914, the year the war first broke out, heralded several important changes in Einstein's life. It was then that he was invited by Max Planck to become director of the Kaiser Wilhelm Institute of Physics, a position he accepted and would retain until 1933. This organization was an opportunity for Einstein to conduct his own science and research, under his own demands, schedules, and guidelines.

Max Planck was a noted German physicist who challenged many notions of classical physics. He developed a quantum theory of physics, which Einstein used in his own explanations of photo-electricity. Planck won the Nobel Prize for physics in 1918. He was appointed president of the Kaiser Wilhelm Physical Institute in 1930.

Like Einstein, Planck was a pacifist. Although projects relating to war were plentiful during his lifetime, Planck refused to work on any project whose research went directly to the war effort. He adamantly opposed Hitler, and anti-Semitism in general. Although he was reluctant to return to Germany at all, Einstein was wooed there by the promise of a prestigious position at the center of the European physics community. In addition to the position at Kaiser Wilhelm, Einstein was also appointed a professor at the University of Berlin in 1914, furthering both his academic and research goals.

Einstein's First Marriage: The Beginning of the End

World War I took an enormous toll on Einstein's marriage. The family moved to Berlin in April of 1914. In the summer of 1914, Einstein's wife and children took a vacation in Switzerland. Separate vacations were not uncommon in the Einstein household. Albert usually went home to visit his family, and Mileva was generally not invited along for those excursions. Similarly, she would often vacation away from him.

FACT

Although Einstein moved back to his native Germany in 1914, he did not immediately reapply for German citizenship. He instead kept his Swiss citizenship, although his official citizenship status would change several more times over the course of his life.

This trip, though, would be different. After the war broke out in August of 1914, Mileva, Hans, and Eduard were unable to travel from Switzerland to Berlin, and they couldn't rejoin Einstein there.

The separation between Einstein and Mileva may have been physically caused by the outbreak of World War I, but the seeds of discontent were probably already there. Einstein's increasing fame aroused some feelings of discontent with Mileva. Jealousy may have played a role, and she could have been resenting him for her own failed career as a scientist. There seems to be a correlation between Einstein's rise in popularity and her own dissatisfaction with him.

Letters from Albert to Mileva showed that he was becoming increasingly demanding of Mileva's time and attention. Their marriage was showing signs of strain, with Einstein demanding that she serve him most meals in his room. He asked her not to speak badly of him in front of their children—well, "ask" may be a polite rephrasing of what was actually said—indicating that appearances were important to Einstein. Such interactions also showed that, despite marital problems, Einstein wanted to be popular with his children, and he tried to keep things positive for them rather than exposing them to the troubles he and his wife were having. After a separation of a number of years, Einstein and Mileva eventually divorced in 1919.

More Life Changes

The years from 1915 to 1920 brought more changes, both personal and scientific, to Einstein's world. From illness to the end of war to scientific triumph, Einstein emerged into the 1920s as one of the world's most preeminent scientists.

Serious Illness

Einstein became seriously ill in 1917. He collapsed, perhaps partly due to pressures from his research and from the new stress of being such a prominent figure throughout the scientific community. He'd been working on developing his theory of gravity during this time, and it's likely that he nearly exhausted himself to death. He'd been separated from his wife since 1914, so she was not by his side during this intense period. Instead, his cousin Elsa was the one who helped Einstein regain his health. She stood by him completely during this time, and their love grew stronger and stronger.

Political Changes

1918 marked the end of World War I. This was also the year in which Einstein was one of the creators of the German Democratic Party, a progressive political party. In order to further show his support for the party, Einstein would eventually reclaim his German citizenship.

Relativity Tested

1919 was another seminal year in Einstein's life—his theory of relativity was put to the test. His earlier predictions of how the sun would deflect passing starlight were proven true by a total solar eclipse that occurred on May 29, 1919. The British sent expeditions to monitor the eclipse, and Einstein's predictions were proven correct. This eclipse, discussed in depth in Chapter 12, proved to be a turning point in Einstein's professional career.

Einstein's Divorce

By 1919, Albert and Mileva's marital discontent (as well as his obvious love for Elsa) reached a point where it could no longer be ignored. They filed a separation agreement, but Mileva was at first reluctant to divorce Einstein. She probably suspected that he would want to marry Elsa at some point, and her jealousy played a factor in wanting to keep the marriage alive. However, eventually she conceded, and the couple was officially divorced.

Einstein didn't exactly sit around in mourning, though. Just a few months after the divorce, Einstein married his cousin Elsa Lowenthal. They would stay married until Elsa's death in 1936. However, Einstein wasn't reputed to be the most faithful of husbands, even to Elsa. He had numerous affairs over the years of their marriage, which Elsa appears to have more or less put up with.

FACT

1920 marked the year that Einstein's mother died after a bout with cancer. Her death led Einstein to focus on his work even more, leading the way to major events in the near future.

The Nobel Prize and International Acclaim

1921 was another seminal year in Einstein's public life. It was then that he was awarded the Nobel Prize in physics "for his services to Theoretical Physics, and especially for his discovery of the law of the photoelectric effect." He did not receive the Nobel Prize for his work on relativity but for his early work from one of his first major papers, in 1905.

Einstein was unable to travel to Sweden to accept the award, since he was traveling in Japan at the time. Einstein and his wife Elsa also toured the United States in 1921. He was world-famous for having won the Nobel Prize, and they were constantly followed by photographers and journalists. Although Einstein's nature was not to pose for the camera, he used his popularity to further the two causes he felt strongest about, Zionism and pacifism.

Einstein and the Bauhaus

In 1924 Einstein actually played a role in the creation of one of the period's most important architectural movements. The Bauhaus School, a daring new school of architecture and design, was founded in 1919 in Germany. Bauhaus design principles influenced most aspects of life: furniture design, photography, typeface, theater, use of color, architectural style, and kitchen dishes are just a few examples. Many of the Bauhaus students and instructors would go on to become famous. Some of the more well-known alumni include Wassily Kandinsky, Marcel Breuer, Paul Klee, and Ludwig Mies Van Der Rohe.

The school was founded in Weimar, and it was headed by Walter Gropius. Gropius would eventually have a worldwide impact on architecture—he served as the chair of Harvard University's Graduate School of Design in 1937. The school relocated to Dessau in 1925. The death of the school came at the hands of the Nazis in 1933, and many of its teachers moved to the United States at that time. Einstein came out in support of this radical new style, and his endorsement helped the school gain popularity.

ALERT!

Who would think that dishes and tablecloths could carry political meaning strong enough to cause someone to fear for his or her life? Nazi misinterpretation severely limited the growth of artistic (not to mention religious) development, showing how important freedom of expression really is.

The Formation of Einstein's Political Life

Einstein and other Jewish intellectuals were increasingly stigmatized during the 1920s. The League of Nations was first founded in 1920, and in 1922 Einstein joined the Committee on Intellectual Cooperation, which formed under the auspices of the League of Nations. Other famous scientists were invited to join this committee, including Marie Curie. Through this group, Einstein attempted to further his attempts to promote world peace, but he resigned from this organization after a year. He didn't feel that they took activism strongly or seriously enough. He did, however, keep attending their meetings throughout the 1920s. He continued to further his political causes, including petitioning for the release of political prisoners. Einstein was adamantly antifascist, and he always promoted democracy.

The Impact of Anti-Semitism

Following 1919, or the end of World War I, the Nazi party gained in strength in Germany. Anti-Semitism would come to its peak during this period. Einstein was a target because he was Jewish, and his theory of relativity was dubbed "Jewish Communist." He was increasingly hounded by the Nazis, actions which led him to become a more outspoken public Jew. Not having been raised in an observant household, he was hesitant to join Jewish organizations, but he was firmly convinced that the Nazi beliefs and implementations were wrong.

FACT

Einstein strengthened his political views throughout the 1920s. He traveled extensively during these years, both observing and protesting inequities. He signed petitions against Italian fascism in 1927. He visited a wide range of countries, including England, France, Austria, Japan, and South America.

The Move to America

Between 1930 and 1933, Einstein alternated between the United States and Europe. He spent summers in Caputh (a town near Berlin), winters teaching at the California Institute of Technology (located in southern California), and each spring in Berlin. (His Caputh home was, incidentally, in the Bauhaus style.) Einstein's life as a Jewish scientist living in Germany, though, was in increasing danger. He worked with antifascist groups in Germany, making himself more and more of a target. Finally he had to leave the country—in 1933 he moved to the United States permanently. He gave up his German citizenship in 1933, at which point the German government took all the property he still had there.

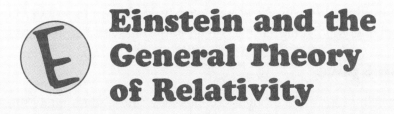

Chapter 12

Einstein and the General Theory of Relativity

The theory of general relativity took Einstein's previous work on special relativity to a new level by including gravity. The results were rather weird, including bent light rays, time changing with altitude, curvature of space, and other strange results—all of which have proven to be true experimentally.

Einstein's Principle of Equivalence

Although his 1905 paper on special relativity had brought Einstein, then an obscure patent clerk, no shortage of fame and controversy, he was not willing to let his theory rest as originally proposed. As early as 1907, while preparing a review of special relativity, it occurred to Einstein that his theory would not fit with Newtonian gravity. He began to wonder how Newtonian gravity would have to be altered to fit with his new theory.

A Chest in Space

Einstein proposed a thought-experiment, as he had so many times before, to consider the problem. In this case, he thought of an observer in a primitive space station—a large chest located far out in space, far enough from everything else that it was not subject to any gravitational forces. Since there is nothing close enough to provide a gravitational attraction, the observer in the chest will float around.

However, Einstein then considered what would happen if a rope were attached to the chest, and some external "being" began to pull on the chest with a constant force. This activity would cause the chest, and the observer inside, to accelerate upward toward the being pulling on the rope. The observer in the chest will no longer float around—he will find himself pulled toward the bottom of the chest, and will have to stand there.

The observer can also perform experiments, dropping objects in the chest or rolling them down ramps, and will find that they accelerate toward the floor at a constant rate. Thus, the observer will conclude that he is in a gravitational field. If the observer knows that he is in a large chest, he will probably wonder why the chest itself isn't falling, and when he discovers the rope (that the unseen being is using to pull the chest along), the observer will conclude that the chest is in fact suspended on the rope.

So, is the observer in the chest just wrong? Einstein stated that, in fact, the perspective of the observer in the chest is just as valid as the perspective of an external observer, or one who can see the whole system for what it is. That is, there is no difference between being in a uniformly accelerating chest (reference frame), and being in a uniform gravitational field.

The Happiest Thought of Einstein's Life

In fact, this simple thought-experiment leads to the basic tenet of general relativity. Remember that special relativity was based on the idea that all inertial reference frames were equivalent, and that an observer could not tell if she was at rest or in a reference frame moving at a constant velocity. General relativity extends this idea. In general relativity, an accelerating reference frame is equivalent to a reference frame in which there is a uniform gravitational field. This idea is called Einstein's principle of equivalence, and Einstein stated that the discovery of this idea, in 1907, was the happiest thought of his life.

Einstein's principle of equivalence says that there is no way to distinguish between an accelerating reference frame and one in which there is a uniform gravitational field. In other words, acceleration and gravity create exactly the same conditions, and an observer in a closed room cannot perform any experiments to distinguish between them.

Einstein's principle of equivalence can also work in reverse. Not only can acceleration create what feels like a gravitational field, but it can also cancel out a gravitational field. For example, passengers in an elevator whose cable was cut, a situation in which the elevator would be falling freely toward the ground, would feel no gravitational field—they would be in "free fall." Of course, they would probably have too much to worry about to enjoy the sensation, but the physics of the situation would be equivalent to the observer who was in the chest far out in space, who experienced no gravitational field.

This effect is also similar to what passengers feel in a "free fall" ride at an amusement park, where a car is lifted to the top of a tower, suspended there momentarily, and then allowed to fall to the ground under the acceleration of gravity. During the fall, passengers feel a weightless sensation as they fall at the same rate as their surroundings, although they are strapped into their seats for safety. Of course, amusement park ride designers include a special part of the track near the bottom to decelerate the car and its passengers. Otherwise, they would be in for an unwelcome surprise when they crashed into the ground.

The reason that observers in free-fall experience no gravity is that the acceleration of their fall cancels out the acceleration of gravity. These two forces cancel each other out perfectly only because the masses involved in both cases, the inertial mass and the gravitational mass, are exactly equal. There is no equivalent way to cancel out an electric field, for example, because there is no constant relationship between charge and mass.

FACT

Scientists at NASA use the principle of free-fall to simulate the weightless conditions of space without going into orbit. They use a special aircraft nicknamed the "vomit comet," which climbs high into the atmosphere, then dives down to Earth, giving the passengers inside short periods of weightlessness to perform experiments and practice moving around without gravity.

Bending of Light in a Gravitational Field

After his 1907 paper on the principle of equivalence, Einstein's next contribution to the study of general relativity did not come until 1911. As part of his principle of equivalence, Einstein had realized that light itself should be bent by a gravitational field. However, when considering only terrestrial measurements, Einstein thought that there was little chance of any kind of experimental verification of this claim.

In his 1911 paper, though, Einstein realized that the bending of light could be seen by way of astronomical observations. The masses of stars and galaxies, Einstein surmised, would be large enough to bend light to a sufficient extent that it could be observed.

Why Should Light Bend?

The bending of light is, in fact, a direct consequence of the principle of equivalence. Think about an elevator in free fall here on Earth. If a laser shines a beam of light from one side of the elevator, it will make a dot on the wall of the opposite side. Since the inside of the elevator is an inertial reference frame, the laser will make a dot of light directly across the elevator from the position of the laser. This is the same behavior that we would expect from a laser located in a nonmoving laboratory.

However, now imagine that there is a window in the elevator and an observer outside the elevator observes the laser beam. The external observer sees that the elevator is accelerating downward, toward the surface of the Earth, due to the Earth's gravity. In order for the beam of light to reach the directly opposite wall of the elevator, then, the beam of light itself must also be accelerating down toward the Earth at the same rate.

If the external observer plotted the path of the beam of light with respect to his nonmoving reference frame, the path would look like a curve. Therefore, even light can be affected by gravity, and a gravitational force will bend the path of light. Since the speed of light is very fast, the bending is very small; however, it is detectable if the mass is large enough and the distance long enough.

Observational Confirmation!

Einstein's bold prediction that light would be bent by a gravitational field was stunningly confirmed by observations made on May 29, 1919, during a total solar eclipse. Astronomers made very careful measurements of the positions of stars near the sun during the eclipse. They saw that their apparent positions were deflected by a distance of 1.7 seconds of arc, a very small distance, but the amount Einstein had predicted. This measurement pushed the boundaries of scientific accuracy at the time, but it was precise enough to confirm Einstein's theory.

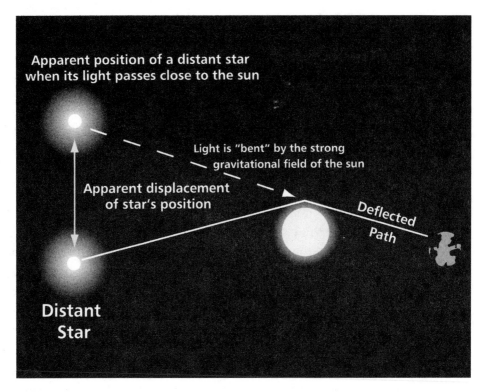

Apparent position of a distant star
when its light passes close to the sun

Light is "bent" by the strong
gravitational field of the sun

Apparent displacement
of star's position

Deflected Path

Distant
Star

▲ Einstein proved that even light could be affected by gravity.

The confirmation of Einstein's theory in 1919 made Einstein an
overnight celebrity, and the myth of Einstein the genius began to build up.
It was only six months after the end of World War I, and the world
embraced the idea that this forty-year-old scientist had made such an
amazing revelation in the realm of pure science, untouched by political or
social conflict.

The 1919 observations certainly launched Einstein and general
relativity into the limelight, but questions still remained about whether his
theory was in fact correct. The eclipse observations could include up to
a 20 percent error, not precise enough to rule out some competing
theories of gravity that conflicted with Einstein's. It was not until the
Hipparcos satellite charted stellar positions with unprecedented accuracy,
from 1989 to 1993, that scientists finally had enough proof to show that
Einstein's predictions were correct to an accuracy of $1/10$ of a percent—

one part in a thousand. That was enough to convince even the most skeptical scientists.

FACT

The elegant bending of light by stars can be seen in astronomical features called "gravitational lenses," in which the light of a faraway star or galaxy is pulled into shapes such as arcs or rings by an intervening mass. Many of such features have been observed by the Hubble Space Telescope and other telescopes, and their configuration can be used to extract information about the masses of the objects.

Gravitational Redshift

Another result of Einstein's principle of equivalence, as discussed in his 1911 paper, is the gravitational redshift. Redshift refers to the fact that when light escapes from a very high-mass body, it loses some energy in doing so, and thus its wavelength is shifted toward the redder, longer wavelength, lower-energy end of the spectrum. For this reason, the feature is called a "redshift."

The Doppler Effect

Redshifts, and accompanying blueshifts, are common in astronomy when the light from stars moving either toward us or away from us is measured. These phenomena are similar to the Doppler effect, which refers to sound waves. In the Doppler effect, if a police car is standing still with respect to an observer, its siren will consist of a sound at a particular frequency (or wavelength). If the police car is moving toward us, however, in the time in between cycles (or waves) of the sound, the police car will have moved toward us a bit. This motion of the police car causes the sound waves to bunch up; this bunching effectively shortens the wavelength, increasing the frequency and resulting in a higher-pitched siren.

Once the police car passes us by, however, in the time in between subsequent cycles or waves, the police car will have moved away from us a bit. The time between waves will be stretched out and wavelength of the sound will be increased, thereby lowering the frequency and resulting in a lower-pitched siren.

Redshifts and Blueshifts

Redshifts in light are similar to Doppler shifts. If an object giving off light at a certain wavelength (or color) is moving toward us, the motion of the light source will cause the distance between subsequent wave crests to shorten. The apparent wavelength is shortened, resulting in light that has been moved toward the blue end of the spectrum. This shifted light is called a blueshift. A redshift is the opposite. A source moving away from us will appear to stretch out its light, moving it toward longer wavelengths at the red end of the spectrum, hence the name redshift.

Back to the Elevator

We can see why the gravitational redshift takes place if we return to the thought-experiment performed with a laser in a free-falling elevator on Earth. Instead of shining the laser beam directly across the elevator, however, we shine it from the ceiling down onto the floor of the elevator. Einstein's equivalence principle once again states that conditions inside the falling elevator are the same as in an inertial frame, so the frequency of the light as measured by an observer on the floor of the elevator will be the same as that measured at the source laser on the ceiling.

However, now consider an outside observer who tries to measure the frequency of the light. If the light pulse were sent at the same moment that the elevator started falling, then the observer outside the elevator would measure the same initial frequency as the observer inside the elevator. However, since the elevator is accelerating down toward the surface of the Earth, the outside observer will measure the frequency of the light when it reaches the bottom of the elevator as having increased. Thus, light shining downward in a gravitational field increases in frequency (and therefore is blueshifted). We could also do the experiment backward, with a laser on the floor of the elevator shining light onto the ceiling. In this case, the frequency of the light would decrease. Thus, light shining upward in a gravitational field decreases in frequency (and is redshifted).

Einstein's prediction here was yet again confirmed by observation. Astronomers measured the characteristic wavelengths emitted by certain elements at the surfaces of massive stars and compared them to the results from elements in a laboratory on Earth. Sure enough, the results from the stars showed a redshift by the expected amount.

Time and Altitude

Having already shown that time was no longer an invariant quantity in his theory of special relativity, Einstein extended this idea (when coupled with the gravitational redshift) to show that time passes at different rates at different altitudes. Remember that gravity decreases with altitude, due to the inverse square law. An object at the top of a mountain is farther from the center of the Earth and thus experiences less of a gravitational force.

Fast Clocks on Mountains

The most accurate clocks are atomic clocks, which are based on the oscillations given off by various atoms (usually cesium). But due to the gravitational redshift, the oscillations of atoms will vary with gravity—that is, their frequency will change depending on the value of the gravitational field they are in. Since higher altitudes have less gravity, the frequency of the atoms will change slightly. Therefore, time runs faster at a higher altitude.

ALERT!

Due to the same effect that makes time run faster at higher altitudes, it would run more slowly in a large gravitational field. So your life might be longer if you lived on the surface of a high-mass planet. You might not be very comfortable, though!

The effect of time running faster at higher altitude has actually been measured. An atomic clock in Boulder, Colorado, 5,400 feet above sea level, gains about 5 microseconds per year as compared to an atomic clock in England (which is almost at sea level). These clocks are both accurate to about 1 microsecond per year, so this result is extremely precise.

Effects on the Global Positioning System

One important application of the time shifts of general relativity is on the satellites that make up the global positioning system (GPS). This network of satellites in orbit around the Earth is carefully engineered so that at least three satellites are visible from most locations on Earth at any particular time. From a careful determination of the positions of the satellites, coupled with an accurate time stamp on each satellite's signal, a GPS receiver can calculate the position of an observer on the surface of the Earth with amazing accuracy. GPS receivers are becoming common tools used by hikers in regions without roads or signs, and they are also used in navigational computers in some cars to help drivers find their way without maps. They are also used in aircraft and military navigation, and as such are critical to the safety of the country.

In order for GPS to work, there must be incredibly precise timing of the signals received by the satellites. To obtain highly accurate positions on the Earth, the clocks on the satellites must make corrections for both the time dilation from the motion of the satellite, due to special relativity, and the general relativity due to the change in gravitational potential in orbit.

When the first test GPS satellite was put into orbit in 1977, the scientists were a bit dubious that the general relativity correction was necessary. They left it out of the main clock, but they put in a special module that could be activated to perform the correction if necessary (just in case Einstein was right after all). Sure enough, after three weeks, the time on the satellite clock differed from a clock on the ground by just the amount predicted by Einstein. The scientists turned on the module and left it on.

The Curvature of Space

Einstein continued his work on what was becoming known as general relativity. Around 1912, he realized that the simple transformations that had worked in special relativity no longer applied to the more general case. He continued trying to find a more general theory, and eventually concluded that if all accelerated systems are equivalent, via his principle of equivalence, principles of Euclidean geometry were not true for all of them.

Euclidean Geometry

Euclidean geometry is the simple geometry of lines, planes, polygons, and curves, familiar to any student who has taken a high school geometry course. Simple, elegant, and full of geometric and mathematical proofs, Euclidean geometry was just the next vestige of pre-twentieth-century math and physics (following Newton's theories) to fall before Einstein's theory of relativity.

Curved Space

In the new curved space as defined by Einstein, the rules are all different. Parallel lines can meet. Triangles can have more or less than 180 degrees. The universe becomes a very weird place! The curvature of space, and space-time, is governed by the distribution of matter and energy. In turn, the curvature of space tells matter how to move.

FACT

A consequence of general relativity is that space is curved. Large, massive objects, such as stars and galaxies, can actually bend and warp the three-dimensional space around them, much as a rock will stretch and distort a rubber sheet.

Einstein's curved space also explains the paradox of the instantaneous gravitational force. Recall that a big problem with Newton's theory of universal gravitation was that it required the impossible—information would have to travel at a speed greater than the speed of light to allow masses to instantaneously respond to a change in the gravitational field.

Curved space solves the problem. Since the curvature of space is caused by the distribution of matter, the motion of a particular mass causes ripples to form in the curvature of space, and these ripples can travel at the speed of light. Since the motion of a mass is just dependent on the curvature of space in its local vicinity, a mass will not feel any instantaneous change in the gravitational force, and thus special relativity (with its universal speed limit) is not violated.

The Perihelion of Mercury

Einstein continued to expand relativity, developing much of the mathematics required to describe it along the way (much as Newton had to develop calculus to describe his laws of motion). Einstein wrote a number of papers in 1913 and 1914 in which he expanded the field of tensor calculus and differential geometry, often in collaboration with the greatest mathematical minds of his day.

The perihelion is the point in a planet's orbit around the sun when it is closest to the sun. Aphelion is the point where a planet is farthest from the sun. The suffix changes depending on what object is being orbited. The closest point in a satellite's orbit around the Earth, for example, is perigee, and the farthest point is called apogee.

In November of 1915, Einstein made a breakthrough when he finally produced a solution to the gravitational field equations for general relativity. At this time, he also solved another problem that had puzzled previous physicists and astronomers, related to the advance of the perihelion of the planet Mercury.

The French astronomer Urbain Jean Joseph Leverrier (1811–1877) first noticed in 1855 that the perihelion of Mercury advanced more per century than could be explained by the theories of the day. Leverrier spent many years searching for moons of Mercury, which could have explained the effect, but he was ultimately unsuccessful. Other theories were proposed, including changes in the shape or density of the inner planets, an extra planet inside the orbit of Mercury, or a breakdown of Newton's inverse square law theory of gravity. None of these theories was borne out by observation. It was not until many years later, in 1915, that the effect was explained.

In 1915, Einstein took a new set of accurate observations of Mercury, which showed that its perihelion advanced by 43 arc-seconds per century, and applied the theory of gravitation from general relativity. Lo and behold, the theory exactly predicted the measured 43 arc-second advance, without the need to appeal to an unseen planet or satellite or other mechanism.

The Final Form of General Relativity

On November 25, 1915, after a number of false starts and other errors, Einstein submitted a paper, entitled "The Field Equations of Gravitation," that finally had the correct field equations for general relativity. Most of Einstein's colleagues of the day were confused and baffled by the quick series of papers between 1912 and 1915, each of which corrected, changed, and extended the previous ones.

FACT

One of the first extensions of general relativity was done by Karl Schwarzschild (1873–1916) in 1916. In this paper, Schwarzschild solved Einstein's equations of general relativity and gravitation, to find the gravitational field of a massive, compact object. This work led to the discovery of black holes, neutron stars, and other astronomical objects (see Chapter 14 for more information).

In March of 1916, Einstein wrote an article that summarized and explained the underpinnings of general relativity in more understandable terms. This article and one he wrote slightly later became the canonical source for general relativity, and both are still widely cited and referred to.

The three main statements of general relativity are as follows:

1. Space and time are not rigid. Their form and structure is influenced by matter and energy.
2. Matter and energy determine how space, and space-time, curve.
3. Space and its curvature determine how matter moves.

General relativity, then, was firmly established in the realm of physics, much to the chagrin of many of the scientists of the day who were resistant to Einstein's new ideas. The theory would prove sound, however, and over the following years as Einstein's fame grew, more and more scientists began to understand and expand on Einstein's groundbreaking theories.

Chapter 13

Quantum Theory and Einstein's Role

Unlike relativity, which was a theory largely created by Einstein alone, quantum theory was a collaborative work by a number of scientists over a period of thirty or more years. Einstein laid some of the groundwork for quantum theory, and he was involved in a number of roles along the way—perhaps most notably, in his disagreement with it!

What Is Quantum Theory?

Quantum theory, or quantum mechanics, is the study of the behavior of the smallest pieces of matter. It involves interactions on a very small scale—at the level of molecules, atoms, and subatomic particles. Quantum theory is mostly interested in the absorption and emission of energy at these tiny scales. In a way, quantum theory is similar to relativity in that it extends the everyday physics of our world to an extreme. In the case of relativity, the classical laws of physics break down at speeds close to the speed of light, or for very massive objects. For quantum theory, the classical laws of physics break down at very small scales.

The Study of the Very Small

In classical physics, as studied by Newton and others before the twentieth century, energy is considered to be continuous. Matter consists of discrete, physical entities with a specific size, location, and motion. In quantum physics, this orderly pattern breaks down into a confusing, statistical world. Energy is quantized, and is only available in tiny, discrete packets rather than at any possible amount in the continuum theory. These quanta sometimes act like individual particles, but they sometimes act like waves, depending on the situation in which they are measured.

In another similarity to relativity, quantum theory takes a few initial assumptions and follows their implications through to the logical conclusions, which turn out to be very odd indeed. Where relativity led to ideas like length contraction and curved space, quantum theory leads to the uncertainty principle and other strange results. In particular, Einstein was never pleased with the statistical nature of quantum theory, perhaps in a similar way to how other scientists felt about Einstein's theory of relativity.

Problems with Classical Physics

Quantum theory was originally proposed to explain a number of inexplicable results from classical physics. For example, classical physics proposed that electrons orbited around the nucleus of an atom. However, if they orbited in the same way that the planets orbited the sun, the prediction from classical physics was that this system would be incredibly unstable, resulting in electrons spiraling in to the nucleus of the atom in just a fraction of a second. Clearly, however, if this were the case, matter itself would be unstable. However, classical physics was unable to propose an alternate way for atoms to be organized.

The Discovery of Quanta

The theory of quantum mechanics began with the first realizations that energy levels at a subatomic scale seemed to be quantized rather than continuous. The first step toward this insight came with the work of Max Planck in 1900 on black body radiation (as described in Chapter 5). Planck suggested that a classic puzzle, that of the amount of radiation given off from a heated body, could be explained if the radiation were emitted in discrete packets he called "quanta." Planck also suggested that the size of the radiation packet was related to the frequency.

The next step in the study of quantized radiation came with Einstein's seminal 1905 work on the photoelectric effect (Chapter 5). Einstein explained a situation relating to the amount and color of radiation given off from a metallic surface that was exposed to light. The odd results, which were measured experimentally, could be explained if the radiation absorbed by the surface of a metal (as well as the radiation given off) were constrained to certain amounts of energy, rather than having continuous possible energy values.

FACT

Einstein also used the idea of quantization, in 1906, to study the relationship between heat and temperature for diatomic gases, those which contained molecules made up of two atoms (such as H_2 or O_2).

The work of Einstein and Planck was at odds with the Maxwell theory of electromagnetism, which had united electric and magnetic waves in an elegant mathematical construct. Instead, in the new quantized view, energies were constrained to particular values. This new view, however, was not too different from the views of the nineteenth century. The concepts of classical mechanics were just adapted slightly to take into account the fact that only certain amounts of energy were allowed.

Atomic Structure

The study of quantum theory took an important step forward with the discovery of atomic structure. This work began in 1911 with the discovery by Ernest Rutherford (1871–1937) of the atomic nucleus. At that time, the atom was thought of as a mixture, with about the same density throughout its volume, and with electrons scattered throughout, like nuts in a brownie. The negatively charged electron, in fact, had only recently been discovered in 1897 by J. J. Thomson.

Rutherford's Experiment

Rutherford was conducting an experiment in which he shot alpha particles, which come from the radioactive element radium, at a very thin sheet of gold foil. A beam of alpha particles was at the time called an alpha ray (to distinguish it from higher-energy rays such as X rays and gamma rays). Alpha particles are now known to actually consist of two protons and two neutrons. They therefore have the same form as a helium nucleus. At the time Rutherford was conducting these experiments, however, they were just thought of as another mysterious form of radiation.

In Rutherford's experiment, he tracked the path taken by the alpha particles as they passed through the very thin sheet of gold foil. Most of them just passed right through the foil, which is what he had expected. However, occasionally, one of the alpha particles would instead bounce back off the foil, just as if it had hit something solid! Rutherford was intrigued by this result, and he investigated it very carefully. Eventually, Rutherford was able to trace back the paths of many particles that had bounced back rather than traveling through the foil, and from these paths he could tell that there seemed to be a central concentration of mass in the middle of each atom.

The Nucleus

From this experiment, then, Rutherford was able to determine that atoms were centrally concentrated rather than having their constituent parts evenly distributed. In addition, he showed that almost all the mass of the atom, as well as all its positive charge, was concentrated in this central region, which he called the nucleus. The nucleus itself was tiny—the atom was in fact about 10,000 times larger than the nucleus! Given that atoms themselves are tiny, an atomic nucleus is unimaginably small. Rutherford surmised that since all the positive charge of the atom was held in the nucleus, that the negative charge must reside in the electrons, which he imagined to orbit around the nucleus just like planets orbit around a larger, massive star.

FACT

Rutherford received the Nobel Prize in chemistry in 1908, before he even discovered the atomic nucleus. His prize was for his work on radioactive materials, regarding radioactive decay and the chemistry of radioactive substances.

Quantum Theory Joins Atomic Theory

While Rutherford's picture of atomic structure was appealing, it had a fatal flaw. The problem was that the structure was not stable, according to classical physics. Orbiting electrons would lose energy as they orbited, and eventually they would spiral down closer and closer to the nucleus until they collided with it. They should also collide with each other on relatively short time scales. Yet most atoms were known to be extremely stable. So what was wrong with this picture?

Bohr's Suggestion

In 1912, Niels Bohr (1885–1962), a newly minted Ph.D., expanded Rutherford's work to include quantum effects. Bohr's research built upon the work done by Planck on quantum theory. Bohr used this body of knowledge to explain why most atoms were much more stable than would be predicted by classical mechanics. First, in studying atoms, Bohr found that when the energy of an electron and the frequency of its orbit around the atomic nucleus were compared, their ratio was equal to Planck's constant. This revelation was Bohr's first clue that quantum effects would be important in the study of atomic structure.

Bohr's most exciting suggestion, however, was in his description of how electrons moved between different energy levels in the outer structure of an atom. It was known that electrons could exist in different energy levels, thought of as orbits with different energies. Orbits that were further out from the nucleus were less tightly bound to the nucleus, and thus energy was required to move an electron from an inner, tightly bound orbit to an outer, less-bound orbit.

Bohr suggested that rather than gradually moving out in distance from the nucleus, electrons instead made quantum jumps from one fixed energy level to another. The odd thing about these jumps was that the electrons never existed in an intermediate energy state at all—they just jumped directly from a higher to lower, or lower to higher, energy level. These jumps corresponded with the atom either absorbing energy or giving off energy. So, if an electron jumps from a higher to a lower energy state, energy is given off in the form of heat or light from the atom, and if an electron jumps from a lower to a higher energy state, that energy must come from the absorption of either heat or light.

ALERT!

Contrary to popular usage, a quantum leap does not mean a huge jump. In fact, a quantum jump is a very, very small change. The important part, however, is that a quantum movement consists of a single, predefined step.

Bohr published his suggestions in 1913. As was the case for much of quantum theory, however, it was not widely accepted at first. The physics community of the time still resisted quantum theory, just as it had initially resisted relativity. After all, classical physics had worked perfectly well for the last 200 years, so there was a lot of resistance to change.

Spectral Matches

However, Bohr's new model had a lot going for it. First, although it was only based on a very simple hydrogen atom, it was able to explain many of the details of its structure. The electrons in Bohr's model, and the amounts of energy they gave off or absorbed while jumping between energy levels, exactly matched the spectrum of light that experimental physicists had measured from hydrogen.

It was known at the time that all elements gave off a particular spectral signature, both absorbing light at a variety of very specific wavelengths and also emitting light at very specific wavelengths. Bohr's theory for hydrogen predicted the amounts of energy absorbed and emitted by electrons in a hydrogen atom as they jumped up and down between energy levels, and these values matched the observed spectrum quite well.

The Periodic Table

Bohr's theory also proved important in understanding the structure of the periodic table. The familiar table of elements that graces every high school chemistry classroom has a very particular structure to it, with elements organized into groups based on various shared properties. Bohr's atomic structure helped scientists understand how these properties are shared between materials with very different masses.

In Bohr's theory, electrons orbited the nucleus in very particular orbits called "shells." Shells of different energies all have different properties, and they can hold only a particular number of electrons before they are full. Once a shell is full, electrons are forced to go to a different energy level. The first shell can only hold two electrons, the second up to eight, the third ten, and so on in a complicated pattern.

FACT

Bohr received the Nobel Prize in physics in 1922 for his work on the new understanding of atomic structure and for his studies of the radiation that came from various atoms.

It turns out that the outer shell is the most important in terms of how a particular element interacts with other elements, since the outer shell is the most readily accessible (and since inner shells are filled first, the outer shell is the one that's most likely to have any vacancies). Atoms whose outer shells are completely full are very stable, and these are called noble gases. These include helium, neon, and argon. Elements whose outer shells are not completely full tend to be much more reactive. Thus, elements with the same number of electrons in their outer shells are aligned in the same column in the periodic table, and it is this shared position that shows their similar properties.

Old Quantum Theory

Work on quantum theory took a hiatus during World War I but resumed in the early 1920s. The new quantum theory became increasingly mathematical, building on new developments in theoretical math at the same time. This mathematical version of quantum theory became known as quantum mechanics.

Bohr's theory of the quantum energy levels of atoms had been expanded by Arnold Sommerfeld (1868–1951) in 1916. Sommerfeld's work included elliptical orbits of the electrons—rather than just the circular orbits in Bohr's initial model—as well as relativistic effects. Bohr, Sommerfeld, and others attracted an array of young, bright students, and they organized a number of centers of study that focused on extending quantum theory to other elements. These attempts, which initially seemed so promising, eventually were unsuccessful.

The main problem was that the "old quantum theory," as it is now called, assumed that the mechanics of a dynamic system, such as electrons orbiting a nucleus, were basically classical dynamics, with some quantum effects tossed into the mixture. These theories assumed circular or elliptical orbits just like those previous physicists had determined for the motion of the planets around the sun.

It turned out that this treatment worked very well for a simple atom like hydrogen, which has only a single electron orbiting a proton in the nucleus. However, the treatment breaks down once there are more electrons orbiting the nucleus, or one electron orbiting multiple nuclear particles.

The Matrix Formulation of Quantum Mechanics

It became increasingly clear that the so-called "old quantum theory" which was still based on classical effects, failed with respect to any elements more complicated than hydrogen. At this point, various physicists began to try to find a theory to replace it. Two important figures in this search were Max Born (1882–1970) and his assistant Werner Heisenberg (1901–1976).

As a new Ph.D., Heisenberg tackled the problem of trying to determine the allowed quantum states of a particular system. After much tedious work, he eventually reached a breakthrough in determining how to describe the quantum state of a system using matrix algebra, which was a very new mathematical field at the time. In fact, it was Born who recognized Heisenberg's work as part of matrix theory.

Heisenberg's new theory, called "matrix mechanics" or "the matrix formulation of quantum mechanics" turned out to be a very complicated and unwieldy mathematical description of quantum theory. It was based on the mathematical construct called a matrix, which is a two-dimensional array of numbers with particular mathematical properties. Despite its complexity, however, Heisenberg's theory was the first complete description of quantum mechanics.

FACT

Heisenberg received the Nobel Prize in physics in 1932 for his work. His award cited his work on the creation of quantum mechanics, which led to the detailed study of atomic and molecular spectra.

The Wavefunction Formulation of Quantum Mechanics

At the same time, parallel work was going on which resulted in the development of a separate theory of quantum mechanics. This theory, developed by Louis de Broglie (1892–1987), asserted that the wave-particle duality (which had been accepted for light) could be extended to all matter, particularly electrons. In this theory, the physics of matter and the physics of radiation were finally joined—according to de Broglie, even solid matter had a wavelength.

The new description of electron matter waves was worked by Erwin Schrödinger (1887–1961) into a comprehensive wave theory. Schrödinger's wave equation is a famous equation that relates wave mechanics to general relativity. In fact, Schrödinger created the second formulation of quantum mechanics, called the wavefunction formulation.

At this point, around 1925, there were not one but two complete, internally consistent theories of quantum mechanics, the wave formulation and the matrix formulation. Fortunately, it was soon proven that the two theories were actually mathematically equivalent to each other, although expressed in different ways.

Einstein's Response

Einstein's response to the new quantum theory seems to have been mixed. On the one hand, he supported the new breakthroughs, but he was worried by the element of chance that seemed to have entered the orderly, predictable world of physics.

In 1924, before the competing versions of quantum mechanics had been reconciled, Einstein bemoaned the fact that there were now not one, but two theories of light, which seemed to have no logical connection with each other. In that same year, Einstein also was resistant to Bohr's solution to the paradox of how the electron can know when to emit radiation.

However, also in 1924, Einstein was instrumental in the successful publication of a paper by Satyendra Nath Bose (1894–1974), which had initially been rejected for publication. When Einstein received the paper from Bose, he immediately realized its importance and pushed to get it published. In his paper, Bose proposed that photons could exist in different states, and that the number of photons was not conserved. This observation led to the property of photons called "spin."

While he was initially resistant to quantum theory, when Einstein read

Schrödinger's wave mechanics formulation in 1926, Einstein wrote to him expressing how impressed he was with his work. He stated that it seemed to be the work of pure genius, and that Schrödinger's research provided a decisive advance in quantum theory.

The Heisenberg Uncertainty Principle

Another major disagreement that Einstein had with quantum mechanics was over Heisenberg's uncertainty principle. As stated in 1927, Heisenberg's principle basically says that the more precisely the position of a subatomic particle is known, the less precisely the momentum can be measured, and vice versa. If an observer can measure the position of a particle with great accuracy, the particle's momentum cannot be measured nearly as well. But if the momentum is measured extremely accurately, then it will be the particle's position that is comparatively unknown.

The Heisenberg uncertainty principle states that the more precisely the position is known, the less precisely the momentum can be measured, and vice versa. This principle means that if you know exactly where a particle is, you can't know how fast it is moving; conversely, if you know exactly what a particle's momentum is, you can't know exactly where it is.

Uncertain Consequences

The uncertainty principle has a number of strange consequences, especially on the idea of causality. In Heisenberg's new indeterminate world, precise knowledge of the present circumstances no longer allowed an observer to exactly predict the future. This result was in opposition to the classical, Newtonian world of physics where if the current conditions of a system, such as a particle's position and velocity, were exactly known, the position of the particle at any future time could be predicted exactly.

The uncertainty principle also resulted in the entrance of probability into much of quantum physics. In particular, the orbits of electrons around a nucleus, which had started out being pictured as solid particles orbiting like planets around a sun, had been revised by the initial quantum theory and the study of electron waves to represent electron density in various locations around a nucleus. Now, with Heisenberg's probabilistic interpretation, these positions became instead merely probabilities. Physicists now showed atomic structure with probability density plots, providing locations around a nucleus where an electron was more or less likely to be found.

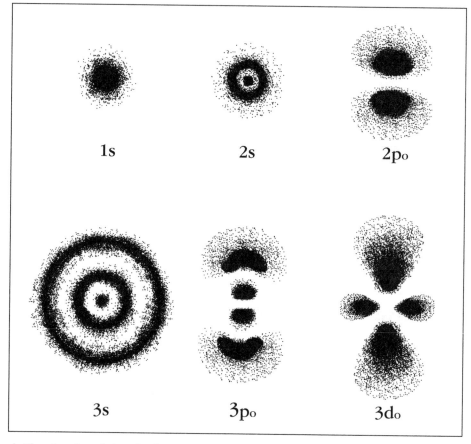

▲ The density of dots in these hydrogen orbitals shows where an electron is likely to be found.

Other Strange Results of Heisenberg

Heisenberg, working with Bohr, continued to formulate quantum mechanics in 1927. This work resulted in many strange conclusions, including the complementary wave and particle descriptions. In this formulation, any object can be either a wave or a particle until the observer, in the act of observing it, seals its fate by considering it to be one or the other. The wave function that describes the object is, in fact, a combination of both the wave and particle pictures until the act of observation takes place. Thus, in making an observation, the observer actually changes the state of the system she was observing. With these and other observations, Bohr and Heisenberg produced a complete picture of quantum mechanics called the "Copenhagen Interpretation," which they presented at the end of 1927.

The Bohr-Einstein Debates

Not everyone agreed with the new interpretation of quantum mechanics, however. Einstein in particular was very resistant to the increased presence of probabilities in the results. Additionally, Einstein was uncomfortable with the idea that physical systems only existed when they were observed and that the act of observing made a fundamental change in the state of a system. Einstein believed that natural systems existed on their own, independent of any observations that might be made of them. Also, Einstein believed that the motions of particles could be exactly calculated based on previous information about them. He was also very uncomfortable with the fact that the theory meant that there was no way to predict exactly when an atom would emit a photon, for example.

Two famous debates took place at the Solvay Conferences, held in 1927 and 1930. On these occasions, Bohr and Einstein got into a series of discussions over the details of the new quantum theory. Einstein raised many objections during these debates, and both men went over and over various points of the theory. Eventually, even after discussions which went on day and night, neither would admit defeat.

The Bohr-Einstein debates served to clarify and strengthen the new description of quantum mechanics. They also led to a 1935 paper by Einstein, along with Boris Podolsky and Nathan Rosen, in which the authors attempted to discredit quantum mechanics by showing a seemingly impossible situation where a measurement of a particle at one location would also reveal information about a particle at a different location. This possibility was called "spooky action at a distance," and actually caused Bohr to back down on one particular point in his formulation of quantum mechanics. However, much later, in 1964, a flaw was found in the Einstein-Podolsky-Rosen formulation showing that matter did indeed behave just as strangely as the three authors had suggested it could not.

FACT

To express his discomfort with the probabilistic nature of quantum theory, Einstein made a famous comment which said, effectively, that God does not play dice with the universe. It is reported that Bohr responded by saying that Einstein should stop telling God what to do!

Einstein's Search for a Better Theory

Eventually, however, by the late 1930s, Einstein accepted that while quantum mechanics was not perfect, it did at least present a consistent picture of subatomic structure and behavior. While classical physics produces satisfactory results for most everyday observations, quantum theory is necessary when observing matter at very small scales, just as relativity proves necessary at very high speeds or large masses.

However, Einstein never accepted quantum mechanics as a complete, finished product. He was still uncomfortable with the fact that the mathematical structure of quantum theory could not predict individual events, just overall probability. Einstein believed that there must be a simpler, more fundamental, way to describe how each individual atom behaved now and would behave in the future. Einstein began the search for such a theory as an extension of the theory of relativity. It would be this ultimately unsuccessful search for a more basic theory, a unified field theory, that would occupy most of the rest of his life.

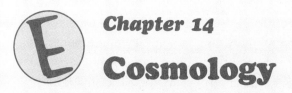

Chapter 14

Cosmology

Cosmology, the study of the universe as a whole, was founded by Einstein in a 1917 paper that used general relativity to model the universe. The theory resulted in the theoretical discovery of black holes, the expanding universe, and the beginning (and eventual end) of the universe itself.

An Extension of General Relativity

Following the success of the publication of his theory of general relativity, published in its final form in 1915, Einstein began to expand his theory by looking for applications to other fields. One paper, published in 1917, single-handedly laid the groundwork for the field of cosmology, which is the study of the universe as a whole. In this paper, Einstein used general relativity to model an entire universe. The results of Einstein's initial modeling produced many interesting cosmological elements that are still hot topics in today's study of astrophysics and cosmology.

Einstein's 1917 paper was titled "Cosmological Considerations on the General Theory of Relativity." In this paper, he applied some basic ideas of cosmology to the general theory of relativity, and in the process he expanded the bounds of astronomy as it was currently known.

In the early twentieth century, astronomers were just beginning to understand the large-scale structure of the universe. In 1917, when Einstein wrote his first cosmological paper, astronomers had yet to realize that some of the fuzzy patches in the sky were in fact whole separate galaxies, distinct from our own. At the time, it was thought that our galaxy was all there was, and that the fuzzy patches, called "nebulae," were just clouds of gas and dust contained within our own galaxy.

QUESTION?

What's a galaxy?
Our sun, and the planets orbiting it, make up our solar system. Each star we see in the night sky could have its own planets orbiting it. All these stars, about 100 billion in all, make up our galaxy, which has a spiral shape and is held together by gravity. Our galaxy, and many billion others, make up the universe.

The Cosmological Principle

Cosmology is basically the study of the universe as a whole. It includes the physics of the universe, and the study of the distribution of objects and matter on all scales and their motions throughout the universe. Cosmology is also concerned with the study of the evolution of the universe, including its origin, age, changes over time, and the ultimate fate of the universe.

A basic tenet of cosmology is the cosmological principle, which states that the universe is homogeneous and isotropic on the largest scales. This is a critical assumption of the study of the universe as a whole, and it underlies the very study of cosmology itself.

The cosmological principle states that the universe is homogeneous and isotropic on the largest scales. There are no special places in the universe, and the universe is the same in all directions—there are no special directions either. It also states that these descriptions are only valid over very large distances and are not valid for smaller-scale systems like our solar system or galaxy.

Homogeneity

What does the cosmological principle mean? To understand it, we can break it down into smaller parts. First, homogeneous means "of uniform structure or composition throughout." As applied to the universe as a whole, this clause means that no matter where you are in the universe, the average density of matter will be about the same. According to this principle, the structure of the universe itself is smooth on very large scales, and its matter is basically distributed evenly throughout space.

This clause does not apply on a smaller scale, however. Local regions with more mass than average certainly exist, such as our own solar system's star and planets. Galaxies themselves represent a higher-than-average distribution of mass. Therefore, on the smaller scale (by the standards of the whole universe), the universe is not a nice smooth distribution of mass but features local enhancements.

Isotropy

The other component of the cosmological principle is that the universe is isotropic. This statement means that the universe looks the same in all directions. There is no one particular direction that an observer can look to see the center of the universe, for example. This means that the universe looks the same to all observers, wherever they are in the universe.

FACT

Similar to the first component of homogeneity, isotropy also does not work on a local scale. When we look up at the sky at night, we see a greater concentration of stars when we look toward the plane of our galaxy, which is visible in the sky as a band of stars called the Milky Way. This is also the name of our galaxy, and as we look toward the center of it, we see more stars there than when we look off in another direction.

A Surprising Result

In his 1917 paper, Einstein took the cosmological principle and applied it to his newly published theory of general relativity. This application resulted in the use of general relativity to model the entire universe, and it was done in conjunction with the astronomer Willem de Sitter (1872–1934). The results of this work, like so much of Einstein's work, were surprising.

A Nonstatic Universe

Einstein and other scientists discovered that when the cosmological principle was combined with general relativity, it resulted in a universe that was not static. Instead, the results showed that the universe must be either expanding or contracting! However, this result went against all the astronomical evidence of the day, which required that the universe be static and unchanging.

The Cosmological Constant

Since astronomers of the day did not observe any general motion in the skies, and thus believed that the universe could not be expanding or contracting, Einstein searched for a way to make his theories fit with the observations. He found that by introducing a term he called the cosmological constant, he could come up with results that supported a static universe, one that was neither expanding nor contracting.

The cosmological constant is a term that balances out the attractive force of gravity. It takes the form of a repulsive gravitational force, and it was added as a constant of integration to Einstein's equations. Unlike the rest of general relativity, this new constant was not justified by anything in the current model of gravity—it was introduced purely to achieve the result that at the time was thought to be proper. With the addition of this constant, Einstein's equations described a static universe, fitting the assumptions of the time.

Not everyone thought that the cosmological constant was necessary, however. De Sitter, for example, believed in Einstein's initial result, that the universe was in fact expanding. He commented that the introduction of the cosmological constant marred the simple elegance of Einstein's original theory, which aside from the cosmological constant had managed to explain so much without introducing any new hypotheses or constants.

The Expanding Universe

Within fifteen years of Einstein's publication of his static model of the universe with general relativity, he would be proven wrong (and de Sitter proven right). The true nature of the universe was initially revealed due to work by astronomers such as Edwin Hubble (1889–1953). Beginning in the early 1920s, Hubble and others began to study the nature of the odd fuzzy patches of light that were called nebulae at the time.

Galactic Distances

Hubble developed a technique to measure how far away objects in the sky were, and he used this technique to reveal that the Andromeda nebula was in fact a hundred thousand times farther away from us than the nearest stars! In fact, Andromeda was a separate galaxy—one that was comparable in size to our own Milky Way, but much farther away. Its great distance is what made it look like a small fuzzy patch of light.

Hubble then measured or estimated the distance to a number of galaxies, showing that many of these nebulae were in fact galaxies in their own right. The Milky Way suddenly became just one of a number of galaxies scattered throughout the universe, rather than the sole location of stars and planets. However, Hubble did not stop with this amazing revelation.

Galactic Motion

Along with his estimates of galactic distances, Hubble noticed that he could also measure the redshift of galaxies. Recall from our previous discussions that objects moving toward us give off light that is shifted in wavelength toward the blue end of the spectrum (blueshifted), and objects moving away from us give off light that is shifted toward the red end of the spectrum (redshifted). Hubble measured the amount that the light from various galaxies was shifted, and he was able to determine that not only were most galaxies redshifted, but that the amount of redshift was correlated with their distance from us. Galaxies that are farther away from us were redshifted more, which corresponds to higher velocities.

Curiously, however, all the shifts were toward the red, meaning that all the galaxies were moving away from us. The only explanation for this phenomenon was if the entire universe were expanding; this expansion would result in everything moving away from everything else as space itself expands. Thus, in 1929, Hubble had provided the first evidence for an expanding universe.

One way to picture an expanding universe is to think of dots drawn on a balloon. As the balloon is inflated, the dots all move away from each other as the surface area of the balloon increases. This is similar to what happens in the universe, except in three dimensions rather than the two present on the surface of the balloon!

Einstein's Greatest Blunder

When Einstein learned of the results of Hubble's work, he realized his mistake in introducing the cosmological constant into his equations. In fact, he had been right in the first place. He later called the introduction of the cosmological constant the greatest mistake of his career. Even geniuses sometimes make mistakes.

A New Model of the Universe

Following the publication of Hubble's 1929 results, Einstein and de Sitter set to work to develop a new model of general relativity that could be applied to an expanding universe. In fact, there turned out to be a simple solution to the gravitational field equations in the case of an expanding universe, and this idea came to be known as the Einstein–de Sitter model of the universe.

In a 1932 paper, Einstein and de Sitter published their results. In this paper, they suggested that there could be large amounts of matter in the universe that had not yet been detected, because this matter did not give off any light. This material has since been dubbed "dark matter," and it has been shown to exist in at least a few situations. Since dark matter cannot be detected directly, its presence has been inferred from the gravitational effects it has on other objects. Dark matter, and the amount of it that may or may not exist in the universe, is a hot topic of study by astrophysicists today.

The Origin, and Fate, of the Universe

Once the expanding nature of the universe was revealed, the next question was one of origins. If the universe were currently expanding, then at some time in the past all the matter in the universe would have been closer together. Extrapolated back in time far enough, this theory leads to the suggestion that at some finite beginning to the universe, all the matter was located at a single point. Since that time, the universe has been expanding until it is in the state it is today.

This theory is called the Big Bang theory. In it, the entire universe came into existence in a giant explosion, which occurred about 15 billion years ago. During the first few seconds of the existence of the universe, all matter was created—subatomic particles joined together to form simple elements like hydrogen and helium. These gases clumped together, eventually collapsing together under gravity and igniting; they thereby formed the first stars. These stars, during their lifetimes and at the end of their lives in spectacular events such as supernovas, created all the heavier elements in the universe.

FACT

The name "Big Bang" was in fact created by astronomer Fred Hoyle as a disparaging way to describe a rival theory. Unfortunately for him, not only did the name stick, but the theory was also shown to be correct and his theory disproved.

Since the Big Bang, the entire universe has continued expanding. Galaxies continue to move away from each other, and matter itself gets more and more spread out. But will this type of motion continue forever? Once the expanding universe was established as fact, scientists studying Einstein's equations of general relativity came up with three possibilities for the universe, depending on how much matter it contained.

If the universe exceeded a certain critical density, then eventually the whole universe would collapse back onto itself, in a scenario called a closed universe. If it had less than the critical density, it would keep expanding forever as an open universe. Only if it had exactly the critical density would it be in a balanced, steady-state condition. This final one is the situation that Einstein had believed, and it's why he had introduced the cosmological constant into his equations to keep the universe from expanding.

ALERT!

Although the universe will someday come to an end, it won't be for some time. In the closed universe case, the universe will collapse in a "Big Crunch" about 100 billion years after the Big Bang, or 85 billion years from now. In the open universe, stars will be around for about a trillion years. Of course, our sun will burn itself out in about 8 billion years, so we probably won't be around to worry about the end of the universe!

The Steady-State Theory Disproved

The Big Bang theory, however, wasn't believed by everyone. In the 1940s and 1950s, the other main competing theory was the steady-state theory, proposed by Fred Hoyle (1915–2001). Hoyle's theory was that instead of having an origin around 15 billion years ago in the Big Bang, the universe had been around forever and was in a steady state. This idea is distinct from the critical density condition, because Hoyle did not believe that the universe originated in the Big Bang.

Hoyle did agree that the universe was expanding, but instead of having galaxies moving away from each other, he proposed that space was constantly being created in between galaxies, giving them the appearance of moving away. He also suggested that in this new space, matter was also created to keep the average density of the universe constant. This aspect of the theory would allow new galaxies to be created in between old ones.

Elemental Abundances

Over the years, however, two pieces of evidence were found that supported the expanding universe theory and disproved the steady-state theory. First, astronomers measured the abundances of various elements in the sun, planets, and other stars, and they came up with a list of the most abundant elements. These abundances matched the amounts in which elements were created in the Big Bang theory very closely, and the steady-state theory was unable to explain these proportions.

Cosmic Microwave Background Radiation

The most compelling piece of evidence in favor of the Big Bang theory, however, is the cosmic microwave background radiation, discovered in 1965. This radiation is a kind of fossilized remnant from the earliest moments of the universe. As the universe formed in a primordial fireball, it gave off radiation. However, as the universe has expanded over time, the radiation has been stretched out to longer and longer wavelengths.

Scientists predicted that the radiation from the beginning of the universe, if still observable, would be at a wavelength of about 7 centimeters. Sure enough, an omnidirectional radiation source was found in 1965 at just this wavelength! The cosmic microwave background radiation was found to come from all directions in the sky, and there are subtle variations in the radiation (as mapped out by the COBE satellite, launched in 1989) that could correspond to the first density fluctuations in the early universe, from which arose matter concentrations and eventually stars and galaxies.

FACT

The cosmic microwave background radiation is at a wavelength of 7 centimeters, which is in the microwave range of the electromagnetic spectrum. This wavelength corresponds to a temperature of about 3 degrees Kelvin. This is an extremely cold temperature, only 3 degrees above absolute zero (the coldest possible temperature, at which all motion stops), corresponding to 454 degrees below zero Fahrenheit!

Black Holes

Einstein's work on general relativity laid the groundwork for the modern understanding of the origin, and ultimate fate, of our universe in the Big Bang theory. It also predicted a number of odd facets of astronomy, including the bending of light by stars. The results of this bending (gravitational lenses) are discussed in Chapter 12. General relativity also suggests the existence of dark matter, a virtually undetectable substance that could fill up much of the universe.

In addition to these results, general relativity also predicts an even more exotic astrophysical object, the black hole. Recall from Chapter 12 that general relativity defines gravity as a curvature of space-time that is caused by the mere presence of matter. The more massive or compact an object, the stronger its gravitational field. The densest, most compact objects in the universe are black holes, which have a gravitational field that is so strong that not even light can escape!

Black holes are just that—their gravity is so strong that not even light can escape from them. No radiation at all is given off by black holes, since nothing can radiate away from one without being trapped by its gravity. Black holes can only be detected by indirect means, through their effects on other objects.

Schwarzschild

Black holes were first studied by Karl Schwarzschild (1873–1916) in 1916. In solving Einstein's equations of general relativity for a perfectly spherical, nonrotating object, Schwarzschild showed that a sufficiently massive object would result in an infinite curvature of space-time, meaning that light would not only be bent, it could not escape at all.

Black holes have a certain radius, called the Schwarzschild radius, that depends on their mass. This distance from the center of the black hole is called the "event horizon." Anything that crosses the event horizon, from matter to light, will inevitably be sucked into the black hole's center. There is no escape!

Einstein reported on Schwarzschild's results at a meeting, but Einstein himself never believed that such an object could exist in reality. Rather, Einstein considered them to be bizarre mathematical constructs. The term "black hole" was coined after Einstein's death, and since the 1960s there has been increasing evidence that these bizarre features could indeed exist in our universe!

One possible way that a black hole might be formed is at the end of the life of a large star. Such a star could gravitationally collapse on itself, and if it had sufficient mass to begin with, it could reach a point of critical density and form a black hole. But how could such objects be detected?

Gravitational Waves

General relativity, which predicts the existence of black holes, also contains a possible method for detecting them. Einstein's theory suggests that disturbances in space-time produce gravitational waves. These waves are produced by the oscillation of the fabric of space-time itself. Gravity waves were a controversial suggestion, and many were skeptical when they were first suggested.

However, recently scientists have found a number of ways to show the possible existence of gravitational waves. First, a binary pulsar system was shown to have a decrease in its orbital period, which is the exact amount that would be suggested if it were giving off gravitational waves and thus losing energy. In the future, a number of experiments are planned to search for gravitational waves directly, including the Laser Interferometer Gravitational-Wave Observatory, or LIGO. Ⓔ

Chapter 15

Later Years—Effects of the Nuclear Age

E instein's life took a complete turn in 1933. He was essentially forced out of Germany by the Nazi regime, and he relocated to the United States. The next twenty years of his life would coincide with many extremely significant world events. World War II took place between 1939 and 1945, and many aspects of the war would fundamentally change Einstein's life.

Einstein in America

As we left off in Chapter 11, Einstein moved to the United States in 1933. The impact of the Nazi regime on German Jews was growing more and more pervasive, and ultimately Einstein was forced to flee the country. Friends and family feared for his safety, and the move was probably none too soon. His leaving was, in addition to a security measure, a sign of protest—Adolf Hitler was appointed chancellor of Germany in 1933.

The move of 1933 wasn't the first time Einstein had visited the United States. He actually visited in 1921 and delivered lectures on relativity at Princeton University as part of the Stafford Little series. He was also given an honorary degree at this time. The main reason Einstein went to America at this point was to promote Zionism, but his scientific lectures proved immensely popular. They were published in a book by Princeton University Press in 1921, *The Meaning of Relativity*.

Einstein returned to America in 1930, and he gave a speech in New York at the Ritz Carlton Hotel. He provided support for those who resisted the military draft and spoke about how it was the duty of all pacifists to convince the general public that war is not only dangerous, but also immoral. At this time, he was firmly convinced that passive, or nonviolent, resistance was the way to defeat an enemy. Einstein stated that not only would he refuse to personally participate in a war, but that he would also encourage all his friends to do the same, no matter what he felt about the causes of the war.

That trip to America provided many other opportunities for Einstein to get to know the country. He met with politicians, musicians, artists, scientists, and others from all walks of life. He went to Pasadena to visit the California Institute of Technology. In a lecture there, he reinforced to students the idea that humanitarianism must be behind science and technology; without a concern for people, science wouldn't make anyone happy. This speech relayed the important fact that Einstein was genuinely concerned with humanity; this aspect of Einstein's personality would become very important in the coming years.

Sowing the Seeds of Pacifism

Einstein was so vehemently opposed to the Nazi regime that he issued a statement after his permanent move to the United States that the rest of Europe should defend itself against Hitler. For the first time, he entertained the possibility that the use of force might be acceptable. This change in his viewpoint did not endear him to more diehard pacifists, once again placing Einstein in between worlds, and aligned clearly with neither side. Some pacifists were shocked at Einstein's apparent reversal. He defended himself, however, by saying essentially that while he still hated violence and armies, that hatred was overridden by his fear of what a successful Nazi regime could do to the world.

Einstein's exposure to the Nazi Party changed his views on war and peace considerably. Earlier, he had been firmly antiwar. Exposure to the Nazis, however, transformed his activism to the extent that pacifism itself was somewhat sacrificed. At first, he hoped that a nonviolent blockade could be used to quell the Nazis, but later he voiced support for a standing militia.

So to America he went, arriving there on October 17, 1933, in his mid fifties. After having moved to the United States with his wife Elsa, Einstein did not have long to wait before finding work. In October of 1933 he found himself once again in Princeton, New Jersey, where the Princeton Institute for Advanced Study was basically created around him. He was offered a position there immediately, which he accepted, and Princeton became his new home.

The Institute for Advanced Study was founded in 1930, originally to study mathematics. Professors from Princeton University were recruited, as was Einstein a couple of years later. Over the coming years, the Institute widened its field to study areas such as economics and politics. Einstein felt at home at Princeton; he lived a couple of miles away and walked to work each day, describing his new life as highly enjoyable. He returned to his previous diversion of the violin, in addition to taking up sailing.

World War II in Summary

The major event of this period of Einstein's life was World War II, both the events leading up to it and what would transpire during the war itself. A bit of background into the war will be very useful for determining choices Einstein would make, some of which heavily influenced the outcome of the war.

Background

Although World War II took place between 1939 and 1945, it arguably began as early as 1933, when Hitler became chancellor of Germany. Germany and Austria united, with German troops being placed into Austria a few years later. The war officially commenced with Germany's invasion of Poland in September of 1939, after which France and Britain declared war on Germany. The United States declared itself neutral, although it did aid the British even during this initial phase.

FACT

The warring countries of World War II were divided into two basic sides. The Axis powers consisted of Germany, Japan, and Italy. China, the Soviet Union, France, Britain, and, eventually, the United States were members of the Allied Forces. Germany fought the war and won key battles in several European countries, including France, Holland, and Belgium.

Truly a World War

Fighting took place all over Europe and beyond. Japan attacked Pearl Harbor in 1941, and this is the point at which the United States formally entered the war. The Nazi killing of Jews in Germany hit full force in 1942, with Jews being killed en masse at concentration camps at Auschwitz and elsewhere. D-day, when Paris was liberated, occurred in 1944. Auschwitz was liberated in 1945, the United States dropped atomic bombs on Japan in 1945, and the war ended shortly thereafter.

Nuclear Research

During the late 1930s, the field of nuclear science grew rapidly. Many advances in physics were made, culminating in the viability of nuclear fission. The beginning of the so-called nuclear age, though, really came from Einstein's 1905 papers. His development of the special theory of relativity was seminal in creating the ideas and science that would later lead to the invention of the atomic bomb. The equation $E=mc^2$ indicated that a lot of energy could come from a relatively small amount of matter (see Chapter 7), and this was one of the founding principles behind the atomic bomb.

Fission

"Nuclear fission," in this context, means that a uranium atom could be split into smaller elements. When this fission turned into a chain reaction, under a controlled environment, energy would be released. Controlled chain reactions became possible, meaning atomic power could be released gradually. Lots of atoms could potentially be split at once, leading to a huge explosion. These ideas struck physicists, and eventually would trickle down to the rest of the world—could this power be contained in the form of a nuclear weapon?

QUESTION?

What is a chain reaction?
A chain reaction (as it relates to nuclear fission) is a technique whereby the end products from one reaction become the reactants in another reaction. For example, neutrons can initially be added to an unstable fuel. Fission occurs (producing more neutrons as well as other products), and these neutrons result in more fission of more of the fuel. This process continues until all the fuel is used up.

The Impact of Szilard

A Hungarian physicist by the name of Leo Szilard (1898–1964) played a major role, along with Einstein, in the militarization of the developing nuclear age. He was in tune with the European research community, and even more aware of the potential danger that advances in physics could have.

Leo Szilard, like Einstein, was Jewish. The son of a civil engineer, Szilard studied engineering at Budapest Technical University in 1916. He served in the Austro-Hungarian army starting in 1917, continuing his studies in 1919. In 1920 he moved to Berlin and began studies at the University of Berlin, and he took physics classes from none other than Albert Einstein.

Szilard and Einstein collaborated on scientific projects during this period, notably a design for a refrigerator pump. By the 1930s, however, Szilard found himself subject to the same terror from the Germans as Einstein. He would eventually leave Europe in 1933 for the same reasons as Einstein—mainly, to avoid the Nazi threat. He would work on chain reactions and nuclear fission throughout the 1930s.

Defense Against the Germans

One of Einstein's primary concerns was, if a nuclear weapon could be made, that the Germans not make it. Many other physicists and intellectuals of the period had the same concern. Szilard actually took the reins in warning the world of such a risk. He informed the United States government of what might happen if the Nazis were able to build and maintain control of something as potentially destructive as a nuclear weapon.

Developing the Weapon First

Research in Germany in 1938 led to the splitting of the uranium atom, and this fact alone caused fear in America. German researchers Fritz Strassmann and Otto Hahn were largely responsible for these developments. Also, German and Nazi hostilities were far from over, making Americans even more fearful that other countries could be making nuclear weapons. Leo Szilard understood these potential threats and discussed them extensively with Einstein, who agreed that those in power in America should also understand them.

The Letter to the President

1939 was a seminal year in world history. Einstein and other physicists (including Szilard, Edward Teller, and Eugene Wigner) would collaborate on a letter addressed to President Roosevelt. Recognizing that they needed support and name recognition for their effort to succeed, Szilard, Teller, and Wigner came to Einstein with the idea of writing to the president; Einstein then joined their effort. In this letter, the scientists informed the president about the state of scientific research into nuclear fission, suggesting that it might be possible to incorporate this new science into weapons of unprecedented power. They recommended experimentation on a large scale before even attempting to create such a device.

ALERT!

Surprisingly, and perhaps frighteningly, fear can be a determining factor in scientific development. Part of the reason the bomb was eventually constructed was the fear that another country was already producing such a device, one that could potentially be used against the United States.

President Roosevelt eventually would create funding and opportunity for the research that could create nuclear weapons. The Briggs Committee was formed in 1939 for the purpose of studying chain reactions with uranium, an essential component of a nuclear weapon. Research went slowly because, at the time, it was still considered fairly abstract research—not something that anyone intended to use in a war. The pace was picked up after a British report in 1941, one that showed that an atomic bomb could in fact be built and ready for use in just a few years.

Einstein opposed using the atomic bomb. He was still fundamentally opposed to war, and he was not in favor of using a nuclear weapon to bomb another country. He stated several times that he thought the United

States should demonstrate the atomic bomb to foreign countries, not use it to destroy them. Despite the unfortunate way that history sometimes remembers Einstein's contribution here, he was quite clear on his intent.

Educating the Public

In the 1940s, scientists launched a public education campaign. They realized the impact of what they were creating, and wanted to make sure that the general public, as well as political leaders from around the world, did as well. Einstein in particular was adamant that while nuclear weapons could be developed, they should not be, precisely because of their destructive capability.

The effort to gather research and design toward the creation of the atomic bomb was managed by Vannevar Bush, an engineer and inventor who was chairman of the National Advisory Committee for Aeronautics in the late 1930s under President Roosevelt. He also proposed, and was named chairman of, the National Defense Resource Committee (NDRC), and would eventually become military science and research advisor to the president.

Einstein himself was very minimally involved in the design and creation of the atomic bomb. Vannevar Bush asked Einstein for a consultation in 1941 on a specific area of nuclear fission, and Einstein provided assistance. However, Einstein had been on record as saying he disagreed with producing such a weapon for military purposes.

Despite the truth of Einstein's involvement (or lack thereof) with the creation of the bomb, many people thought that he was entirely responsible for its design. Some even thought that $E=mc^2$ represented a formula for building a bomb. How did such a misunderstanding become prevalent? Possibly because Einstein was so famous at the time, people who didn't understand the science of nuclear fission simply thought that Einstein must be responsible for it. Perhaps there was some latent anti-Semitism at play as well. However, time and fact would prove these rumors false, and the true nature of Einstein's involvement with the project, or lack thereof, would come to light.

Vannevar Bush's role in the development of the atomic bomb, on the other hand, cannot be underestimated. It was he who convinced the president that other countries could create such a bomb, and that the United States must develop one first. December of 1941 marked the year that manufacturing plants, ones where fissionable material could be created, were starting to be built. In June of 1942, responsibility for the development of the atomic bomb was given to the U.S. Army.

Los Alamos and the Manhattan Project

The government looked long and hard for a suitable place to build such a plant. It couldn't be located near any international borders, and it also couldn't be too near major residential areas. Everyone understood what could happen if there was an accident, and officials wanted to minimize any potential risks to American citizens. Los Alamos, New Mexico, was eventually decided upon as the best location, and a scientist named J. Robert Oppenheimer was chosen to lead the endeavor that would come to be called the Manhattan Project.

Einstein wasn't the only person rejected for this project. It was done in complete secrecy, and even the families of the scientists working on it had to be kept in the dark. There were over 600 scientists working on the creation of the atomic bomb—that's a lot of people to try to keep quiet. Their mail was screened, their cars had special license plates so they could easily be identified, and family photos couldn't show anything about their location. The government took all these precautions because they were so worried that Germany or another foreign enemy would discover their location.

Einstein also wasn't the only Jewish person involved in some way with the Manhattan Project. Several of the other scientists were German Jews as well, including Edward Teller (who helped write the letter to President Roosevelt that started the entire campaign). Felix Bloch and Otto Frisch were instrumental in the creation of the bomb, as was Enrico Fermi (an Italian scientist who would go on to become extremely famous for his work on quantum mechanics and atomic structure). Fermi actually won the 1938 Nobel Prize in physics for his work in this area.

Leading to Hiroshima

The bomb was first tested in the middle of 1945. President Roosevelt died in April of 1945, though, and was succeeded by President Harry Truman. Political leaders in America became convinced that they had to attack or invade Japan in order to win the war, and Truman decided to use the atomic bomb. General Dwight Eisenhower, who would later become president, was commanding the Allied forces in Europe at this time. President Truman gave the order to drop the atomic bomb over Hiroshima in August of 1945, despite the fact that large-scale testing had not been conducted. No one was sure exactly what would happen.

A World-Altering First Bombing

The impact, of course, was monumental. An incredibly bright explosion ensued, and some estimate that as many as 80,000 people were killed instantly. Consider that next to the fact that close to 55 million people were killed throughout all of World War II. Winds and fires followed, destroying much of the Japanese-style wooden architecture in the area. Nagasaki was bombed as well, and Japan surrendered the following week.

FACT

The atomic bomb dropped on Hiroshima was carried by the U.S. bomber *Enola Gay.* Four square miles of the city were destroyed upon impact. Close to 70 percent of the city's buildings were destroyed. The bomb dropped over Nagasaki destroyed approximately 40 percent of that city.

Einstein's Reaction

Einstein's reaction to the bombing of Hiroshima and Nagasaki came nearly a year after the events. In a 1946 article published in *The New*

York Times, Einstein said that he didn't think President Roosevelt would have authorized the bombings, had he still been alive.

Einstein would later declare that the one great mistake of his life was signing the letter to then-President Roosevelt, suggesting that atomic bombs could be made. Had he known about the devastation that would ensue, he said that he would have rather spent his life as a shoemaker. His ongoing justification of having signed that letter was that, to the end, it was better than what would have happened if Germany had developed the atomic bomb first.

Legacy of Hiroshima

One of the most far-reaching legacies of American atomic bomb development was the ensuing arms race. Now that the United States had this capability, other countries wanted the same weapons to be able to compete on the same level, should it ever become necessary. While one of the United States' primary nuclear rivals became the Soviet Union, other countries also hurried to develop their own nuclear weapons, thereby increasing tension felt throughout the world.

Background to the Cold War

By 1943 the Soviets, having learned of the Manhattan Project, set about researching and developing their own atomic bomb. After World War II ended, the United States implemented a policy of disarmament, where all materials that could be used for nuclear fission would be given to an international agency. The Soviet Union, in contrast, wanted to completely destroy all nuclear weapons already in existence, a policy the United States didn't agree with.

Additional tensions between the Soviet Union and America were fueled by this disagreement. The USSR was a Communist country, while the United States was a democracy; most at the time agreed that these two types of government were completely incompatible with each other. The United States declared a sort of general war against Communism by providing funding for non-Communist countries, and the Cold War was informally declared by the stating of these ideas in the Truman Doctrine of 1947.

The Formation of NATO

The North Atlantic Treaty Organization (NATO) was created in 1949. Its initial member countries were the United States, France, Britain, the Netherlands, Belgium, and Luxembourg. One of the main goals of NATO was to unite against Stalin, whom many thought could become the next Hitler. In 1950, the United States passed a resolution called NSC-68, the gist of which was to increase national defense spending dramatically and to not allow the Soviets to dominate the world the way Germany had tried to. All these factors contributed to the Cold War, which would last until the early 1990s, when the Soviet Union dissolved.

ALERT!

Not all battles are fought with weapons. The definition of a "cold war" (the term invented by Bernard Baruch in 1947) is one in which there is no actual fighting, but there can be a very high level of hostility between the countries involved. Rather than fighting with guns or bombs, cold-war battles could involve propaganda, spying, and attempts to ruin other countries economically.

American experimentation into new kinds of warfare certainly didn't end with World War II. In 1952, Americans set off the first hydrogen bomb at Enewetak Atoll. The Soviets followed with a thermonuclear weapon, and the British succeeded with their own in 1957. The United States followed the Soviet launch with the creation and deployment of the world's first nuclear-powered ship. Other experiments by other countries would follow.

Einstein's Reaction to the Cold War

Einstein feared that the growing Cold War would threaten democracy, even within the United States. His fears were realized by the creation of the House Un-American Activities Committee (HUAC) in 1938, lasting until

1975. This committee was part of the House of Representatives, and its goal was to investigate anyone and anything considered disloyal to the United States, nominally in the name of anticommunism. People were questioned and trials were held. Einstein was generally correct that this sort of extended fear of Communism really threatened the freedom that had once characterized America.

Bertrand Russell

Meanwhile, public opposition to the increasing nuclear arms race was growing. In the spring of 1955, shortly before his death, Einstein collaborated with Bertrand Russell (1872–1970). Russell was a British philosopher and mathematician who publicly condemned the hydrogen bomb tests of 1954; he would work with Einstein a year later.

This campaign was his last attempt to try to convince the world that nuclear weapons posed a threat. The two issued the Russell-Einstein Manifesto, in which they urged governments from all nations to stop considering the use of nuclear weapons in war. This document set up two choices: ending the human race, versus an agreement to end all wars. The latter option was combined with a caveat that no new wars be started. They suggested nuclear disarmament and wrote that, as scientists and humanitarians, they strongly favored peace.

Russell would go on to continue this work after Einstein's death in 1955. In 1958 he became the founder and president of the Campaign for Nuclear Disarmament. He would also participate in antinuclear protests, getting himself jailed more than once in the process.

While Einstein had little to do with the actual creation of the atomic bomb, then, he was part of the initial effort. And, of course, his scientific discovery from decades earlier laid the groundwork that other scientists would use to develop the bomb itself. It's hard to say how much responsibility Einstein ultimately felt for the devastation in Hiroshima and Nagasaki. Scientists cannot possibly predict every way in which their results will be used, nor are they necessarily responsible for what others choose to do with their results. For Einstein to have "taken it all back" he would have had to undo the discovery of $E=mc^2$, and that alone would have changed the entire course of history. Ⓔ

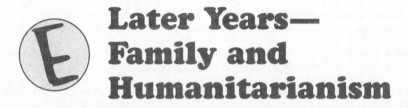

Chapter 16

Later Years— Family and Humanitarianism

The years between 1933 and Einstein's death in 1955 would be filled with more than professional commitments. Einstein's children grew up and went on to lead interesting lives themselves. Their trials and tribulations affected the direction Einstein's life would take as well. Einstein's political and scientific goals took many turns during his later years.

Einstein's Children

In the earlier part of his life, when Einstein was still married to Mileva, married life treated him well. He was cared for, and in turn he loved his children deeply. They seem to have responded well to him, and they respected the work and research that he was a part of. When he moved to Berlin in 1914 and his wife and children, vacationing in Switzerland, were unable to join him, the separation must have been difficult for father and sons alike.

By 1933, when Einstein moved to the United States with his second wife Elsa Lowenthal, Hans was twenty-nine years old and Eduard was twenty-three. Einstein's children, like most people's kids, were a source of both pride and dismay at various points throughout their lives. They achieved various goals, and undoubtedly they provided Einstein with a source of much pride. They followed their father's example of science and humanitarianism to varying degrees. While neither of them achieved the fame that Einstein did, they accomplished goals in their own rights.

Hans Albert Einstein

Hans Albert (1904–1973) lived an interesting life that followed partially in his father's footsteps. After completing his elementary school education in Zurich, Hans received a diploma in civil engineering from the Swiss Federal Institute of Technology in Zurich in 1926. He then received a doctor of technical sciences degree from the same university in 1936.

Between 1926 and 1930, Hans actually lived in Germany. He worked in the town of Dortmund as a steel designer. As a graduate student in Zurich, he was fascinated by the problem of transporting sediment via flowing water, and wrote his doctoral thesis on this issue. That thesis is still in use today by scientists and engineers worldwide.

Hans married a woman named Frieda Knecht in 1927. She was a German instructor at the University of Zurich. They moved to the United States in 1938, several years after Albert Einstein moved. Hans would continue his research into sediment transportation at the U.S. Agricultural Experiment Station in South Carolina until 1943. At that point, he moved to the U.S. Department of Agriculture Cooperative Laboratory, which was part of the California Institute of Technology.

Hans remained a researcher there until 1947, at which point he became a faculty member at the University of California. He started off as an associate professor, and later became a full professor of hydraulic engineering. Hans fulfilled multiple roles while at the university—he was a teacher, a researcher, and also a practicing engineer. He was well-known during his career and received numerous awards and honors, including the Certificate of Merit given by the U.S. Department of Agriculture in 1971.

FACT

Hans Albert Einstein and his wife Frieda would eventually have three children. Their son Bernard became a physicist, like his grandfather. Daughter Evelyn became an anthropologist. They also had another son, Klaus, who died as a child.

His first wife Frieda died in 1958. Shortly afterward, Hans married a second time to Elizabeth Roboz. She worked as a biochemist at the Stanford University Medical School. She later became a professor of neurology at the San Francisco Medical Center, part of the University of California.

Professional inclinations aside, Hans enjoyed the same sort of entertainment as his father. He was a big fan of music, as well as sailing and walking. Sailing on San Francisco Bay was one of his favorite pastimes. Hans was known for being willing to spend time with his family and friends. More social than his father, Hans spent much time with his graduate students and was known for his patience and devotion. Like his father, though, Hans also understood the importance of making professional connections in his field, and he made every effort to be in touch with current experts in the field of sedimentation transport.

After suffering a heart attack in June of 1973, Hans Albert Einstein died in July of that same year. Albert and his older son had a good relationship. Both being scientists, they could relate to each other on multiple levels. Over the years and despite various separations, they seem to have gotten along well most of the time. They had a mutual respect for each other's intelligence and abilities.

Eduard Einstein

Eduard was born in 1910. Unlike his older brother, Eduard did not excel in the sciences. He enjoyed reading the works of Shakespeare as a child and shared his father's abilities with music, but he does not appear to have particularly excelled in any one area. Eduard was always considered the most sensitive of the Einstein clan.

He ended up studying pre-med in college and was interested in becoming a psychologist. Unfortunately during this period, he suffered a mental breakdown that would later be determined to be either the onset of schizophrenia or a serious case of depression. Albert Einstein returned to Switzerland to be by his son's side, although he doesn't appear to have been of great use.

Albert and Eduard's relationship does not seem to have been that close. Einstein was not physically living with Eduard for his early and formative years (the period coinciding with the time when Einstein and Mileva were separated, and later divorced), and his son spent much more time with his mother. In letters written to his father, Eduard indicated that he identified strongly with his mother on several levels—both felt Albert had abandoned them, and both were hesitant to recognize their own intelligence.

Of course, part of their connection could have been that after Albert and Mileva formally separated, she had no one to dote on except for the children. Eduard, being less like his father than Hans, was the more likely target for her abundance of affections. Eduard lived with his mother until her death in 1948, and then he was placed in a psychiatric institution. He died in an institution near Zurich in 1965.

Lieserl Einstein

Lieserl was born in January 1902. The general theory is that she was given up for adoption shortly after her birth, probably because of the damage that having had an illegitimate child could have done to both

Mileva and Albert's burgeoning careers. Almost nothing is known about Lieserl's life. Some think she might have been born with Down syndrome. Some think that, based on letters from Einstein to his wife, the baby died as a young child from scarlet fever. Others think that, unable to put her up for adoption, Mileva left her with relatives in Serbia. Not that a lack of information is cause for a lack of speculation! Authors have written fictional novels involving Lieserl, wondering about what her life might have been.

Ilse and Margot Einstein

Albert Einstein also had two stepdaughters, Elsa's daughters from her first marriage. They were Ilse (1897–1934) and Margot (1899–1986). Einstein formally adopted them after his marriage to Elsa, and both legally changed their last name to Einstein. Albert probably never had the opportunity to know Ilse very well. She died early, in 1934, due to an illness. Margot, however, became an artist, and she apparently shared Einstein's fascination with nature and music. She would live with him in Princeton, New Jersey, after her move to America.

Einstein's Sister

Einstein's sister, Maria (Maja) was his closest friend as a child. Born in 1881, she was two years younger than Albert, and he was always protective of her. They explored the German countryside as children, and both loved nature. She was his constant companion until he separated from his family, and the two would always be close.

FACT

Much of what's known about Einstein's childhood, in fact, comes from Maja's writings; she produced a biography of her famous brother in 1924. Maja eventually married Paul Winteler, son of the headmaster of the school Einstein had attended in Aarau.

In 1939, Maja was living in Florence but was rapidly becoming ostracized, due to Mussolini's rule. After moving to the United States that year, Maja moved in with Einstein. Her husband Paul moved to Geneva at this time. Maja would continue to take up residence with her brother until her death in 1951. Einstein was completely devoted to his sister, and he remained so until the end of her life. Unfortunately, she never saw her husband again after her move to America. The couple planned to reunite after the war, but a stroke that Maja suffered left her unable to travel.

Einstein's Grandchildren

Einstein had two living grandchildren by his son Hans: Bernard and Evelyn. Bernard became a physicist as well as an author. He has written a foreword to a book about his grandfather entitled *The Fascinating Life and Theory of Albert Einstein.*

Evelyn Einstein currently resides in Berkeley, California. She is what's known as a cult deprogrammer. Her job is to deprogram people who have been members of cults. She had a somewhat dubious honor, as well. In 1955, Dr. Thomas Harvey, chief pathologist at Princeton University, autopsied Einstein's brain in the hopes of learning about what had gone into creating the genius that was Einstein. Years later, granddaughter Evelyn became the recipient of part of Einstein's brain. If you're interested in more information on this subject, Michael Paterniti has written a book entitled *Driving Mr. Albert: A Trip Across America with Einstein's Brain.*

Citizenship

Albert Einstein officially became a United States citizen in 1940. In order to do so, he had to declare that he wouldn't return to Germany.

Citizenship had advantages for Einstein, especially since he was living and working in the United States. Citizens are entitled to certain rights and privileges that noncitizens are not, and Einstein made full use of these benefits.

Professional Affiliations

One example is membership in professional societies. The National Academy of Sciences is an organization devoted to scientific and technological research. It was first chartered by Congress in 1863, and part of its responsibility is to advise the government on how technology and science apply to the general public welfare. The group consists of members, who are citizens, and foreign associates. Einstein was elected to the NAS as a foreign associate in 1922, and he was able to finally become a member after he became fully naturalized as a U.S. citizen.

The group encompasses a wide array of scientific fields. Chemistry, physics, and biology are of course included, as are geology, mathematics, psychology, and much more. Today, members outnumber foreign associates by about six to one. Einstein's election as a member was symbolic of his acceptance into the American scientific community. While this shift came near the end of his life, Einstein's impact on both worldwide and American research would remain enormous.

Assisting Others with Immigration

After his move to the United States, Einstein spent a great deal of time in the 1930s helping others in Europe to escape from Nazi Germany. He wrote affidavits for Jews from other European countries as well, helping them to immigrate to America.

FACT

Einstein was the kind of activist who would spend his own time and energy helping others. Jews and other minorities the world over would benefit from Einstein's humanitarian achievements in his later life.

Ties to Israel

In 1952, Einstein was actually offered the presidency of Israel. Israel's first prime minister, David Ben-Gurion, asked Einstein to become the country's second president (a largely symbolic role) when its first president, Chaim

Weizmann, died. Einstein and Dr. Weizmann had been friends, working together on fundraising efforts for Israel. In fact, Einstein's first trip to the United States, in 1921, was with Dr. Weizmann. Einstein regretfully declined the invitation from Ben-Gurion.

Was his age the only reason Einstein didn't become president of Israel? Probably not. Throughout his political career, he'd hoped that Jews and Palestinians would be able to share the land they both inhabited. His views in this area were widely misunderstood. While he may not have been explicitly opposed to the idea of creating a Jewish state, if it were to be done through warfare he probably would not have supported it. Becoming president of Israel, even as a figurehead, might have pushed his involvement into acquisition through force, something Einstein probably wanted no part of.

The offer for Einstein to take over the presidency of Israel came toward the end of his life. His health wasn't the best, and he was comfortable in his Princeton, New Jersey, home. He turned down the offer, although he remained active politically during this time.

Support of Israeli Education

Even before being offered the presidency, Einstein's relationship with Israel was certainly not new. He was on the board of governors that planned what would come to be Hebrew University in Jerusalem. His support of Israel throughout World War II, as well as his active protest of the Nazi regime, solidified his Jewish ties to Israel. He had been active professionally there as well. Einstein was president of the Technion Society, Israel's first official institute of science and technology. Einstein supported the project from the very beginning, and the Technion would go on to become Israel's first university, also called the Israel Institute of Technology.

In 1925, Einstein also became the first president of the World Union of Jewish Students. This organization was founded by a Jewish man from Austria, Zvi Lauterpacht. It came about because, in some European countries, there were quotas for how many Jewish people could attend university. The match up with Einstein was obvious. Einstein was also concerned about Jewish education, as well as about fighting anti-Semitism in all its forms. Einstein was involved in these and similar projects during their inception, and he truly had a huge range of influence across a variety of Jewish causes and organizations.

ALERT!

The policy of affirmative action, as applied to university admissions today, has been seen by some scholars as encouraging quotas of certain ethnicities. The World Union of Jewish Students had to fight against the Numerus Clausus, a quota that worked specifically against Jews. A rose by any other name, perhaps?

Ties to the IRC

Then, in 1933, Einstein helped found the International Rescue Committee. The IRC is a nonprofit group still in existence today. It exists to help refugees from around the world, and especially helps people who are trying to escape racial and religious persecution. The American branch of this organization (known in Europe as the International Relief Association) was started to help Jews fleeing from Hitler's Germany. The American and European branches came together under one organization in 1942.

A Canceled Synopsis of Einstein's Life

In July of 2002, Israel canceled an Albert Einstein exhibit planned to be on display in China in September. The exhibit had been scheduled to premiere in Beijing, then travel to Shanghai and other Chinese cities. It would have been quite a production, lasting four months. It was to have consisted of thirty display boards, all with photographs and information about Einstein's personal and professional life.

The exhibit was canceled because the Chinese Ministry of Culture wanted to remove all references to Einstein's Judaism. Especially in the later part of his life, Einstein and his identity with the Jewish people were inseparable. To remove this aspect of his life would have been telling only part of the story behind who he was and why he made the decisions he did.

Commitment to Peace

Einstein's pacifism was truly a lifelong endeavor. As world politics underwent huge changes in the last years of his life, Einstein continued to be involved and aware. Substantial events occurred in the 1950s that would have impacted Einstein even more had he lived to the end of the decade and into the 1960s. Can you imagine Einstein in tie-dye? Seriously, while many people associate these years with hippies and free love, there were important political changes going on, and Einstein was a part of them to the extent that he was able.

QUESTION?

What is Communism, anyway?
Communism is, like democracy, a theory of a type of government. Communism is a political system that supports the idea of everyone being equal, to the point where there is no private ownership. Goods and land are owned communally, generally by the government, and given to citizens as needed.

McCarthy and the Red Scare

1952 marked the year that Senator Joseph McCarthy threw much of the United States into a panic. He alerted the nation to an alleged "Red Scare," and made high publicity of the search for Communists inside the United States government and military. A blacklist, or list of names of possible suspects, was created; McCarthy claimed to have a list of 205 Americans in the state department who belonged to the American Communist Party. With the ongoing Cold War, many Americans were more than willing to believe the Communist threat.

McCarthyism, as it would come to be called, affected all aspects of American life. The famous Arthur Miller play *The Crucible*, written in 1953, serves as a political satire of the times. While the play was about the Salem witch trials, it was clearly written to reflect the growing comparison to current American politics. McCarthyism played on the post–World War II fear that Americans had of Russians, and of Communism taking over. The Red Scare prompted a general change in both American pride and people's tolerance for those who were unlike themselves.

FACT

The primary danger with the Red Scare lay in the means to escape it. Those who were blacklisted could save their own lives in exchange for pointing out other alleged Communists. Sound like the Salem witch trials? Not a bad comparison to make. Many non-American citizens (and even some Americans) feared for their lives during this period.

For Einstein, this period resonated with similarities to Nazi Germany. While the circumstances were different, he was reminded of the suspicion, blacklisting, and fear that accompanied the earlier period. The Federal Bureau of Investigation was rumored to have had a file on Einstein. He protested McCarthyism vigorously, which didn't exactly make him less of a suspect himself.

Einstein's Role in the Emergency Committee of Atomic Scientists

After World War II, in 1946, Einstein became president of the Emergency Committee of Atomic Scientists. The goal of this group was to increase public awareness of the atomic bomb's potential in peacetime, and about how atomic energy could and should be used for peacetime activity. They also focused on the immorality of using atomic power for weapons. Einstein cofounded this group with his friend and previous collaborator Leo Szilard.

Einstein actually inspired famed scientist Linus Pauling (1901–1994) to join this group in 1946. Unlike most of his friends and scientific colleagues, Pauling was born in the United States. His main contribution to the scientific community came in the form of his work with protein structures, as well as the description of chemical bonds. He performed groundbreaking research into the causes of sickle-cell anemia, and he is the only person to have won two Nobel Prizes (one for chemistry in 1954 and one for peace in 1962) by himself. Needless to say, his contributions to the Emergency Committee were critical in spreading their message of how peace and technology could be compatible.

Einstein and the Idea of World Government

One of Einstein's lifelong goals was to see the creation of a world government. Rather than individual states and countries having their own separate institutions of power, he favored the idea of a worldwide organization that could be devoted to solving conflicts and problems peacefully, without war. Einstein was a primary player in the World Government Movement, an attempt to create just such a coalition.

The main problem Einstein saw with localized governments was the fear and insecurity that he witnessed in McCarthy-era America. Fighting and conflict abounded due to these fears, and Einstein was strongly antiwar. Individual governments, he thought, would need to assume that war might erupt at some point, hence the need for military buildup. Given that assumption, he presented two choices: either be prepared for war, or create a worldwide government so that war would not be necessary. He saw the United Nations as a step in the right direction, but one that was insufficient by itself.

Einstein's life came to an end in a Princeton, New Jersey, hospital on April 18, 1955. His humanitarianism followed him almost literally to the grave. His final project, which he worked on at this hospital, was a speech marking Israel's seventh Independence Day. Ⓔ

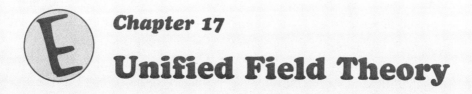

Chapter 17

Unified Field Theory

After spending the first part of his career working to define general relativity, Einstein's final quest was to unite all aspects of physics into one unified field theory. Was he successful in his attempts? Has anyone ever succeeded in tying up the world of science into a neat package? Read on to find out.

A United Theory

Einstein devoted the last years of his professional career to the unified field theory. The quest began in 1928, but it would occupy his thoughts for years to come. The general definition of a unified field theory is an attempt to create one theoretical framework that describes all the fundamental elements of physics. Sounds neat, doesn't it? Such a theory would provide one way to define everything, and one method by which all of science would make sense. Does such a thing exist?

It certainly didn't exist in the time of Einstein, and the quest for a unified field theory turned into an all-out obsession for him. He felt strongly enough about the unified field theory to allow it to consume the remainder of his scientific career.

Einstein had an intense desire to explain all aspects of physics with a single, simple, elegant theory. This theory had to include seemingly disparate concepts—general relativity, particle-driven quantum mechanics, electromagnetism, gravity, and the space-time continuum would all have to be explainable under the same set of rules.

The Basics

For starters, what's so hard about uniting these ideas under a single theory? Were these scientific concepts really so incompatible? Unified field theory is sometimes called the "theory of everything"—for good reason! It basically tries to link together all the known methods of explaining science and nature. A "field" is anything that's acting under the influence of a force, like gravity. Gravity is what keeps us safely on the surface of our planet and what governs the orbits of the planets around the sun. General relativity expands the notion of gravity to deal with very large masses and very high speeds. The space-time continuum represents an infinite series of interactions, taking place in an ever-expanding environment.

As with many aspects of mathematics and science, Isaac Newton started the ball rolling toward the development of an inclusive way to understand the universe. He was one of the first scientists to use mathematics to describe motion. His theories developed into modern-day calculus, which would become the first way of describing the universe—classical field theory.

Newton's discovery that force equaled mass multiplied by acceleration would become a key part of developing later ideas about gravitation. His laws of motion could be applied not just to objects, but to fluids and strings as well. In applying these ideas to spatial volumes, in addition to finite objects, the transition was made from mechanics to fields—hence the term "field theory." Newton's law of gravitation, then, was a precursor to the first official field theory.

The formalized idea of a field theory came about first from James Maxwell, in the early nineteenth century. His work in the area of electro-magnetism, a specific kind of force, is generally considered to be the first field theory. Much of his research focused on proving that electromagnetic waves provided an answer to the current great mystery of the day—how light worked. After Maxwell, Einstein's work with general relativity and gravitation would come to be known as the second field theory.

Einstein's Difficulty

It was Einstein himself who would first coin the term "unified field theory." His quest began with an attempt to prove that electromagnetism and gravity were just different manifestations of the same basic field. Later, his findings were summarized into an effort to bind together the four main forces that many scientists thought governed the world. These were electromagnetism, gravity, a "strong force" (the force that held together the nucleus of an atom), and a "weak force" (the force that dealt with nuclear processes such as decay).

The four main forces that unified field theory attempts to unite are these:

- Electromagnetism
- Gravity
- Strong force
- Weak force

Then, however, quantum theory had to be thrown into the mixture. Quantum science is the study of particles, atoms, and other aspects of the universe on a microscopic level. Atoms are studied in terms of subatomic particles such as protons and electrons, and things are studied on the smallest possible scale. Relativity, on the other hand, is almost the opposite. It examines the universe macroscopically. Elements are studied on a large scale, certainly large enough to be visible without the aid of microscopes, and they are often viewed with telescopes instead!

One of Einstein's largest challenges with the unified field theory was to find some way to describe both quantum theory and relativity under the same umbrella—in other words, to find a way to have both systems make sense under the same set of rules. Einstein never accepted quantum theory. He would never believe that the lack of a rigid causality could describe the behavior of atoms on a quantum level. This disbelief is, perhaps, one reason why his unified field theory never reached fulfillment.

The most difficult aspect of Einstein's quest was trying to unite electromagnetism and gravity. The causes and attributes of these two forces were different enough that none of his attempts to unite them, bridging the gap between particles and photons, made sense.

Einstein did make several predictions that would help mobilize his research toward solving the quest for a unified field theory. One such prediction was that energy in the form of electromagnetic radiation and gravitational energy travels at the speed of light. This very important fact eventually led to the discovery of the weak and strong force fields that accompany nuclear reactions. These forces, combined with the electromagnetic photons they emit, lead to Einstein's equivalence of mass and energy, $E=mc^2$. These diverse elements comprised several of the major forces that Einstein would ultimately try to unite; however, the existing force field model of the day wouldn't permit a union of the interaction between particles and photons.

Einstein's great disappointment was that he never managed to unite all of physics in one grand scheme. In fact, in his later years he was regarded by younger scientists as having wasted much of his career. They saw Einstein as chasing an unattainable dream while the rest of physics passed him by. However, Einstein never regretted his quest for a "theory of everything." Although such a theory has still not been found, even today, Einstein laid some of the groundwork for today's cutting-edge research.

The Standard Model

Although uniting all of nature's forces still remains an elusive search, some aspects of these different forces have been successfully unified in today's view of the physics of the universe. For example, there is a theory called the "standard model." This concept is one that unites the strong force, the weak force, and electromagnetism.

There are two main types of particles: boson and fermions. Fermions make up the composition of matter, and bosons transmit forces. Fermions are divided into categories based on electric charge, and many types (including taus and neutrinos) have been observed in a laboratory.

Particles, as they are studied today, fall into a standard model of analysis. This system is actually a mathematical model that explains the physics of particles, and it is accepted by the scientific community.

The standard model divides particles into one of two basic types: bosons (the particles that transmit forces) and fermions (ones that comprise matter). Gravitons and photons are examples of bosons, whereas electrons are one type of fermion.

However, this model serves to define only particle physics—only one aspect of what Einstein would hope to uncover. This description doesn't provide an opening for gravity into the equation. As such, it falls short of ever being a truly unified field theory, because it doesn't take all fields into account.

Einstein's Contemporaries

Einstein was not the only scientist to try to develop a unified field theory. Other physicists working at about the same time had similar interests. Their main discoveries, though, were in other aspects of science and physics. Erwin Schrödinger and Werner Heisenberg were two scientists whose work would be fundamental to the furthering of Einstein's thinking in terms of a unified field theory.

ALERT!

Don't expect to find unified field theory headlining the newspapers anytime soon. It has not been proven, and it currently exists solely as a scientific hypothesis. But perhaps ongoing research will one day turn unified field theory into fact.

Schrödinger (1887–1961)

Erwin Rudolf Josef Alexander Schrödinger was an Austrian scientist, one of Einstein's contemporaries. He entered the University of Vienna in 1906 and studied theoretical physics, such as Maxwell's equations, thermodynamics, optics, and mechanics. He received his doctorate degree in 1910 and, after a brief stint in the military, took a job working in experimental physics. This break from theoretical physics would prove invaluable to his later work in theory because it provided him with a practical backdrop for his research.

Beginning around 1921, Schrödinger engaged in studies of the nature of the atom. He worked with quantum statistics in the mid-1920s, and he was aware of the work of Louis de Broglie. Schrödinger began conversing with Albert Einstein in 1925, and the two exchanged letters on the subject of physics and contemporary scientists. By 1926 Schrödinger had published new papers on wave mechanics and was gaining worldwide fame. He won the Nobel Prize in physics in 1933.

By the 1940s, Schrödinger was starting to work actively on creating a unified field theory. He published a paper on it in 1943, and in 1946, Schrödinger corresponded with Einstein on the subject. Although he never reached a conclusion of any significance, he would continue this elusive quest for the remainder of his life.

FACT

"The Present Situation in Quantum Mechanics," Schrödinger's work from 1935, discusses his famous cat paradox. A cat placed inside a closed box would live or die depending on a quantum event, Schrödinger rationalized. The paradox was that, until the box was opened, both scenarios existed.

Heisenberg (1901–1976)

Werner Heisenberg was one of the primary physicists responsible for discovering quantum mechanics. As such, his contribution to the creation of a unified field theory was enormous, because he laid the foundation for one of its four corners. Heisenberg's research focused on developing the "uncertainty principle" of quantum theory, which states that as the position of a subatomic particle is known with more and more certainty, its momentum is known with less and less precision. Position and momentum are therefore coupled, and only one can be known with any certainty. This idea forms the basis for many aspects of quantum theory.

Heisenberg would go back and forth with Schrödinger, as the two scientists developed competing theories. Heisenberg's idea of uncertainty lent itself to an explanation of quantum theory known as the "matrix form," while Schrödinger actively pursed his research in wave mechanics. Schrödinger would eventually come up with a proof, showing that the two methods arrived at the same conclusions.

Heisenberg's uncertainty principle would later be paraphrased into the notion of the "probability field," the idea that particles had a tendency to exist at certain places in the space-time continuum, although the exact position of any single particle was impossible to determine. Probability was seen as a potentially unifying factor of all the forces of nature. It couldn't be created or destroyed, and its total amount held constant. While this idea never gained universal recognition or proof, it fed into Einstein's idea that such a universal binder might exist.

Current Research: Symmetry Theories

Ongoing work in this area attempts to combine this model (combined electromagnetic and weak forces) with the strong force. Symmetry theories are employed in this endeavor. At its most basic level, a symmetry theory is the idea that everything and nothing coexist on the same plane. Scientifically, symmetry theories have been broken into several categories—gauge symmetry, string theory, supersymmetry, and M-theory are a few examples of types of symmetry theories.

Gauge Symmetry

One of the most significant advances toward the creation of a working unified field theory came in the mid-1960s in the form of a theory called "gauge symmetry." Two physicists, Steven Weinberg and Abdus Salam, unified electromagnetism and the weak force by breaking both forces down into their components. They showed that electromagnetic forces consisted of photons, whereas the weak force consisted of particles called bosons, which were part of the same family as photons.

String Theory

String theory is one of the most popular modern offshoots of the unified field theory. The concept for string theory came about because quantum theory provides an acceptable explanation for particle behavior in the form of the probabilistic behavior of individual particles. It does not, however, provide such an explanation for gravity! String theory can be seen as a balance to particle theory, or quantum theory; it is sometimes called a theory of "quantum gravity."

The basic idea behind string theory can be visualized by imagining a violin. Different musical notes are produced depending on how the strings are plucked (or stroked), and how much tension someone's finger places on the strings. This idea actually dates back to Greek musicians and scientists such as Pythagoras.

There are two major types of string theories—closed loops that can be broken into open strings, and closed loops that can't be broken. Think of an open string as one where a wave strikes a line, and goes off the end of the line (literally!) once it reaches the terminus. A closed-string vibration, on the other hand, would be one where the wave just oscillates back and forth, from end to end. String theory posits that one of the fundamental units is a particle called a graviton, the fundamental unit of gravity.

String theory is basically an attempt to provide a unifying explanation for particle forces in nature, including gravity. String theory provides the string model for interaction and propagation. It is seen in contrast to particle theories, which provide for varied interaction between elements.

To make things even more complicated, there are many subsets of string theories. Bosonic string theory involves only the particles that transmit forces. Particles that involve matter belong to the realm of "superstring theory." There have been up to five types of superstring theories discussed. They're named somewhat mysteriously—type I, type IIA, type IIB, and then there are also two heterotic string theories. Current thinking now is that they're all part of the same fundamental idea.

Supersymmetry

So what of Einstein's dream of uniting all four main types of forces? There is current work in progress that tries to bring together grand unification theory with the fourth and final force—gravitation. Several offshoots of string theories work toward uniting all these different forces.

There are several flavors of supersymmetry. Supergravity combines particle theory with supersymmetry and relativity. There is also a version of supersymmetry that tries to align string and quantum theory, although they are fundamental opposites.

The effort to unite string theory with gravitation has spawned a branch called supersymmetry. Supersymmetry is a subset of string theory that actually tries to relate two kinds of particles—those that comprise matter, and those that transmit forces. Supersymmetry is, by definition, a branch of symmetry theory that includes fermions as well as bosons. It's fundamentally different from traditional quantum theory because, with supersymmetry, there is no notion of infinity. Fermions and bosons eventually cancel each other out.

M-Theory

Can bosonic string theory, supersymmetry, and other string theories all be united to save the world? Or if not that, could they be joined in an attempt to fulfill Einstein's dream of a unified field theory? Scientists and theorists today are working on just such a unification, and it's called M-theory—named such because it would be the "mother of all theories." So far, there is a long way to go in proving M-theory viable. However, theories such as supersymmetry are considered to be potential candidates for inclusion in such a new unified field theory.

Grand Unified Theory

There are several offshoots of Einstein's unified field theory under development today. Most of them try to unite some of the main forces. None of them, however, has yet been successful in creating a true theory that unites all of nature's elements. But some are coming close.

Grand unified theory posits that energetic matter is responsible for wave formation. Under this principle, the Big Bang that created the universe is an example of just such a wave. Surf's up, and in a major way!

Attempts have also been made to unite the weak force with the strong force. The grand unified theory presents a mathematical model that describes this potential relationship. Energetic matter is seen as the element that creates wave formation, and thus it is the factor that ties together all other elements of nature. In wave terminology, more energy creates waves; less energy creates particles. If proven to be true through experimentation and evidence, the grand unified theory could provide an amazingly coherent explanation for the diverse aspects of the world that so intrigued Einstein.

How Unified Field Theory Affects Us

Are string theories forever to remain in the realm of the theory? There are many actual experiments being done, and research is currently underway that attempts to prove string theory as a viable component of a unified field theory. Some of the work being done today involves work with particles to prove their interrelationships with gravity and motion.

The Importance of Particles

Particle experimentation has a rich history, some of which affects our daily lives. The electron, discovered in 1895, went on to form the basis of the cathode ray tube (or CRT, as it's more commonly called). This invention would make possible the television and computer monitor, among other things. The neutron and positron were first observed directly in the early 1930s, and quark theory of the 1960s would describe the composite nature of protons. The process by which particles are discovered and harnessed is a slow and thorough one, and it definitely bodes well for future advances in particle theory.

The Search to Connect with Quantum

Einstein never liked quantum mechanics, and he famously stated that God doesn't play dice with the universe. Quantum theory meant that everything was based on probabilities, and it wasn't possible to predict the behavior of particles with complete certainty. Einstein wanted the definite. His cosmological and spiritual view of the universe was that it should be an organized, orderly place. Although he never found the answer to this question that occupied many of his later years, scientists today persist in searching for a simple, elegant way by which the universe makes sense.

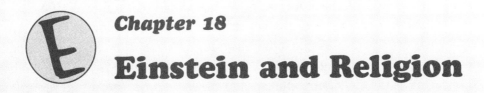

Chapter 18

Einstein and Religion

Particularly in his later life, Einstein and religion were inseparable topics of discussion. While his earlier years were largely characterized by his research, much of his later life was devoted to social causes. There is, of course, a difference between religion and religious observance. There is also a difference between religion and spirituality, and these distinctions would come to the fore with Einstein.

A Primer on Judaism

Some background into Judaism is essential for understanding Einstein's complex relationship with the religion into which he was born. The Jewish religion is one of the world's oldest, and is the foundation for many other religions. The holy work of Judaism is the Old Testament of the Bible, called the Torah. In the books of the Torah, which were handed down through the generations by an oral tradition (and eventually written down, of course) the basic principles of the religion were set forth. These include the idea that God exists, there is just one God, and God is the only entity that should be prayed to. God would reward people who believed in him and followed his word, and would punish those who did otherwise. God allowed for a prophet (named Moses) to communicate his will to the people—to spread the word, as it were.

In an effort to give people some basic rules to live by, God issued the Ten Commandments through Moses. These rules have come to be the guiding moral principles that Jews try to live by. They include such ideas as not killing, not stealing, not coveting, honoring your father and mother, not committing adultery, and keeping the Sabbath day holy. They also included honoring one and only one God, and making no graven images or other idols to worship.

FACT

Going back to the earliest roots in the Bible, Jews were wanderers. Between being ordered out of Eden and having to wander the desert, Jewish people were habitually in search of a homeland. Jewish nomads resided in Germany, Poland, and many other European countries.

Zionists Find a Home

As seen already, Jews suffered greatly at the hands of the Nazis, as well as other groups who were determined to curtail their religious freedom. The Jewish religion is, to some extent, one with a long history of persecution. Partially in response to this persecution, the establishment of the Jewish state of Israel occurred in 1948. The United Nations actually voted to carve an Israeli homeland out of Palestine a year earlier. Jews had far-reaching ties to the region as their homeland. David Ben-Gurion (1886–1973), who was then the president of the World Zionist Organization, formally established Israel as a separate and independent entity for the first time.

The United States was among the first to formally recognize the new state. President Harry Truman responded to the Tel Aviv declaration eleven minutes after it had been made. There was argument both for and against the United States' support for the creation of a Jewish homeland inside Palestine. Particularly after the Holocaust and the terror of World War II, Truman was loathe to suggest that Jews be given anything but a top priority. On the other hand, Arabs controlled much of America's access to oil at this point, and supporting the creation of Israel might have been seen as a threat to the relationship that the United States had with oil-producing countries. Fortunately, Truman made the decision he thought best, and his immediate support of the Zionist nation created the groundwork for future ties and relationships with Israel.

Ben-Gurion, the driving force behind Israel's statehood, was born in Poland. He studied in a Jewish school as a small child, and this education fomented the seeds for Jewish pride from a very early age. By 1906 he had arrived in what would later become Israel, and he was involved in Zionist activism throughout most of his life. He worked as an agricultural laborer, slowly getting more and more involved in politics. He studied law in 1912 in Istanbul, but was deported during World War I. He spent time in the United States, learning more about how Zionism was being realized abroad.

Much of Ben-Gurion's work after 1948 lay in fulfilling his roles as prime minister and defense minister of Israel, as well as in building the new country economically, agriculturally, culturally, and militarily. It was he who, in 1952, offered Einstein the presidency of Israel upon the death of Chaim Weizmann. (See Chapter 16 for more information.) Although Einstein didn't accept this position, the fact that it was even offered to him is testimony to what a profound impact he had on the Jewish people, and the strength of the impression he made.

Chaim Weizmann had an important impact on a number of facets of Israeli life. While his presidency was surely one of the most influential, he also served as one of the founding members of Hebrew University, along with Albert Einstein.

What Makes Judaism Unique?

Much comparison is made of the similarities and differences between Judaism and Christianity. After all, these two religions share the same Bible. The basic tenet of all religions is fundamentally the same—the belief in something, be it a deity or group of deities, that acts on a higher plane than individual humans.

However, the differences between the major world religions are fairly clear. Judaism and Islam worship one God and only one God, whereas Christianity involves a Holy Trinity.

One of the defining characteristics of Judaism, compared to other religions, is its very lack of definition. While the basics of Judaism are clear (worship God and no one else), much of the rest of the religion is left undefined. There is no official Jewish doctrine on the afterlife (that is, there is no concept of Heaven or its less-friendly alternative) or, other than the Commandments, on how people should pray or otherwise live their lives.

In this respect, the Jewish faith presented an interesting conflict to Einstein. On the one hand, there are a few hard-and-fast tenets of the religion that are basically nonnegotiable. On the other hand, Judaism leaves much to interpretation, and each Jew is responsible for figuring certain things out for herself. Judaism is also a cultural tradition as well as a religious one, due to the shared cultural values and mores passed down through generations of Jews. These include foods, language, charity, and many others.

Einstein was more of a cultural Jew than a religious one. Although he was born Jewish and raised in a Jewish household, the religion did not dominate his upbringing. Quite the contrary, in fact. Einstein was raised in Ulm, Germany, a town known for its Jewish residents who assimilated enough into German society not to be persecuted. Einstein's family didn't raise him to be a closet Jew, though—they simply don't seem to have been active practitioners of the religion.

When the Einstein clan moved to Munich during Einstein's early years, in fact, they didn't fit into the Jewish community there because they were so unobservant. Einstein never had a bar mitzvah. (A "bar mitzvah" is a Jewish confirmation and recitation, performed by Jewish male children at the culmination of their Hebrew education, around their thirteenth birthday.) The fact that he didn't participate in this Jewish ritual indicates his desire to interpret and create his own Judaism, even at a young age.

Einstein never practiced stereotypical Judaism in his adult life. He didn't seem to have attended regular synagogue services, and he definitely took issue with many aspects of Torah-based Judaism, including its conception and definition of God. However, as will be seen later in this chapter, Einstein was extremely connected to Jewish views on values, ethics, and morality. The emphasis on personal responsibility for religion also appealed to Einstein's fundamental nature. Had Judaism been more stringent the way some religions are, Einstein might have rejected it altogether. Throughout his life, he developed his own approach to Judaism, which is entirely in keeping with the very spirit of the religion.

A Call to Action

Judaism is concerned with action. Jews are to behave according to the Ten Commandments, and they are explicitly forbidden from committing the sins set forth. In other ways, though, Judaism is a religion of action over word. For example, suppose a Jewish person were to be involved in a car accident and accidentally ended up responsible for killing someone else. The Jewish person who was responsible (depending on his or her degree of commitment to the religion, of course) would be expected to actively make up for that person's life to the extent that he or she was able. If the person who died was the breadwinner for a family of four, the individual who caused the accident would have to support that person's family.

Judaism is a nonproselytizing religion, and Jews will not be found going door-to-door and recruiting new members. While Einstein may not have explicitly supported all the rituals and observances of Judaism, he was eerily in sync with many of its social tenets. This connection is especially true in the Jewish tendency to express emotion and morality through action. While Einstein was a prolific writer and theorist, he believed firmly in supporting his causes through direct action.

When a Jewish person does something wrong, even when it's not her fault, she is expected to make amends in the best way she can. Some religions allow "sinners" to admit to their wrongdoing and simply be forgiven; Judaism offers no such forgiveness. Jews are called to act, and it is their obligation to right wrongs wherever they find them. This aspect may explain some of Einstein's outspoken activism later in his life.

Einstein traveled extensively to raise money for Jewish organizations. In 1922, for example, Einstein sailed to Singapore as part of a larger trip, and he used the opportunity to raise funds for Hebrew University, one of his pet projects. Much of Singapore's Jewish community was reputed to have met Einstein's boat when it docked. He was very famous by this point, and he used that fame to attract both attention and funding to his Jewish causes. In the late 1930s, Einstein spent much time raising funds for the United Jewish Appeal, a general advocacy and awareness group for Jewish people.

In the interest of perpetuating his philosophy through action, Einstein also gave many public speeches and public appearances to garner attention for various Jewish organizations. He believed that his physical presence would create more of an influence than words alone. This notion is in direct accordance with Jewish ethics; there's nothing like giving a human touch to furthering a cause. He gave public speeches in New York in 1930, Chicago in 1931, and London in 1933, to name just a few of his many appearances geared toward raising public awareness of the issues about which he felt strongly.

Einstein and Jewish Values

Einstein believed in and associated with the values of Judaism. Going back as far as the religion itself, Jews have traditionally been hard workers. They wandered the desert, built their homes and cities, and took responsibility for creating a life for themselves (with God's blessing, of course). Einstein certainly adopted his work ethic from the Jewish religion. Throughout his life he dedicated himself to intellectual labor, rarely letting up and never diminishing his goals. He continued work and research literally up until the day he died. On his deathbed in Princeton, New Jersey, Einstein was working on a speech for Israeli Independence Day.

Cultural Judaism

In some ways, Einstein identified with Judaism more culturally than religiously. For example, the idea of extended family is very strong in the Jewish culture. All Jews are considered family. Homes are extended to those in need, and Jews tend to bond closely with other Jews. It's a cultural phenomenon that seems somewhat out of place in a fast-paced modern world, but it is nonetheless true. Einstein extended himself to offer protection and hope for maligned Jews throughout the world. For example, in 1933 Einstein founded the International Rescue Committee, a group devoted to helping refugees from around the world. That sort of familiarity and association is a definite part of the Jewish culture that Einstein absorbed.

Social Justice

Social justice is another Jewish value that Einstein took and made his own. Judaism teaches that all people have a right to be treated equally, regardless of race, gender, religion, or other factors. Einstein shared this belief wholeheartedly. The Jewish religion doesn't discriminate in this sense, and neither did Einstein. He was an associate of several organizations devoted to peace, as well as equal treatment for all. One example was the Jewish Peace Fellowship, a group of Jews that promotes worldwide peace through positive action. The group was founded in 1941 to support Jews who didn't want to serve in the military. Einstein believed it was their right to be supported as Jews, and again simply as citizens who chose a certain path. For Einstein, social justice meant that Jews should be allowed to express themselves as Jewish, and also as people, and he worked toward protecting both sets of rights.

FACT

The term "social justice" was coined in 1840 by a Sicilian priest named Luigi Taparelli d'Azeglio, and it is generally defined as the idea that everyone should be treated equally well.

Humanitarianism

Humanitarianism is another value that is strongly encouraged within the Jewish faith. Judaism is different from religions such as Christianity, some sects of which might pass around a collection plate at services to gather funds for the church or for a specific cause. Judaism doesn't generally support outright charity in this sense. It's consistent with the idea of personal responsibility, which comprises a major core of the Jewish faith. Rather, Jews tend to devote time, energy, and personal attention to particular causes.

Humanitarianism, or having a concern for people's general welfare, is therefore part of Judaism's core foundation, and Einstein certainly followed that tenet. His work with the International Rescue Committee is just one example of his devotion to an organization that was devoted to protecting people's rights. Einstein possessed and embodied the values of Judaism. He believed firmly in the rights of Jews worldwide, and he didn't hesitate to act in support of his beliefs.

Einstein's Place in the Jewish Ranks

Religious observance and spirituality are interrelated topics. Being an observant Jew involves obeying many principles and rituals, some of which can take an entire lifetime to devote oneself to. While Einstein rejected many details of the Jewish orthodoxy, a brief primer in the practice of Judaism is useful here because it will show precisely which aspects of the religion Einstein disagreed with. For starters, observant Jews (those who follow the rituals of Judaism) generally belong to one of several categories. The main branches of Judaism include Orthodox, Conservative, Reform, and Reconstructionist. The groups are not always completely compatible, though they all observe the same basic tenets.

Orthodox

Orthodox Judaism is one of the most rigorous branches of Judaism. Those who live as Orthodox Jews obey all the Jewish food laws. They do not eat pork or shellfish, do not combine meat and dairy, and generally only eat food that has been certified as kosher. They keep the Sabbath holy, meaning they do no work from sundown Friday to sundown Saturday. Socially and culturally, some Orthodox Jews do not ascribe to all modern beliefs. Orthodox women don't have all the same rights as non-Orthodox, and other aspects of modern culture have not been accepted. Orthodox Jews take the Bible literally as portraying the word of God.

FACT

Orthodox Jews do no work from sundown Friday to sundown Saturday—including driving a car or using a pencil. Being an Orthodox Jew requires much more commitment to ritual than other branches of Judaism.

Conservative and Reform

Next down the line is Conservative Judaism. Conservatives observe Judaism with the same rigor as Orthodox Jews, but often it does not require that all the rituals be performed. Women take on the role that they have in the rest of modern society, and Conservative Judaism is generally practiced by those who attend weekly services. Reform Judaism breaks with both Orthodox and Conservative in that it believes that Judaism has evolved over time. Literal interpretation of the Bible plays less of a role in the Reform tradition.

Reconstructionist

In response to changes in society, new offshoots of Judaism were created. People had less time to observe all the rituals that comprise strict Orthodox Judaism. Also, lifestyle changes and nontraditional relationships created a demand for a type of Judaism that more people could relate to. Reconstructionism emerged as a branch only in the second part of the twentieth century, so it is by far the newest thread of Judaism. Reconstructionist Judaism basically believes that Judaism can be enlightened with social, political, and cultural influences of the times, so it presents by far the least stringent interpretation of the Bible. While the core teachings of Reconstructionist Judaism remain the same, these teachings are combined with a modern emphasis on community, spirituality, and ethical values.

Other

There are various other branches and flavors of Judaism as well. Hasidic Judaism, for example, was the predominant form of Judaism throughout much of central Europe. The movement spread to the United States and other countries toward the end of the nineteenth century. Hasidic Jews studied the Torah, but they also brought happiness and spirituality to their study of religion. All in all, then, the Jewish faith is not a simple one, nor is there one blanket way to "be Jewish."

QUESTION?

Into which branch of established Judaism did Einstein fit?
None of the above. If anything, he probably would have liked the emphasis that Reconstructionism placed on ethics and intellectual endeavors. However, even this branch of Judaism would probably have been too "religious" for him, since it does still emphasize the importance of the Torah in religious education.

Einstein's God

In terms of his belief in the Jewish notion of one God, Einstein veered once again from the traditional. In this area he followed the teachings of Baruch Spinoza (1632–1677), a European rationalist philosopher. Spinoza was himself Jewish, although he rejected many of the principles of Orthodox Judaism. Philosophically he held that humans were driven by the desire to stay alive. Self-preservation outlawed free will almost completely. Thinking and understanding separated good (intelligent) people from evil (and, consequently, unintelligent) ones. He described God as true thought, and the only way to know God was through thought and understanding.

Einstein's view of God followed that of Baruch Spinoza: All nature was considered God. It just goes to show that great minds, even throughout time, think alike!

As part of this system of beliefs, all nature was considered God. Einstein had always had a secondary interest in nature, loving outdoor activities and simply taking in all that nature had to offer. However, "nature" meant more than trees and waterfalls. For Einstein, nature represented order, harmony, and unity. He once said that he believed in Spinoza's God, one who concerned himself with the physicality of the world rather than with determining the fate of mankind.

Einstein's fascination with Spinoza, while not representing a complete break with the Jewish tradition, was enough of a stretch that he would never have been considered a proponent of "true" Judaism. This idea is not entirely inconsistent with the New Age approach to religion, which holds that God is a part of every creature.

Judaism and Science

Judaism and science were, without question, two of the most important aspects of Einstein's life. Religion and science have historically been at odds with each other; Einstein, however, had a unique take on religion that would allow him to reconcile these two distinct aspects of his personal and professional life.

So how did he do it? First off, Einstein believed that emotion was the primary motivator behind human action. Desire led people to act, in his rationale, as did fear, happiness, guilt, and other human characteristics. Love and fear were perhaps the two most powerful motivators for Einstein. Children loved and feared their parents, and these emotions stimulated their actions and the communities they formed. Similarly, religious adults (or those who believed in the existence of a God) exercised these same emotions toward their God of choice.

The Morality of Science

Einstein saw Judaism predominantly as a "religion of morals," one in which people were urged to behave ethically because it was the right thing to do. His alternative, the "religion of fear," was one in which God was a terrible figure who forced people to behave against the threat of punishment, either now or in the afterlife. The Jewish scriptures, though setting out certain guidelines about God, were quite open to interpretation. Their lack of fear-inducing dogma left interpretation of morality up to the individual, something Einstein intensely appreciated about Judaism.

Following from this idea that Judaism and ethics are compatible, Einstein also argued that science and Judaism could influence each other beneficially. Religion and science were historically incompatible, he argued, because either events happened for scientific reasons, or a God intervened to make events happen. How could both ideas exist simultaneously?

Einstein reasoned that a religious scientist like himself was one who, while incredibly awestruck at the magnitude of the Earth's creation, was completely driven by the desire to understand it. In Einstein's world, faith could belong to both nature and science, to both God and technology. Einstein himself wrote that he longed to understand God's actions as well as his thoughts. He wasn't necessarily concerned with dissecting mysticism and faith, but he wanted to know how God had created the universe. He believed and accepted the idea of a power higher than himself. Being

Einstein, though, he wasn't content to leave it at that! He was always searching for comprehension, and this desire for understanding was not limited to the realm of hard science.

Judaism was not the only religion that Einstein considered in his multifaceted approach to science. He made connections between science and other religions as well. He thought Buddhism reflected science and research quite accurately. This idea is actually not surprising in light of Einstein's theory of relativity. For Einstein, waves and vibrations replaced the hard substance that other scientists liked to attribute to the world, and this notion of the world (as more conceptual than absolute) fit well with the teachings of Buddhism. In addition, Buddhism transcends the notion of an individual, all-powering God, and Einstein agreed with this aspect.

The Great Debate: Creation Versus Evolution

One of the most typical divides between religion and science occurs with the subject of how life began, or the debate between evolution and creationism. To briefly summarize the major players here, the debate focuses on either a scientific or a religious explanation for the formation of the universe. Evolutionists believe that life began through a series of events beginning in the Big Bang, followed by the formation of the Earth and primitive life here, after which point humans eventually evolved from more primordial ancestors. This theory, championed by Darwin, goes along with the idea of natural selection—those who are most fit to survive, will.

ALERT!

Einstein never claimed to solve the debate between creationism and evolution, nor did he claim to have bridged the gap between science and religion. His theories, however, show that his thinking definitely brought the two areas together.

Creationists, on the other hand, believe that God created the world. While the precise explanation varies according to the religion, most creation myths involve the notion of a main deity who was responsible for generating both Earth and the life that inhabits it. In the Jewish religion, for example, in the first book of the Old Testament (Genesis),

God creates the world in seven days. During those days, the Earth, heavens, people, and animals are all created.

What did Einstein think about this great debate? His theory of relativity worked toward defining space and time, two of the most abstract concepts there are. A true creationist would probably consider such research blasphemous, since to some extent it subverts the notion of an infinite God and an equally infinite universe. However, Einstein seems to have held with the existence of some force that was responsible for creating the universe, though probably not the traditional Judeo-Christian one. He was constantly amazed by the miracle of the world as it was shown through science and understanding.

Religion and Government

Einstein was able to successfully reconcile his interests in religion and science. So what of his third major occupation—politics? Could government and religion coexist in Einstein's world of activism?

In the United States, religion and politics have been legally separated since the early nineteenth century. In a letter to the Danbury Baptist Association in 1802, President Jefferson informed the people that there would be a separation of church and state and that America would have no one official denomination of any particular religion. Since the writing of this famous document, church and government have been at least nominally separate throughout America's history, and religious freedom is one of America's defining characteristics.

It was no accident that Einstein ended up in America. By moving to the United States, he was free to practice (or not practice, as the case may have been) Judaism as he saw fit. More importantly, perhaps, he was free to continue his life's work without having to fear religious persecution. Had America been an officially Catholic country, for example, Einstein might never have immigrated here, or his activism might not have been tolerated. Einstein had contact with members of the United States government in many different capacities, and that degree of involvement might not have even been possible if not for the separation of church and state.

Organized religion was, however, never something that Einstein took a major interest in. The last synagogue he appeared to have been a member of was in Berlin in 1924. He did, though, attend services occasionally, and he certainly visited Jewish holy sites. In 1935, he was awarded a golden mezuzah by an Orthodox congregation, the Tifereth Israel Synagogue in San Diego, California.

FACT

A mezuzah is a small box with a piece of parchment in it, on which is written an excerpt from the Torah in Hebrew. The Torah includes a commandment to affix a mezuzah, containing the commandments of God, on the doorposts of every Jewish home. A mezuzah is supposed to offer divine guidance and protection.

Einstein, then, took full advantage of America's separation of church and state. For him, Orthodox and Conservative Judaism were not the way to go. However, he never protested other people's rights to express their own Judaism. While he may not have believed in all the tenets of the Jewish religion, he fully supported any other Jew's rights to do so. Religious tolerance, a hallmark of America, suited Einstein quite well.

Judaism and Education

In keeping with another traditional Jewish notion, Einstein placed an extremely high value on education. Believing that Jews had the same right to receive high-quality, persecution-free education as anyone else, he made significant contributions to the Jewish educational world.

Hebrew University

One of his major educational projects was Hebrew University in Jerusalem. The school officially opened in 1925, and it was founded by many different scholars and government officials—including Einstein. He actually went to the United States in 1921 largely to raise funds for the creation of the school. Hebrew University initially offered courses of study in Judaism, chemistry, and microbiology. They expanded their course offerings, and the university is today one of the most respected in Israel.

Yeshiva University

Einstein also affected educational institutions that he wasn't directly affiliated with. Yeshiva University was founded in 1886, and it is the oldest Jewish university in America. In determining a name for the college of medicine, university president Dr. Samuel Belkin was highly influenced by important scientists and politicians of the time. He ultimately chose to name the school after Einstein (called, appropriately, the Albert Einstein College of Medicine). Einstein agreed to let the school use his name in 1953, and it opened in 1955.

FACT

Jews have traditionally placed much emphasis on education. Perhaps this attitude stems from Nazi Germany, where Jewish students were forbidden to attend university at all. Education became all the more cherished when it was taken away.

Chapter 19

Applications of Einstein's Theories

Einstein's theories have weathered the tests and ravages of time, but to varying extents. Many of his ideas were ahead of their time, and others never reached completion. How does his work hold up to modern research, and how are his theories being applied today?

Gravity Probe B

Einstein's theories about general relativity, gravity, space, and time will be given the ultimate test in 2003. The National Aeronautics and Space Administration (NASA) has been developing a mission since 1964. The goal of this mission is to test the effects predicted by Einstein's theory of relativity.

Background

Recall that, in the seventeenth century, Newton posited that gravity was a force acting between objects anywhere on Earth. In his theory of universal gravitation, Newton thought that the strength of this universal gravitational force changed immediately whenever the mass of an object changed. The equation for Newton's theory is stated as $F = GmM/r^2$, where F (force of gravitation) equaled G (a constant) multiplied by the masses of two objects, divided by the square of their distances apart.

Einstein later proposed that the speed of light was the fastest speed at which anything could travel. Under this logic, a major question arose: How could the gravitational force change so quickly? Einstein's solution lay in his description of the space-time continuum. The typical analogy is that space and time are like a fabric, woven inextricably together. Large objects (like the Earth and other planets) entering the continuum have a tendency to warp, or dent, this fabric. The Earth's daily rotation also causes the space-time fabric to change.

QUESTION?

What is space-time?
Scientists used to define the universe in terms of three dimensions: length, width, and height. A fourth was added, time, and together these dimensions make up space-time or the space-time continuum.

General relativity provides an explanation for the way light and matter behave under the influence of gravity. Observing these principles in action, though, provides even more information because it allows scientists to "see" proof of relativity. The theories of space-time and relativity were expanded upon in 1918 by two physicists named Joseph Lense and Hans Thirring. They researched and calculated gravity's effect on rotating masses (such as the Earth), and they evaluated the way rotating matter dragged inertial frames through gravity.

The Lense-Thirring effect, or "frame-dragging," as it would come to be called, was actually predicted by general relativity. It's basically the idea that as a small object rotates around a larger one in space, the orbit of the small body is changed slightly by the rotation itself. This effect is thought to be responsible for powering theoretical objects like quasars. Near Earth, though, it's difficult to measure because it is thought to be fairly weak.

The Search to Prove Relativity

Detecting and measuring gravity and related effects around Earth became a popular quest. Scientists in the 1960s started to think about how it could be done. Two physicists, Leonard Schiff and George Pugh, came up with the idea of sending gyroscopes into space via a satellite. The idea was that if Einstein were correct in his theory that a rotating Earth was actually warping the space-time fabric, then a spinning gyroscope placed in space would drift and change directions. When measured, this change in the gyroscope would give scientists a much firmer idea about how space-time actually works.

FACT

Was there a Gravity Probe A, you ask? There was indeed, and it consisted of a two-hour space flight in 1976. It tested Einstein's principle of equivalence, where he showed how acceleration was inseparable from the gravitational field. Relativity is based on this principle.

Scientists spent the next forty years trying to figure out how to design such an experiment. The gyroscopes would need to be inside a vacuum and couldn't be affected by temperature or vibration—no small task aboard a spacecraft. The satellite itself would be in constant motion, and temperatures in space change wildly.

The cost for the mission grew over the years, and it has actually been canceled seven times (so far). While most NASA missions are designed to perform multiple tasks, this mission had only one goal. And what a goal—if successful, some of the most basic properties of space will be measured, for the first time.

FACT

Gravity Probe B, dubbed "The Relativity Mission," is currently set to be launched in November 2003. It will use a Delta II rocket to propel it into space, and is scheduled to launch from Vandenberg Air Force Base in Southern California.

Perihelion of Mercury

Another area in which Einstein's research was continued after his death is in calculating the perihelion of Mercury. Remember that "perihelion" is the location of a planet's orbit when it is closest to the sun. As the closest planet to the sun, Mercury is also the swiftest traveler, taking just eighty-eight Earth days per orbit around the sun.

Before Einstein, in the late 1800s, scientists first noticed that Mercury's orbit wasn't quite what it had been predicted to be. Newton's law of universal gravitation was applied to calculate the perihelion, but what they observed didn't match the calculations. There was a mystery afoot.

Einstein's Prediction

While Einstein was alive, he actually recalculated the position at a particular time of the perihelion of Mercury. He predicted that, because of general relativity, the perihelion would be slightly different than one would expect, and this anticipated difference would be based on orbital mechanics. Because space-time was curved, in accordance with the principles of relativity, Mercury's orbit was precessed from what Newton had predicted. The planet's orbit was not statically elliptical, Einstein argued, but rather there should be a discrepancy from the purely elliptical orbit.

It turned out that, because of the effects of general relativity, Einstein was absolutely right. Scientists in the 1960s and 1970s were able to use radar and various telescopes to measure Mercury's orbit with extreme precision, and Einstein's predictions were proven accurate.

Upcoming Space Missions

Two planned missions to Mercury will study its orbit in precise detail, and they will give Einstein's theory a chance to be proven yet again. Bepi Colombo is a mission planned by the European Space Agency, which is scheduled to be launched in 2009 or 2010. This mission will send two spacecraft into orbit around Mercury, and they will study many different aspects of the planet. A second mission, "Messenger," is planned for launch by NASA in 2004, and it should reach Mercury's orbit around 2009.

Unified Field Theory

While no one has managed to create a unified field theory in modern times, Einstein's ideas are definitely alive and well in this pursuit. Einstein's attempt to formulate a unified field theory was discussed in depth in Chapter 17. What's relevant here is acknowledging that his quest is still being carried out by various scientists and philosophers around the world.

One of the most significant modern incarnations of the unified field theory lies in the development of symmetry theories. They try to explain the universe as consisting of different elements, which somehow manage to coexist symbiotically. There are several types of symmetry theories, including gauge symmetry, string theory, and supersymmetry. None of them has been able to achieve Einstein's goal of uniting all pieces of the universe into a single formula that makes sense—but the work forges ahead, and new theories are being developed literally as we speak.

Black Holes and Cosmology

Einstein's theories of gravity and relativity paved the way for modern cosmology. As seen in Chapter 14, the entire field of cosmology came about because of the work Einstein had done in setting the stage.

In particular, Einstein's research actually predicted the existence of black holes, one of today's hottest topics.

What Is a Black Hole?

Black holes are, by definition, extremely dense points in the space-time continuum. When a very large star collapses and compresses into itself, a black hole is formed. As long as stars are able to emit heat and light, they can resist their inward gravitational pull; upon collapse, however, they resist no longer. This inward gravitational pull is so intense that nothing can escape from a black hole, not even matter or light.

The first "actual" black hole scientists believe to truly exist was found in 1970, Cygnus X-1. Indirect evidence has been found for other black holes, as well. Without Einstein's theory of gravity and the space-time continuum, black holes could never have been conceptualized, let alone discovered.

Einstein's Effect on Cosmology

Einstein's influence into research on the space-time continuum went beyond black holes, though. General relativity paved the way for the development of the Big Bang theory, the event many scientists now believe was fundamental to the creation of the universe. Russian mathematician Alexander Friedmann, working in the 1920s, used relativity to create an equation whereby the Big Bang and the world's subsequent expansion made sense. Without Einstein's formulation of relativity, our conceptualization of where we all came from might be completely different today.

ALERT!

Contrary to popular fiction, Einstein neither invented nor discovered the black hole. Einstein never truly believed in the existence of black holes. His denial of them is extremely ironic, since it was his theories on gravitation and relativity that made their discovery possible in the first place.

Gravitational Lensing

Another area in which Einstein's theories would bring about future advances concerns gravitational lensing. In a paper he published in 1936, Einstein predicted that gravitational fields of large strength could bend light, in the same way that a lens does. According to his conception of the space-time continuum, any large mass would deform the space-time fabric, thus bending light.

The idea of gravitational lensing comes from this description: Large objects, such as a cluster of galaxies, act as a lens that consists of gravitational forces. As light passes through this object or cluster, it's bent and focused as it would be through an optical lens. The gravitationally lensed image could then be magnified or distorted, depending on the location of the source.

The definition of "gravitational lensing" is the focusing effect that a large object or cluster has on light, often causing it to bend. The resulting image can be distorted or magnified when seen by an observer, depending on where the observer is positioned.

If an observer and the lens are perfectly aligned, the image that results is called an Einstein ring, named appropriately after the scientist who predicted the existence of this effect. An Einstein ring was discovered in 1998 by observations conducted by the Hubble Space Telescope and a telescope array at Jodrell Bank Observatory, located at the University of Manchester in England. When the alignment is imperfect, on the other hand, multiple images can be formed. One type of object consisting of multiple images is called an Einstein cross.

Bose-Einstein Condensate

Einstein's predictions found yet another application in the study of subzero temperatures. Satyendra Nath Bose (1894–1974) was an Indian physicist who studied how light was transmitted in small packets called "quanta." Einstein took this idea and applied it to atoms, but he found that strange things happened when atoms were exposed to extremely low temperatures. He used Bose's calculations to predict that matter would enter a new phase when it reached absolute zero. At this point, atoms would become part of an ideal system, where their quantum and mechanical properties would equal out.

At this level, Einstein predicted that a special kind of condensation would form. At this lowest of possible temperatures, atoms would join together to act as a single entity. The discovery of a new phase of matter was incredibly significant, since, at that time, it was believed that matter could exist only in one of four phases (solid, liquid, gas, and plasma). This new phase was dubbed the "Bose-Einstein Condensate." One of the results of this prediction was that quantum physics could be examined on a larger scale, since larger groups of atoms could now be studied as representative of their smaller, constituent atoms.

FACT

Absolute zero is the coldest temperature possible. It's measured at negative 459.69 degrees Fahrenheit. This is the temperature at which all atomic motion ceases.

The prediction of this new phase of matter would go on to be proven in 1995, when a team of scientists actually created a Bose-Einstein Condensate. A team of scientists led by Eric Cornell and Carl Wieman conducted this research, and they shared the 2001 Nobel Prize in physics for their work.

Global Positioning Systems

Do you have a new car with a fancy global positioning system in it? Ever eye the handheld GPS units for sale in trendy tech shops and wonder if your neighborhood has been mapped for all the world to see? Thank Einstein for making these nifty new devices possible!

Relationship with Relativity

General relativity led to a number of scientific breakthroughs and theoretical changes, but it also made its way down to personal technology that affects people in their everyday lives. One "side effect" of relativity is the idea that time passes at different rates depending on your altitude. This effect had to be taken into account when GPS systems were designed.

How Does It Work?

Global positioning systems work by receiving signals from satellites in orbit around Earth. Signals are transmitted by multiple satellites, and there's a time delay due to the fact that signals are emitted in intervals. These signals are encoded so that the GPS device (usually a handheld unit, or one inserted into an automobile, airplane, or other means of transportation) knows exactly where the satellite was (and how it was positioned) at the time the signal was emitted. The speed of light is used to translate the time delays between satellites into distances, and the GPS system is able to figure out exactly where it is at any given time.

To accurately determine a position on the ground, the clocks on GPS satellites must run with an accuracy of 1 nanosecond (1 billionth of a second). However, the satellites are moving with respect to observers on the ground. So both special and general relativity must be taken into account. The designers of GPS satellites must account for both the time dilation from special relativity, and the fact that time moves at different rates depending on altitude, from general relativity.

Thanks to Einstein, these effects can be calculated exactly and built into the clocks on the GPS satellites. Without the relativistic corrections, the GPS satellites would fall out of synch within minutes, and positional errors on the ground would start to build up by about ten kilometers every day! Without Einstein's theory of relativity, GPS positioning would not be possible, and airplanes and hikers would have a lot more trouble finding their way around our planet.

Cosmological Constant

One of the areas in which Einstein's theories did not withstand the test of time is with the cosmological constant. (This concept was discussed in depth in Chapter 14.) To summarize briefly, when developing his theory of relativity, the currently accepted idea was that the universe was unchanging and static. Einstein thought that relativity should support this idea. However, evidence didn't support his claim.

In order to make relativity reign supreme (and, at the same time, keep the universe from expanding,) Einstein added an extra term to his equations of general relativity. This term was expressed by the Greek letter "lambda." As with all constants, lambda would have the same value at all points within the universe. This value has sometimes been dubbed the "antigravity term."

However well-intentioned Einstein was in attempting to maintain the model of the universe as static and unexpanding, he was wrong. The cosmological constant tried to force the universe into a model that simply wasn't valid, and lambda was seen as shaky not long after Einstein introduced the idea in 1917.

The Friedmann equation works within the larger framework of general relativity, but it excludes the cosmological constant in an effort to represent the universe as dynamic. Energy conservation is maintained by using the idea that solving this equation for one particle is equal to solving it for all particles.

By 1922, a Russian mathematician named Alexander Friedmann was working on creating a model of the universe that didn't require the cosmological constant, and he met with success. He accurately recognized the universe as expanding and came up with a dynamic equation called Friedmann's equation that expressed the changing nature of the cosmos.

Additionally, Einstein was further proven wrong by Edwin Hubble. A scientist at the Mount Wilson Observatory, Hubble discovered evidence proving that the universe was, in fact, expanding. He studied the Andromeda galaxy and formulated equations that related a galaxy's velocity to its distance from Earth. Hubble used these equations to deduce that the universe is actually expanding, and it does not remain static.

The cosmological constant that Einstein had introduced to force the universe into stability hadn't been necessary after all. Einstein called the cosmological constant one of his greatest mistakes. He officially retracted it as a theory in 1932.

Quantum Theory

Quantum theory remains of the largest areas of theoretical physics that Einstein was never able to reconcile. In reality, his theories of general relativity actually cannot handle a quantum universe. When examined closely enough, quantum theory requires that matter breaks down into probabilities, and this aspect of quantum theory was one that Einstein always resisted.

Quantum theory is basically the idea that if a particle's position and momentum are known, there is an exclusion between the two. Only one of those two quantities can be known precisely. The more accurately a particle's position is known, the less accurately its momentum is known, and vice versa.

That idea forms the basis of quantum mechanics. Another way of stating it is that the behavior of matter at a subatomic level forms a purely statistical set of behaviors. A certain percentage of the time, there will be a certain behavior. However, one can never know the behavior of any individual particle, precisely because its properties can only be known on a statistical, or average, basis.

Einstein never liked quantum theory. He refused to believe in a purely statistical description of events, which effactually comprised the basis for quantum theory. Einstein was uncomfortable with quantum theory's inherently statistical nature—he thought that the universe should be more orderly, and more precise.

Despite Einstein's rejection of quantum theory, he was ahead of his time in recognizing the fundamental problem with all existing theories—they couldn't take everything in the universe into account. Quantum theory explained some aspects of the world we all live in, while relativity explained others. Could all the forces that act in the universe be explained under one coherent theory? Einstein spent the latter part of his life experimenting with his unified field theory, which attempted to wrap up the universe under a single overarching idea. As discussed in depth in Chapter 17, he was never successful in this attempt. Currently, theoretical physicists use string theory to try to find a "theory of everything."

Generally, then, Einstein's theories have had varied application in modern times. From ongoing space missions to the technology in your car, the impact of relativity and other aspects of Einstein's work has been enormous. Stephen J. Hawking, one of today's most brilliant cosmologists, bases his research on that of Albert Einstein. Much of Einstein's work has increasing relevance in the twenty-first century, and it will continue to allow scientists to make advances as history moves forward. Ⓔ

Chapter 20

Einstein's Other Science

Einstein is clearly best known for his most famous work and research into the theories of general relativity and special relativity. This work alone would have been enough for a lifetime, but Einstein also developed a number of other ideas. He was an inventor, and he held patents on a number of items. He also created and solved an array of theoretical puzzles.

The Noiseless Refrigerator

Beginning in 1926, Einstein and his friend Leo Szilard united on a project that was completely unrelated to atomic energy. Einstein and Szilard met in the early 1920s, and the two scientists collaborated on many projects over the course of their lives. Einstein even tried to get Szilard a job at the patent office. Perhaps fortunately, Szilard declined the invitation, but the two continued to create and innovate together. One of their more interesting inventions was a new type of refrigerator.

Why a Refrigerator?

The motivating factor for developing the refrigerator actually came from a news story about a German family living in Berlin. The refrigerator seal in the family's house broke, leaking toxic gases into their home and killing the entire family. Einstein set out to develop a safer, more family-friendly refrigerator that didn't have moving parts (at least, one that didn't have parts that could rupture).

The main thrust of Einstein's concept for the new design was to remove the part of the pump that had leaked in the famous example in Berlin. The pump was used to compress refrigerant as part of a heat pump cycle. Others had also tried to create new designs as well, notably two Swedish inventors named von Platen and Munters; they would later sell their design to the Electrolux Company.

How Did It Work?

Einstein and Szilard set out to improve upon the designs of von Platen and Munters, and they came up with their own plan for a noiseless, nonleaking refrigerator. They would come up with three main variations. The core of this refrigerator was the Einstein-Szilard pump, which was based on electromagnetism and diffusion. This pump was designed for home (noncommercial) refrigeration, and it was the first such device to dramatically improve safety by having no moving parts.

Some have suggested that the idea for this refrigerator pump actually began with Szilard. He used magnetic fields and coils to force the liquid metal through the pump. The major problem he ran into was corrosion.

This appears to be the point in the process where Einstein was brought in. Einstein changed the fundamental methods behind which the liquid metal was moved, and the team brought their designs into reality.

Once the ideas became a proven success, the Electrolux Company bought two of their designs. After years of trying, they finally sold the design for the pump itself to the General Electric Company of Germany in 1928. Einstein and Szilard would eventually hold eight major patents together. In total, they held forty-five patents for three different models of the home refrigeration unit.

QUESTION?

What's the difference between a patent, a trademark, and a copyright?
Patent gives the owner exclusive right to make and/or sell something. Trademark protects distinctive words or designs that are sold or used commercially. Copyright prevents others from copying something that's been created (art, music, and so on).

Einstein's Other Inventions

In addition to his work on the noiseless refrigerator, Einstein also worked on a number of other inventions that were later patented. These include several compass ideas and a new type of hearing aid. Einstein also held a patent for a light intensity self-adjusting camera.

Compasses

In his innovations on compasses, Einstein had come full circle from his first scientific inquiry. Einstein was reputedly given a compass as a small boy, and he spent quite some time trying to figure out the scientific principles behind its operation.

There are two main types of compasses—magnetic compasses and gyrocompasses. As seen in Chapter 2, magnetic compasses have a needle (which is actually a magnet) that's balanced around a pivot point. The end of the needle labeled "North" always points north because it works with the Earth's magnetic core. This is the simple type of compass used by hikers to find their way around, and is the type that Einstein was given as a child.

A gyrocompass, on the other hand, doesn't find north through a bar magnet. It uses a rapidly spinning wheel, along with friction and the rotation of the Earth, to find north. It gets its name from the gyroscope— a device that is basically a mounted, spinning wheel that can orient itself toward any direction. The law of conservation of angular momentum dictates that, in the absence of other forces, a freely spinning wheel will keep its original orientation or direction. What makes a gyrocompass work is the additional force of friction. Because it is actually not free to spin in any direction, it orients itself toward true north.

The gyrocompass is used mainly on ships. Why not just use a regular magnetic compass on a boat? There are two main reasons. First, gyrocompasses find true north (not magnetic north, the way a magnetic compass would). Also, some large ships are built mostly of metal, which can interfere with a magnetic compass. This device was first invented by a Dutchman, Martinus Gerardus van den Bos, in 1885. Later iterations were produced by a German scientist, Hermann Anschütz-Kaempfe, and an American, Elmer Sperry. Einstein developed a compass of his own design in 1926, followed by an airplane gyrocompass in 1935.

The Hearing Aid

Did you know that Einstein worked on developing a hearing aid as well? There were, of course, precursors to the modern electric hearing aid. The earliest of these was probably a device known as the ear trumpet, a shell-like contraption that users would hold up to their ears to amplify sounds. Such a device was simply for people who had "trouble hearing," and didn't address any specific type of hearing problem. Some of the earliest ear trumpets were manufactured in the 1880s by various companies in Germany, London, Philadelphia, and New York.

The first electric hearing aids were produced around the turn of the century. The Akouphone Company was established in 1899. Its founder, Miller Reese Hutchison, held a patent for an electric hearing aid that used a transmitter and a battery. The history of the battery is, in and of itself, a long and very interesting one. Thomas Edison introduced the first nickel-iron battery in the United States in 1901. Einstein's design, while not directly related to models currently in use, showed the true breadth of his interest and ability in the realm of design.

Why Is the Sky Blue? Solving the Riddle

Einstein was a major proponent of the "thought experiment," the idea that by letting his mind wander and explore, he could determine answers to questions that were seemingly unsolvable. One such thought-experiment was in the area of solving a common riddle: Why is the sky blue?

ALERT!

Even trying to verify Einstein's theory is not a good excuse to stare into the sun. Always wear proper ultraviolet eye protection and never look directly at the sun, especially during an eclipse, or you risk retinal burns and permanent eye damage.

In 1911, early in his career, Einstein thought extensively about this problem. In a paper on critical opalescence, he calculated a formula for the way that light molecules scattered, and his equations were proven true experimentally. As scientists now know, the different colors of light are distinguished by their wavelengths. The sky looks blue on a cloudless day because molecules scatter blue light in the air more than red light. When we look at the sun, it appears white because it's a mixture of all colors along the spectrum.

Einstein, of course, wasn't the first scientist to try to tackle this problem. In the seventeenth century, Isaac Newton used prisms to determine how light is split on the spectrum. John Tyndall, a scientist working in the mid-nineteenth century, discovered that blue wavelengths, which are relatively short, are scattered more strongly than red. Einstein built upon these previous scientists' research and provided one of the first concrete ways in which this age-old riddle could be solved.

Critical opalescence is a topic Einstein discussed in a paper he wrote in 1911. This concept has to do with the way light scatters near the liquid-gas critical point. Density fluctuations can be extreme, and the point at which a fluid becomes almost opaque is called "critical opalescence."

Later Developments in General Relativity

In addition to his early work, Einstein also produced some interesting new developments later in his career. Though much of his later work was devoted to the search for a unified field theory, which united general relativity with quantum mechanics, he also performed a variety of extensions of his previous work. One interesting topic that Einstein explored was an extension of his original work on general relativity.

In 1937, Einstein collaborated with Leopold Infeld and Banesh Hoffman on a paper entitled "On the Motion of Particles in General Relativity Theory." This paper showed that geodesic equations of general relativity can actually be derived from field equations. Thus was formed the Einstein-Infeld-Hoffmann (EIH) approximation procedure for general relativity.

The main significance of the Einstein, Infeld, and Hoffman paper was that, for the first time, it was shown that equations for bodies in motion can be explicitly derived from the equations of general relativity.

Solving Einstein's Field Equations

An extension of Einstein's previous work, which continues to be an area of hot research today, involves new solutions to the equations of general relativity. Einstein's theory of general relativity was, as you know, sometimes called the theory of gravitation. This theory led to a series of formulas that would become known as Einstein's field equations. These equations describe how gravity operates around any given mass, such as the Earth. In coordination with Einstein's idea of the space-time continuum as a woven fabric, his field equations provide a means for measuring how an object bends and curves space-time. They also define precisely how such an object is affected by space itself.

QUESTION?

What is a tensor?
In general relativity, a tensor is an extension of the idea of vectors. In mathematical terms, a vector is any physical quantity that has both a direction and a magnitude. Force and momentum, for example, are examples of vectors. Tensors add extra components, all of which have a magnitude and direction.

Einstein's field equations are derived from the main formula of general relativity, G = 8T. In this equation, G is the Einstein tensor, and T is the stress-energy tensor. The Einstein tensor is defined as a tensor which describes how, under the principles of general relativity, the space-time continuum curves and behaves. The stress-energy tensor is a tensor describing energy and momentum.

The field equations are of clear importance to the scientific community because they could, in effect, describe every aspect of space. The definition of black holes is a prime example of their application. However, these equations are exceedingly complex, and the mathematics behind solving them is prohibitive to most. Einstein himself admitted this problem to pose a major stumbling block in the application of gravitational theory. Today, scientists and researchers are able to harness computer processing power toward solving these equations, and significant headway is being made in just this area.

Geodesic Equations

One possible group of solutions to the Einstein field equations takes a geodesic form, and thus the geodesic equations of general relativity can be deduced from the Einstein field equations. A geodesic is, by definition, a solution for a group of ordinary differential equations. What this definition means in terms of relativity is that a geodesic can be considered as the straightest path, or distance, that travels along a curved surface (such as space). Because space-time is curved, the shortest path between two objects in space will always be a curved one; this curved path is a geodesic.

This aspect of relativity has been taken and advanced by other scientific fields. One example of a modern application of geodesics can be found in the airline industry. Airplane flight paths typically follow a geodesic path, not a straight line, in order to more closely follow the surface of the Earth. This path results in faster travel time and increased fuel efficiency. Einstein probably never envisioned his theory of relativity being adapted to this specific purpose, but it has affected everyone who travels by airplane.

Two-Body Problem

The so-called "two-body problem" of general relativity is another example of further work done on Einstein's theory of relativity. Two-body problems exist in a variety of interrelated scientific fields. In general, two-body issues represent a dynamical problem where a scientist is trying to predict the motion of two interacting bodies, such as one planet orbiting around another. From the time Kepler first discovered planetary orbits, through Niels Bohr and his modeling of the atom, the two-body problem has provided the basis for many analogies and descriptions in physics.

The two-body problem has an analytic (exact) solution, whereas a three-body problem (or higher) typically does not. For example, scientists can write down equations that govern a three-body problem, but they can't solve it precisely without making approximations. Such an approximate solution is called a numerical solution.

As we learned from our earlier studies, relativity provides an explanation for the gravitational effects on objects with mass. These effects are described by sixteen partial differential equations, and these are collectively referred to as the Einstein field equations. The two-body problem as applied to relativity was further developed in the 1960s, after Einstein's death, in the area of cosmology. Einstein's equations of relativity were used to study the motion of particles as they orbited black holes. The collision of two black holes is actually a different modification of the two-body problem.

Work in the 1990s also attempted to reconcile the two-body problem with Einstein's experiments in general relativity. Unified field theory, for example (discussed in depth in Chapter 17), attempts to provide one cohesive, overarching explanation for all the world's forces, combining electromagnetism and gravity with the strong and weak forces. The two-body problem remains a central part of this dilemma. Relativity, along with Einstein's field equations, can provide some cohesion, but not enough to act as a blanket unifier. Unified field theory has yet to come to fruition, and as such, the two-body problem as it relates to general relativity is still unresolved. There remains much work to do in this area, but new computer techniques hold great promise.

Gravitational Waves

Work on unified field theory in general constitutes one of the largest attempts to improve upon Einstein's theory of relativity. There have been other ongoing research efforts that strive to improve on relativity in the area of gravitational waves. The theory of general relativity predicts that waves exist and that there is a type of wave that can transmit gravity. However, such gravitational waves have not been proven experimentally to exist, as they have not yet been detected. To find such a proof would lend tremendous validation to general relativity, and it would add to the potential application of relativity to the scientific world.

FACT

Learn more about the LAGEOS III mission at the LAEFF Web site, located at ✍ *www.laeff.esa.es*. The founding organization is the Laboratorio de Astrofisica Espacial y Fisica Fundamental (Laboratory for Space Astrophysics and Theoretical Physics, in English).

There are current plans in space exploration to detect just such waves. Gravity Probe B, as discussed in Chapter 19, is a satellite planned to be launched in November 2003. Its main goal will be to detect and measure gravitational waves related to the Earth.

Another project is the LAGEOS III mission, which stands for the Laser Geodynamic Satellite Experiment. This is a project of several nations, including Spain, the United States, France, Germany, Italy, and England. Its purpose is to measure another prediction of Einstein's theory of relativity—the gravitational magnetic dipole moment of the Earth.

Einstein's Scientific Impact

Einstein, while most famous for his theory of general relativity, actually worked on a number of other projects during his lifetime. He held numerous patents and collaborated with other scientists on a variety of inventions. The main backbone of his scientific legacy is certainly relativity. Following his initial work on general relativity, Einstein continued developing relativity over the years. Many scientists have continued his research, applying it to different projects and areas of study. Astronomers and physicists seek to send space missions into orbit, further pushing the boundaries of what we know about how relativity affects all aspects of our lives.

Einstein's varied scientific interests are clear from the huge list of contributions he made to many areas of physics. Even his lesser-known scientific accomplishments, such as his patents for items such as a noiseless refrigerator and a new type of hearing aid, show the breadth of his scientific knowledge. In fact, perhaps his lesser-known inventions better exemplify the humanitarianism that marked Einstein's later career. Both his refrigerator and hearing aid idea were meant to improve the health and safety of ordinary people, a far stretch from the universe-shaking ideas of relativity. From the mundane refrigerator to the seemingly simple study of the blue sky to the mathematical formulas of relativity, which are still too complicated for even today's supercomputers to solve directly, Einstein's genius improved every field that it touched upon.

Chapter 21
Einstein's Legacy

Albert Einstein has had tremendous impact on both the scientific community and everyday people. His science would lay the groundwork for many important discoveries in the future, and it changed the way the universe was conceived of. His legacy is felt in just about every aspect of modern society.

Impact Within the World of Science

Einstein's impact on the world of science was monumental, to say the least. He touched just about every area of mathematics and physics, and set new standards in terms of the breadth and caliber of his scientific research. His discovery of relativity was perhaps one of the most significant scientific advances of all time because it changed fundamental ideas about the universe we live in.

His formulation of the equivalence of mass and energy, as stated by the famous relationship $E=mc^2$, is probably the most recognized scientific equation in the world. Einstein's extensions of general relativity laid the groundwork for the entire field of cosmology. Time and space are woven together as a fabric. The space-time continuum curves as a result of the presence of matter, and matter experiences a reciprocal effect expressed as motion. His theory of gravitation gave rise to the eventual formulation of the theory surrounding black holes, and research in this area became possible largely because of Einstein's discoveries.

Awards and Honors

Rewards and accolades followed Einstein's work, and they reassured the rest of the world about the validity of his findings. Perhaps the most famous is the Nobel Prize in physics in 1921, which was awarded for his research on the photoelectric effect. That was not the only formal recognition of Einstein's work, though.

He was awarded medals from several other institutions. In 1925 he won the Copley Medal from the Royal Society of London. This organization was started in the mid-seventeenth century by a group of scientists who wanted to share their experimental research. Founding members included such famous scientists as Robert Hooke, Christopher Wren, and Robert Boyle. The Copley Medal is the highest award given by the Royal Society, and it was received in later years by Niels Bohr and Max Planck.

Einstein went on to receive the Gold Medal from the Royal Astronomical Society in 1926. The Royal Astronomical Society is England's primary group of astronomers, geophysicists, and planetary scientists. It was begun in 1820 and was originally established to promote the relatively new sciences of astronomy and geology. Today the group houses an immense library and produces some of the scientific community's more respected publications. Other famous winners of the prestigious Gold Medal include Charles Babbage, Henri Poincaré, and Edwin Hubble.

In 1935, Einstein earned another award from a well-known institution. He won the Franklin Medal from the Franklin Institute, a unique organization dedicated to one of Einstein's lifelong goals—learning. Primarily established to celebrate achievement in science and technology, the Franklin Center's mission includes informing and educating the public about advances in the sciences. The awards program was begun in 1832 as a way to encourage scientific invention and discovery. Einstein's particular award was given for his work with both relativity and the photoelectric effect.

Einsteinium

Einstein's legacy appears in the periodic table as well. Einsteinium (symbol Es, atomic number 99) was discovered in 1952 as a byproduct of the first hydrogen bomb explosion. It was discovered in Los Alamos, as well as in Berkeley, California, by a team of scientists led by Albert Ghiorso. The actual isotope the team uncovered, called einsteinium-253, has a half-life of twenty days. It produces radiation, but has yet to be found to serve any practical purpose.

FACT

Einstein, of course, was not the only famous scientist to have an element of the periodic table named after him. Bohrium (Bh, 107) is named for Niels Bohr, fermium (Fm, 100) is named after Enrico Fermi, and mendelevium (Md, 101) corresponds to Dmitri Mendeleev, to name just a few.

Einsteinium has the following characteristics:

- **Element symbol:** Es
- **Atomic number:** 99
- **Atomic mass:** 254
- **Room temperature state:** Solid
- **Melting point:** 860 degrees Kelvin
- **Electronegativity:** 1.3
- **Electron affinity:** 50 kJ/mol

Impact on the World at Large

In addition to his contributions and lasting legacy in the world of science, Einstein impacted the rest of society to an extent that has been paralleled by few scientists. He is widely regarded as a symbol of intellectual ability. How pervasive has his influence been?

A Cultural Icon

Albert Einstein has done for science what few scientists have managed in the past—he's turned science into a cultural phenomenon. Einstein's face adorns consumer products to an extent that no scientist in history has equaled. Posters of Einstein are readily available in a variety of stores, from museum shops to poster stores at the local mall. Similarly, T-shirts and coffee mugs that bear Einstein's likeness can easily be found. The phrase "everything's relative" enjoys popular usage, even if it bears little relation to the theory of general relativity.

What's important here is not that Einstein has been commercialized throughout time. Rather, it is significant that a scientist has made it into the realm of popular culture to take on the same level of cultural importance as rock stars or other teenage idols. It is, of course, a two-way street. Because the merchandise is available, Einstein's name becomes even more well-known. The reverse is true as well. Einstein's increased social popularity creates a market for Einstein merchandise.

And so the cycle goes, providing Einstein with name recognition in a market in which few scientists enjoy large-scale success.

ALERT!

Although commercialization brought Albert Einstein's name into the general public, he wouldn't necessarily have approved of it. Seeing Einstein's face on a coffee cup doesn't mean that he personally sanctioned that adaptation of his likeness.

All for Science

Why does it matter that everyone knows Einstein's name? One of the major benefits of his large-scale popularity is that it brought science out of obscurity and into the view of the general public. Scientific invention and discovery resided, for a long time, within a fairly small community of scientists, academics, and other intellectuals. While their major discoveries made public headlines, many of their frontrunners were somewhat invisible to the public at large. With funding based in part on legislative whims, the scientific community needs all the help it can get in increasing public awareness, so that voting citizens will be more interested in allocating funding toward scientific endeavors. Einstein brought science into the public arena and increased general awareness and appreciation for science, and that alone is one of his most important legacies.

Person of the Century

Einstein's impact on society clearly goes beyond coffee mugs and T-shirts. One of the all-time great honors bestowed upon Einstein was given by *Time* magazine, when it announced Albert Einstein as the Person of the Century in 2000.

In earning this most prestigious honor, Einstein beat out two of the twentieth century's most important figures. Franklin Delano Roosevelt was one of the top runners-up who lost this award to Albert Einstein. FDR (1882–1945) was elected president of the United States in 1932. He was already a skilled politician and one who had gained the respect of both his peers and the general public. He was elected during the midst of the Great Depression. FDR connected directly with the people via his "fireside chats," introduced New Deal legislation to help the economy recover from the Depression, and was re-elected president in 1936 and 1940. He led the country in World War II, and interacted with Einstein on the subject of atomic development. (See Chapter 15 for more information.) Franklin Roosevelt's impact on the country's economy, involvement in the war, and development of atomic and nuclear weapons was monumental.

FACT

Franklin Roosevelt succeeded as president despite being afflicted with polio in 1921. He was paralyzed from the waist down, but he never let his disability affect his energy, enthusiasm, determination, or spirit.

The other runner-up for the Person of the Century Award was Mohandas Gandhi (1869–1948). Gandhi was an activist from India, who worked most of his life toward achieving nonviolent, peaceful unification of the Indian state. After living in London and South Africa for a number of years, he returned to India to commit himself fully to helping his native country. His main goal was lifting India out from under British rule, but he wanted to do so through love and peaceful noncooperation, not violence. His commitment to his cause was truly extraordinary, and India was granted independence in 1947 (a year before Gandhi was assassinated).

It was, then, no small achievement for Einstein to have won this award. He was chosen over candidates who were incredibly influential in their fields and who made their own indelible marks on history. The fact that Einstein won proves how large an influence he had, and over what a wide-reaching area.

Einstein in Popular Media

One of the major ways in which the public is made aware of advances in all fields is through the media. Newspapers, books, television, and film help "spread the word" concerning just about every aspect of modern society. Aside from relaying information about Einstein's scientific advances, the media has adapted Einstein's name and character in a variety of public-interest situations that have tremendously increased people's general awareness of Albert Einstein.

The movie *Young Einstein* was directed by an actor/director named Yahoo Serious. While Einstein was known for having a good sense of humor, the liberties taken by this film might have gone a bit too far.

Movies

One of the first popular films to capitalize on Einstein was a comedy film from 1988 entitled *Young Einstein*. In this movie, which is sometimes billed as an "alternative biography," Einstein's inventions (both real and fictionalized) were described and his contribution to history was explained. This movie took more than a few liberties with his life—he's credited with, among other things, splitting the "beer molecule" and inventing rock and roll.

Literature

Einstein's popular influence extended into literature as well. *Einstein's Dreams*, a book by Alan Lightman, discusses Einstein's place in history accurately, then delves into the unknown with thirty discussions of some of Einstein's most salient theoretical quests. Many largely nonfictional books have also been written about Einstein's life. Some of the more prominent include *Einstein in Love: A Scientific Romance,* by Dennis Overbye and *Einstein's Daughter: The Search for Lieserl,* by Michele Zackheim.

Music

His foray into popular culture extended into the realm of music as well. Philip Glass produced the music and lyrics to *Einstein on the*

Beach, a modern four-act opera, that created an entirely new type of musical piece. A five-hour-long production (without intermissions,) "Einstein" was designed with a series of "knee play" interludes that alternated with the text of the story. Glass gave this piece its name because Einstein was one of his childhood heroes. Growing up with the aftermath of World War II, he wrote, it was next to impossible to be unaware of who Einstein was and what his impact on the world had been. His opera was intended to examine all aspects of Einstein— physicist, musician, and humanitarian.

Einstein truly became a pop-culture icon with a recent Pepsi commercial entitled "No Brainer." This commercial (which aired during an Academy Awards presentation) forced Einstein to choose between two leading soft drinks, Pepsi and Coca Cola.

Educational Products

The extent to which Einstein's name and abilities are respected is further emphasized by the commercial products that bear his name. One of the most well-known is a series of educational products sold under the Baby Einstein label. They offer videos, books, and toys designed to stimulate a baby's intellectual development from the earliest ages. Although it's questionable whether or not Einstein would have personally stood behind such a use of his name, it speaks to his legacy that his name has become more or less a household word, to people of all ages.

Fellowships and Monuments in Einstein's Name

As yet another testament to the profound effect Einstein had on the world, a number of scholarships, monuments, foundations, and other functions have been dedicated in honor of one of history's greatest scientists. There are far too many to list each one individually. However, looking at a few highlights gives an idea of how far-reaching this aspect of his influence has been.

Fellowships

One of the most well-known fellowships to bear Einstein's name is the Albert Einstein Distinguished Educator Fellowship. It provides educational fellowships in math and science, for teachers at both the elementary and secondary school level. This program is administered by the United States Department of Energy, and it lets teachers who win the award spend time in either a Congressional office or a federal agency (such as the National Science Foundation or NASA). The winners of this award are primarily responsible for helping to shape the path that math and science education in America takes, and, as such, they contribute enormously to developing the minds of the next generation of future scientists.

Monuments

One of many visible tributes to Albert Einstein can be seen in the Albert Einstein Memorial Statue, located in conjunction with the National Academy of Sciences building in Washington, D.C. This statue, created by artist Robert Berks, was unveiled in 1979 to commemorate the 100-year anniversary of Einstein's birth. This bronze work of art shows Einstein holding papers that discuss his most important contributions to science—general relativity, the photoelectric effect, and $E=mc^2$.

FACT

The enormous Albert Einstein statue in front of the National Academy of Sciences building is a favorite photo shoot, particularly for children on field trips from schools in the Washington, D.C. area.

Although not built as a monument to Einstein, Yeshiva University in New York City bears the Einstein name in a very tangible form. Yeshiva University, founded in 1886, honors the great scientist through its Albert

Einstein College of Medicine. The school first opened in 1955, and Einstein gave his approval to the name shortly before that. Yeshiva University also offers an Albert Einstein Award; Harry Belafonte is one famous recipient.

Awards

Various other organizations and societies offer Albert Einstein awards. Usually they are for either academic merit, achievements in the sciences, or civil service. One of many examples is the Albert Einstein Technology Medal, given by the State of Israel. The purpose of this award is to recognize individuals who made significant creative contributions in the technology industry. Recipients of this prize have included Margaret Thatcher and Steven Spielberg. Another is the Albert Einstein Award, given by a Jewish institution called the American Society of Technion.

It is almost impossible to go through life not knowing who Einstein was. While his discoveries certainly were capable of standing on their own, a large part of the reason we all know his name is that it has been recycled so often through the media. Incredible intelligence coupled with a successful (though unintended!) marketing campaign served to bring Einstein's name to the fore, thereby allowing his immense legacy to continue growing.

QUESTION?

What's the difference between a fellowship and an award?
A fellowship, in this sense, is usually money or another benefit given to someone to encourage his or her study or research in a specific area. A fellowship is one type of award.

Einstein as a Representative for Scientists

Einstein was unquestionably one of the most popular scientists of his day—and he's generally regarded as one of the most popular scientists of all time! As such, he has become a de facto representative for scientists in general. His distinguishing looks, especially the wild, bushy hairstyle, became a hallmark appearance for eccentric physicists, and Einstein's physical attributes would lend themselves readily to depictions of scientists in popular novels and movies.

Of course, what history often chooses to forget is that when he was actually developing his theories of relativity, Einstein appeared much more "normal" and less what we have come to think of as eccentric-looking. During his years at the Swiss patent office, Einstein wore a traditional suit and tie to work, and his hair was of a more normal length. It was in his later years that his signature appearance began presenting itself, and also during this time that Einstein's popularity and fame increased.

Perception Changed

When examining Einstein's legacy, it is important to note that the general public's perception of Einstein has changed over time. When he first came out with his papers on relativity, and then later won the Nobel Prize for his work with the photoelectric effect, Einstein was regarded as a scientist of incredible intelligence. That is predominantly his legacy, and that aspect has survived the ravages of time.

FACT

Popular rumor during World War II was that Einstein's famous equivalence of mass and energy, $E=mc^2$, was a formula for making an atomic bomb! Of course, it was not, but this erroneous rumor served to tarnish Einstein's reputation during the war years.

However, there was a period when Einstein was less than popular. During the atomic age, for a number of reasons, Einstein was falsely associated with the development of the atomic bomb. His involvement with nuclear development was minimal, but his name was already so well-known that people tended to inflate the role he actually played. His reputation was somewhat tarnished because of his perceived involvement with the bombing of Hiroshima, and it would be many years before history corrected itself. In recent times, his reputation has been completely restored, and Einstein is generally regarded as the quintessential symbol of absolute intelligence.

Fundamental Reasons Behind Einstein's Popularity

So why did the media pick Einstein to capitalize upon? There were hundreds of other scientists of the period who also made significant contributions. Why do people wear T-shirts of Einstein instead of Niels Bohr, for example?

One of the reasons that Einstein became such a legend was that his writings, if not his actual research, were accessible to many. Einstein was a very clear writer and speaker, and he presented his ideas in such a way that just about anyone could understand them. Although his research might have been over the head of the general public, the way he presented it was clear, concise, and easy to understand. Almost anyone who tried could understand Einstein's general accounts of his research, and this accessibility served to spread his popularity.

Einstein has such a strong legacy because his general ideals appealed to the masses. He dreamed of creating a world government, where people were humane, and had an acute sense of moral responsibility. He dreamed of a better world and of creating this world through science and understanding. In his ideal world, not only would the arcane laws of physics be united in a universal theory, but all the people of the world would also be united under one common government. These goals are simple ones, and they are difficult to disagree with. While his aspirations may have seemed naïve or idealistic, they give people hope and something to strive for as we move through the twenty-first century, and that kind of appeal is everlasting. Ⓔ

Appendices

Appendix A

Glossary

Appendix B

Timeline of Einstein's Life

Glossary

absolute zero: the coldest temperature possible, measured at negative 459.69 degrees Fahrenheit.

acoustics: the science of the transmission and reflection of sound waves.

albedo: a measure of the fraction of light that hits the surface of a planet and is reflected back.

atom: a particle of matter, usually consisting of a nucleus surrounded by electrons.

atomic mass unit (amu): the units for expressing the mass of an atom.

atomic weight: for an element, the average of the atomic masses of the element's isotopes.

Avogadro's number: the number of molecules in a gram mole of a particular elemental substance; by definition, this amount is 6.022×10^{23}.

bar mitzvah: a Jewish confirmation and recitation, performed by Jewish children at the culmination of their Hebrew education, around their thirteenth birthday.

black hole: an extremely dense point in the space-time continuum, formed when a very large star collapses and compresses into itself.

black body radiation: radiation emitted by a black body, a dark-colored object that absorbs almost all of the light that hits it.

blueshift: when light comes from an object that is traveling toward the observer, such that the light waves appear to be shifted toward shorter (blue) wavelengths.

Bose-Einstein condensate: a state of matter where, at a very low temperature, the quantum and mechanical properties of atoms become equal.

boson: particles that obey Bose-Einstein statistics; have a zero spin.

Brownian motion: a type of movement observed by Robert Brown, where tiny particles are seen in constant motion.

categorical imperative: an idea espoused by Immanuel Kant which meant that morality depended on one single command; morality was absolute.

chain reaction: in physics, a technique whereby the end products from one reaction become the reactants in another reaction.

changing electromagnetic field: a type of electromagnetic field that takes on a wave motion as it propagates. Radio waves, gamma rays, X rays, and microwaves are all examples of changing electromagnetic fields.

communism: a political system that supports the idea of everyone being equal, to the point where there is no private ownership.

congruent: the state something's in when it agrees with its surroundings.

Conservative Judaism: A branch of Judaism that is not as rigorous as Orthodox Judaism; followers do not obey all Jewish rituals, but generally attend weekly services.

cosmological constant: an extra term Albert Einstein added to his equations of general relativity in order to make the universe appear to be static and unexpanding.

cosmological principle: the idea that the universe is homogeneous and isotropic on the largest scales.

cosmology: the study of the nature of the universe.

de Broglie wavelength: wavelength defined by a particle's motion using the equation $\lambda = h/p$ where λ is wavelength, h is Planck's constant, and p is relative momentum.

democracy: a political system where the nation involved is ruled by its citizens.

diffusion: the movement of molecules from areas of higher density to lesser density.

Doppler effect: the idea that, to a stationary observer, waves appear to change in frequency (or wavelength) if they are emitted by something moving.

Einstein ring: an image that results when an observer and a gravitational lens are perfectly aligned.

Einstein cross: an image that results when the alignment between an observer and a gravitational lens is imperfect; can form multiple images.

einsteinium: an element on the periodic table, named after Einstein, that was discovered as a byproduct of the hydrogen bomb explosion.

electromagnetism: the theory of how electricity relates to magnetism.

electromagnetic field: the field generated by the acceleration of charged particles.

electromagnetic radiation: radiation that is propagated at the speed of light; includes such types as X rays, ultraviolet radiation, radar waves, and radio waves.

electromagnetic spectrum: the full range of frequencies of electromagnetic radiation.

electron: a negatively charged particle that partially comprises an atom.

element: a single, indivisible chemical substance.

energy: in physics, the ability to do work.

entropy: a measure of the degree of order, or disorder, in a system.

ether: an undetectable medium that nineteenth-century scientists proposed that light could travel through.

evolution: the theory, developed by Charles Darwin, that all species of plants and animals have developed and changed over time.

fermions: particles that obey Fermi-Drac statistics; have a positive spin.

field: in physics, anything that's acting under the influence of a force, like gravity.

force: an action that causes a mass to accelerate; generally measured in Newton's law of universal gravitation.

frame-dragging: also called the Lense-Thirring effect; the idea that as a small object rotates around a larger one in space, the orbit of the small body is changed slightly by the rotation itself.

frequency: the number of waves or other oscillations per time, measured in waves per second (called hertz).

friction: a force that provides resistance to motion when two surfaces move over each other.

galaxy: a group of dust, stars, and gas that obeys the laws of gravity and has a higher-than-average distribution of mass.

genius: someone who possesses extraordinary intellect or capability, especially as shown through creative activity.

gravitational force: the force exerted by gravity.

gauge symmetry: a branch of symmetry theory which shows that the so-called "strong force," or electromagnetic force, consist of photons, where the weak force consisted of particles called bosons.

general relativity: also called Einstein's law of gravitation; an extension of the theory of special relativity that includes gravitational effects.

gravitational lens: the focusing effect that a large object or cluster has on light, often causing it to bend; the resulting image can be distorted or magnified when seen by an observer, depending on where the observer is positioned.

gravitational potential energy: energy stored by a gravitational field; also known as the potential energy due to gravity.

gravity: one of the fundamental forces of physics; gravitational attraction is responsible for the attraction of bodies on the surface of a planet to the mass of the planet.

gyroscope: a device consisting of a wheel mounted to a rotating disk, that's also free to rotate around other axes; the axel keeps the device spinning in a constant direction once it is set into motion.

Heisenberg uncertainty principle: the fact that the more precisely a position is known, the less precisely the momentum can be measured, and vice versa.

heliocentrism: a view of the solar system in which the planets orbited around the sun rather than around the Earth.

heterogeneous: of diverse composition.

homogeneous: of uniform structure or composition throughout.

humanitarianism: having a concern for people's general welfare.

hypothetical imperative: an idea espoused by Immanuel Kant that stated that morality is conditional. "If your foot hurts when you kick the wall, stop kicking the wall" is an example of a hypothetical imperative.

imperative: a command.

inertial observer: an observer (or reference frame) that is either fixed or is moving at a constant speed in a constant direction.

isotope: atoms of the same element, but having different numbers of neutrons.

isotropic: the same in all directions.

kinetic energy: the energy that comes from motion.

length contraction: a side effect of special relativity where, at speeds close to the speed of light, lengths seem to get shortened in the direction that the observer is moving.

Lense-Thirring effect: also called frame-dragging; the idea that as a small object rotates around a larger one in space, the orbit of the small body is changed slightly by the rotation itself.

M-theory: a modern attempt to create a valid unified field theory through the incorporation of string theory and supersymmetry.

Mach number: the ratio of an object's speed to the speed of sound.

Mach's principle: an idea coined by Albert Einstein that refers to Ernst Mach's idea that the inertia of one body is related to all other bodies in the universe.

macroscopic: a description of objects that are visible to the naked eye.

mass: the amount of matter in an object, measured in kilograms.

matrix: a two-dimensional array of numbers that can be manipulated mathematically in certain ways.

matrix theory: a theory of quantum mechanics that uses matrices.

McCarthyism: a political tactic utilized in the 1950s in which people were publicly accused of subversive behavior.

mezuzah: a small box with a piece of parchment in it, on which is written an excerpt from the Torah in Hebrew.

microscopic: a description of objects or particles that are only visible with the aid of a microscope.

Milky Way: the galaxy that we on Earth inhabit; the first galaxy known to ancient astronomers.

mole: in science, a small mass; its mass (in grams) equals the atomic weight for a given element.

molecule: either an atom or a group of atoms; one of the smallest, fundamental units that has all the physical properties of a substance.

molecular weight: the sum of the atomic weights of all the atoms in a given compound.

momentum: the mass of a body multiplied by its velocity.

nebula: a cloud of gas and dust particles, existing in space.

neutron: a neutral subatomic particle located inside the nucleus of most atoms; simple hydrogen is the exception.

Newton's first law: an object in motion will tend to stay in motion.

Newton's second law: the force applied to an object is equal to the object's mass multiplied by its acceleration.

Newton's third law: every action has an equal and opposite reaction.

nuclear fission: the breaking up of a large nucleus into smaller nuclei.

nuclear fusion: the combining of smaller nuclei into one large nucleus.

nucleosynthesis: the process by which the sun generates energy through nuclear fusion, by burning its hydrogen fuel into helium.

optics: in physics, the study of light as a wave (as opposed to a ray).

orbit: the path a body takes as it revolves around another body.

Orthodox Judaism: one of the most rigorous branches of Judaism; followers obey all the Jewish food laws and do no work on the Sabbath.

parallel postulate: also known as the fifth postulate; the idea that that for every line and point that is not on that line, there is another unique, nonintersecting line that passes through that point.

particle physics: the branch of physics that works with particles, the basic units of matter and energy.

perihelion: the location of a planet's orbit when it is closest to the sun.

photoelectric effect: the emission of electrons from a metal that is exposed to light. The surface of the metal absorbs enough energy from light that some electrons are freed from their atoms and fly off the surface.

photon: a unit of light intensity, or a quantum when referring to electromagnetic radiation.

Planck's constant: A symbol, h, added to relate the energy of a photon's electromagnetic radiation with its frequency; defined as 6.626176 x 10^{-34} joule-seconds.

positivism: a major philosophical idea in Europe during the early twentieth century; the theory basically said that knowledge was sensation—all objects were understood by their sensations.

postulate: a theory or idea that is claimed to be true.

potential energy: the energy that comes from position.

precession: the motion resulting when a rotating axis is torqued so that the axis of rotation changes.

principle of equivalence: Albert Einstein's idea that an accelerating reference frame is equivalent to a reference frame in which there is a uniform gravitational field.

probability field: the idea, as developed by Werner Heisenberg, that particles have a tendency to exist at certain places in the space-time continuum.

proton: a positively charged subatomic particle that is located inside the nucleus of an atom.

Pythagorean theorem: developed by Pythagoras in ancient Greece; the idea that the sum of the squares of the sides of a right triangle is equal to the square of the hypotenuse.

quanta: individual units of energy.

quantum theory: a explanation of theoretical physics that describes how matter and energy behave on a subatomic level; essentially, the idea that if a particle's position and momentum are known, then there is an exclusion between the two.

radiation: the emission of energy from a source, generally in the form of electromagnetic waves.

Reconstructionist Judaism: a branch of Judaism that is enlightened with social, political, and cultural influences of the times; offers the least stringent Biblical interpretation of other branches of Judaism.

redshift: when light comes from an object which is traveling away from the observer, so the light waves appear to be shifted toward longer (red) wavelengths; supports the idea of a constantly expanding universe.

Reform Judaism: a branch of Judaism that breaks with both Orthodox and Conservative in that it believes that Judaism has evolved over time.

rest mass: the mass of an object that's not moving.

shell: in physics, a region surrounding the nucleus of an atom in which an electron has a certain probability of being found; similar to orbit.

social justice: the idea that everyone should be treated equally well.

special relativity: Einstein's theory that the speed of light, as well as Newtonian laws of motion, are equal for all inertial frames of reference; from this theory Einstein developed time dilation, length contraction, and the equivalence of mass and energy ($E=mc^2$).

spin: a particular property of subatomic particles.

stationary electromagnetic field: a type of electromagnetic field where the field itself remains bound to its origin.

string theory: a modern branch of unified field theory that provides an acceptable explanation for particle behavior based on the probabilistic behavior of individual particles.

subatomic particles: particles that are smaller than atoms; includes neutrons, protons, and electrons.

supersymmetry: a branch of symmetry theory that attempts to unite nature's strong and weak forces with gravitation.

symmetry theory: one of a number of attempts to unify nature's forces into a singular explanation; the idea that everything and nothing coexist on the same plane.

time dilation: the fact that moving clocks run more slowly than stationary clocks.

thermodynamics: the branch of physics that studies heat and interparticle collisions in terms of how energy is converted between forms.

uncertainty principle: in quantum theory, the idea that as the position of a subatomic particle is known with more and more certainty, its momentum is known with less and less precision.

unified field theory: a "theory of everything" that takes all of nature's forces into account; attempted by Einstein but never completely developed.

wave-particle duality: the idea that if waves can exhibit particle-like behavior, particles can also act like waves.

wavefunction theory: a theory of quantum mechanics that uses particular properties of waves.

wavelength: the length of one wave of light or other electromagnetic radiation, measured in distance from peak to peak.

weight: the amount of matter in an object measured under acceleration such as a gravity field; measured in pounds.

work: in physics, force multiplied by distance.

Appendix B

Timeline of Einstein's Life

1879: Albert Einstein is born in Ulm, Germany, to Hermann and Pauline Einstein.

1881: A sister, Maja (Maria), is born.

1884: Albert is given his first compass after being bedridden with an illness, and has his first lessons in cosmology.

1889: Begins secondary school at the Luitpold-Gymnasium.

1892: First studies the philosophy of Immanuel Kant.

1894: Einstein joins his family in Pavia, Italy.

1895: Fails the entrance examinations to the Eidgenössische Technische Hochschule (ETH) in Zurich and goes to study in Aarau, Switzerland.

1896: Einstein successfully matriculates at the ETH; renounces his German citizenship.

1900: Graduates from the ETH; Max Planck lays foundation for quantum theory.

1901: Einstein is granted Swiss citizenship; works as a teacher.

1902: Einstein's first child, Lieserl, is born out of wedlock; Einstein starts work for the Swiss patent office.

1903: Albert Einstein marries Mileva Maric.

1904: Einstein's second child, Hans Albert, is born.

1905: The *annus mirabilis* (miracle year) during which Einstein publishes the three major papers for which he will become famous; theory of special relativity is developed; equivalence of mass and energy ($E=mc^2$) is formulated, as well as the photoelectric effect.

1908: Einstein begins teaching part-time at Bern University.

1909: Resigns from the patent office and focuses his full attention on scientific research and teaching.

1910: His third child, Eduard, is born.

1911: Einstein moves to Prague, becomes a full professor of theoretical physics at Karl-Ferdinand University.

1912: Moves to Zurich, becomes a professor at the ETH.

1913: Commences work on his theory of gravity.

1914: Becomes a professor at the University of Berlin; is appointed director of the Kaiser Wilhelm Institute of Physics (lasting until 1933); start of World War I.

1915: Completes theory of general relativity; works on the relationship between space, time, energy, and matter.

1917: Publishes first paper on cosmology, puts forth the cosmological constant; becomes seriously ill, reacquaints himself with cousin Elsa Lowenthal.

1918: End of World War I.

1919: Divorces Mileva Maric and marries Elsa Lowenthal; general relativity is proven by a solar eclipse; the Bauhaus School is founded.

1921: Einstein visits the United States, delivers lectures at Princeton University.

1922: Einstein is awarded the Nobel Prize in physics for his work with the photoelectric effect, won in 1921; joins the Committee on Intellectual Cooperation.

1925: Einstein becomes president of the World Union of Jewish Students.

1926: Collaborates with Leo Szilard on the design for a refrigerator pump.

1927: Starts to develop quantum mechanics with Niels Bohr.

1928: Begins developing the unified field theory.

1933: Moves to the United States; declares he will not return to Germany; works with the Institute for Advanced Study in Princeton, New Jersey; helps establish the International Rescue Committee.

1936: Einstein's second wife, Elsa Lowenthal, dies.

1938: The splitting of the uranium atom by German scientists occurs.

1939: Einstein signs a letter to President Roosevelt, warning of the dangers of using the atomic bomb in a wartime situation; beginning of World War II.

1940: Einstein becomes an American citizen.

1941: Provides a consultation in nuclear fission for research related to the atomic bomb.

1945: President Roosevelt dies; Harry Truman becomes president, drops bomb on Hiroshima in August; World War II ends.

1946: Einstein becomes president of the Emergency Committee of Atomic Scientists.

1948: Einstein's first wife, Mileva, dies.

1949: The North Atlantic Treaty Organization is created.

1952: The first hydrogen bomb is detonated in Enewetak Atoll, led to discovery of einsteinium; Einstein is offered (and declines) the presidency of Israel.

1955: Albert Einstein dies in Princeton, New Jersey.

Index

THE EVERYTHING GREAT THINKERS BOOK

The Everything Great Thinkers Book
Exploring the minds of the men and
women who have changed the
way we see the world
James Mannion

Trade paperback
$14.95 ($22.95 CAN)
1-58062-662-9, 304 pages

By James Mannion

What do Jesus Christ, Albert Einstein, Margaret Thatcher, Ayn Rand, Charles Darwin, and The Beatles have in common? They are just a few of the men and women who have enlightened us, challenged us, and paved the way to progress, innovation, and human accomplishment. *The Everything® Great Thinkers Book* introduces you to the larger-than-life artists, philosophers, religious leaders, pop-culture visionaries, and scientists whose ideas have altered and shaped our way of life. Their genius challenged the ideology of their times, and these thinkers often risked their lives and reputations to fight for their theories and beliefs.

OTHER *EVERYTHING®* BOOKS BY ADAMS MEDIA CORPORATION

BUSINESS

Everything® **Business Planning Book**
Everything® **Coaching and Mentoring Book**
Everything® **Fundraising Book**
Everything® **Home-Based Business Book**
Everything® **Leadership Book**
Everything® **Managing People Book**
Everything® **Network Marketing Book**
Everything® **Online Business Book**
Everything® **Project Management Book**
Everything® **Selling Book**
Everything® **Start Your Own Business Book**
Everything® **Time Management Book**

COMPUTERS

Everything® **Build Your Own Home Page Book**

Everything® **Computer Book**
Everything® **Internet Book**
Everything® **Microsoft® Word 2000 Book**

COOKBOOKS

Everything® **Barbecue Cookbook**
Everything® **Bartender's Book, $9.95**
Everything® **Chinese Cookbook**
Everything® **Chocolate Cookbook**
Everything® **Cookbook**
Everything® **Dessert Cookbook**
Everything® **Diabetes Cookbook**
Everything® **Low-Carb Cookbook**
Everything® **Low-Fat High-Flavor Cookbook**
Everything® **Mediterranean Cookbook**
Everything® **Mexican Cookbook**
Everything® **One-Pot Cookbook**
Everything® **Pasta Book**

Everything® **Quick Meals Cookbook**
Everything® **Slow Cooker Cookbook**
Everything® **Soup Cookbook**
Everything® **Thai Cookbook**
Everything® **Vegetarian Cookbook**
Everything® **Wine Book**

HEALTH

Everything® **Anti-Aging Book**
Everything® **Diabetes Book**
Everything® **Dieting Book**
Everything® **Herbal Remedies Book**
Everything® **Hypnosis Book**
Everything® **Menopause Book**
Everything® **Nutrition Book**
Everything® **Reflexology Book**
Everything® **Stress Management Book**
Everything®**Vitamins, Minerals, and Nutritional Supplements Book**

All Everything® books are priced at $12.95 or $14.95, unless otherwise stated. Prices subject to change without notice.
Canadian prices range from $11.95–$31.95, and are subject to change without notice.

HISTORY

Everything® **American History Book**
Everything® **Civil War Book**
Everything® **Irish History & Heritage Book**
Everything® **Mafia Book**
Everything® **World War II Book**

HOBBIES & GAMES

Everything® **Bridge Book**
Everything® **Candlemaking Book**
Everything® **Casino Gambling Book**
Everything® **Chess Basics Book**
Everything® **Collectibles Book**
Everything® **Crossword and Puzzle Book**
Everything® **Digital Photography Book**
Everything® **Family Tree Book**
Everything® **Games Book**
Everything® **Knitting Book**
Everything® **Magic Book**
Everything® **Motorcycle Book**
Everything® **Online Genealogy Book**
Everything® **Photography Book**
Everything® **Pool & Billiards Book**
Everything® **Quilting Book**
Everything® **Scrapbooking Book**
Everything® **Soapmaking Book**

HOME IMPROVEMENT

Everything® **Feng Shui Book**
Everything® **Gardening Book**
Everything® **Home Decorating Book**
Everything® **Landscaping Book**
Everything® **Lawn Care Book**
Everything® **Organize Your Home Book**

KIDS' STORY BOOKS

Everything® **Bedtime Story Book**
Everything® **Bible Stories Book**
Everything® **Fairy Tales Book**
Everything® **Mother Goose Book**

EVERYTHING® KIDS' BOOKS

All titles are $6.95
Everything® **Kids' Baseball Book, 2nd Ed.** ($10.95 CAN)
Everything® **Kids' Bugs Book** ($10.95 CAN)
Everything® **Kids' Christmas Puzzle & Activity Book** ($10.95 CAN)
Everything® **Kids' Cookbook** ($10.95 CAN)
Everything® **Kids' Halloween Puzzle & Activity Book** ($10.95 CAN)
Everything® **Kids' Joke Book** ($10.95 CAN)
Everything® **Kids' Math Puzzles Book** ($10.95 CAN)
Everything® **Kids' Mazes Book** ($10.95 CAN)
Everything® **Kids' Money Book** ($11.95 CAN)
Everything® **Kids' Monsters Book** ($10.95 CAN)
Everything® **Kids' Nature Book** ($11.95 CAN)
Everything® **Kids' Puzzle Book** ($10.95 CAN)
Everything® **Kids' Science Experiments Book** ($10.95 CAN)
Everything® **Kids' Soccer Book** ($10.95 CAN)
Everything® **Kids' Travel Activity Book** ($10.95 CAN)

LANGUAGE

Everything® **Learning French Book**
Everything® **Learning German Book**
Everything® **Learning Italian Book**
Everything® **Learning Latin Book**
Everything® **Learning Spanish Book**
Everything® **Sign Language Book**

MUSIC

Everything® **Drums Book (with CD)**, $19.95 ($31.95 CAN)
Everything® **Guitar Book**
Everything® **Playing Piano and Keyboards Book**

Everything® **Rock & Blues Guitar Book (with CD)**, $19.95 ($31.95 CAN)
Everything® **Songwriting Book**

NEW AGE

Everything® **Astrology Book**
Everything® **Divining the Future Book**
Everything® **Dreams Book**
Everything® **Ghost Book**
Everything® **Meditation Book**
Everything® **Numerology Book**
Everything® **Palmistry Book**
Everything® **Psychic Book**
Everything® **Spells & Charms Book**
Everything® **Tarot Book**
Everything® **Wicca and Witchcraft Book**

PARENTING

Everything® **Baby Names Book**
Everything® **Baby Shower Book**
Everything® **Baby's First Food Book**
Everything® **Baby's First Year Book**
Everything® **Breastfeeding Book**
Everything® **Father-to-Be Book**
Everything® **Get Ready for Baby Book**
Everything® **Homeschooling Book**
Everything® **Parent's Guide to Positive Discipline**
Everything® **Potty Training Book**, $9.95 ($15.95 CAN)
Everything® **Pregnancy Book, 2nd Ed.**
Everything® **Pregnancy Fitness Book**
Everything® **Pregnancy Organizer**, $15.00 ($22.95 CAN)
Everything® **Toddler Book**
Everything® **Tween Book**

PERSONAL FINANCE

Everything® **Budgeting Book**
Everything® **Get Out of Debt Book**
Everything® **Get Rich Book**
Everything® **Homebuying Book, 2nd Ed.**
Everything® **Homeselling Book**

All Everything® books are priced at $12.95 or $14.95, unless otherwise stated. Prices subject to change without notice.
Canadian prices range from $11.95–$31.95, and are subject to change without notice.

Everything® **Investing Book**
Everything® **Money Book**
Everything® **Mutual Funds Book**
Everything® **Online Investing Book**
Everything® **Personal Finance Book**
Everything® **Personal Finance in Your 20s & 30s Book**
Everything® **Wills & Estate Planning Book**

PETS

Everything® **Cat Book**
Everything® **Dog Book**
Everything® **Dog Training and Tricks Book**
Everything® **Horse Book**
Everything® **Puppy Book**
Everything® **Tropical Fish Book**

REFERENCE

Everything® **Astronomy Book**
Everything® **Car Care Book**
Everything® **Christmas Book, $15.00** ($21.95 CAN)
Everything® **Classical Mythology Book**
Everything® **Einstein Book**
Everything® **Etiquette Book**
Everything® **Great Thinkers Book**
Everything® **Philosophy Book**
Everything® **Shakespeare Book**
Everything® **Tall Tales, Legends, & Other Outrageous Lies Book**
Everything® **Toasts Book**
Everything® **Trivia Book**
Everything® **Weather Book**

RELIGION

Everything® **Angels Book**
Everything® **Buddhism Book**
Everything® **Catholicism Book**
Everything® **Jewish History & Heritage Book**
Everything® **Judaism Book**
Everything® **Understanding Islam Book**
Everything® **World's Religions Book**
Everything® **Zen Book**

SCHOOL & CAREERS

Everything® **After College Book**
Everything® **College Survival Book**
Everything® **Cover Letter Book**
Everything® **Get-a-Job Book**
Everything® **Hot Careers Book**
Everything® **Job Interview Book**
Everything® **Online Job Search Book**
Everything® **Resume Book, 2nd Ed.**
Everything® **Study Book**

SELF-HELP

Everything® **Dating Book**
Everything® **Divorce Book**
Everything® **Great Marriage Book**
Everything® **Great Sex Book**
Everything® **Romance Book**
Everything® **Self-Esteem Book**
Everything® **Success Book**

SPORTS & FITNESS

Everything® **Bicycle Book**
Everything® **Body Shaping Book**
Everything® **Fishing Book**
Everything® **Fly-Fishing Book**
Everything® **Golf Book**
Everything® **Golf Instruction Book**
Everything® **Pilates Book**
Everything® **Running Book**
Everything® **Sailing Book, 2nd Ed.**
Everything® **T'ai Chi and QiGong Book**
Everything® **Total Fitness Book**
Everything® **Weight Training Book**
Everything® **Yoga Book**

TRAVEL

Everything® **Guide to Las Vegas**
Everything® **Guide to New England**
Everything® **Guide to New York City**
Everything® **Guide to Washington D.C.**
Everything® **Travel Guide to The Disneyland Resort®, California Adventure®, Universal Studios®, and the Anaheim Area**
Everything® **Travel Guide to the Walt Disney World Resort®, Universal Studios®, and Greater Orlando, 3rd Ed.**

WEDDINGS

Everything® **Bachelorette Party Book**
Everything® **Bridesmaid Book**
Everything® **Creative Wedding Ideas Book**
Everything® **Jewish Wedding Book**
Everything® **Wedding Book, 2nd Ed.**
Everything® **Wedding Checklist, $7.95** ($11.95 CAN)
Everything® **Wedding Etiquette Book, $7.95** ($11.95 CAN)
Everything® **Wedding Organizer, $15.00** ($22.95 CAN)
Everything® **Wedding Shower Book, $7.95** ($12.95 CAN)
Everything® **Wedding Vows Book, $7.95** ($11.95 CAN)
Everything® **Weddings on a Budget Book, $9.95** ($15.95 CAN)

WRITING

Everything® **Creative Writing Book**
Everything® **Get Published Book**
Everything® **Grammar and Style Book**
Everything® **Grant Writing Book**
Everything® **Guide to Writing Children's Books**
Everything® **Screenwriting Book**
Everything® **Writing Well Book**

Available wherever books are sold!
To order, call 800-872-5627, or visit us at everything.com

Everything® and everything.com® are registered trademarks of Adams Media Corporation.